The British
in Northern Nigeria

ROBERT HEUSSLER

London
OXFORD UNIVERSITY PRESS
NEW YORK   TORONTO
1968

Oxford University Press, Ely House, London W. 1

GLASGOW NEW YORK TORONTO MELBOURNE WELLINGTON
CAPE TOWN SALISBURY IBADAN NAIROBI LUSAKA ADDIS ABABA
BOMBAY CALCUTTA MADRAS KARACHI LAHORE DACCA
KUALA LUMPUR HONG KONG TOKYO

*Printed in Great Britain by Richard Clay (The Chaucer Press), Ltd.,
Bungay, Suffolk*

To
Ten Broeck Jackson Heussler

Acknowledgements

THIS book was made possible by generous grants from the American Philosophical Society and the Social Science Research Council and by the kindness of John B. Howard in arranging the equivalent of a research leave at the end of my time in the Ford Foundation. For writing those irksome letters that scholars have to compose in aid of junior colleagues, I warmly thank Dame Margery Perham and Professors P. J. Bohannan and L. Gray Cowan.

St. Antony's College, Oxford, and the Institute of Administration, Ahmadu Bello University, Zaria, provided rooms and in countless other ways helped the research along. I am especially indebted to the Warden and to the Bursar of St. Antony's and to S. S. Richardson and C. Butler-Stoney, director and secretary respectively of the Institute in Zaria. J. J. Tawney and his staff at the Colonial Records Project, Oxford, aided directly by providing a variety of archival assistance and indirectly by discovering and rescuing for scholarship large amounts of valuable material on Northern Nigerian history. L. B. Frewer, superintendent of the Rhodes House Library, was always ready with advice and help, as were Bernard Cheeseman, librarian of the Colonial Office, and J. C. Enwere, archivist at the National Archives, Kaduna.

The following people, among others, gave verbal or written assistance of great value, as regards both particular points and matters of more general pertinence: Salihu Abdullahi, Ali Akilu, J. P. Attenborough, J. E. A. Baker, J. Ballard, J. D. Bejide, the late Sir Ahmadu Bello, Alhaji Muhammadu Bello (Magajin Rafin Gwandu), Lady Bourdillon, the late H. M. Brice-Smith, T. G. Brierly, Dr. R. M. East, C. J. Hanson-Smith, Alhaji Haruna (Emir of Gwandu), T. Hodgkin, A. H. M. Kirk-Greene, Professor K. Kirkwood, Dr. D. M. Last, T. E. Letchworth, Dr. V. Low, J. A. H. Maund, M. S. Minjibir, Muhammed Monguno, E. L. Mort, D. J. M. Muffett, Umaru Nassarawa (Wazirin Gwandu), St. E. D. Nelson,

Sir John Patterson, Dame Margery Perham, M. T. Pitts, D. A. Pott, J. H. Smith, Muhammadu Tsadu, Alhaji Muhammadu Tukur (Emir of Yauri), H. D. Tupper-Carey, P. J. Wallace, L. S. Ward, S. White, and the late C. A. Woodhouse. My gratitude to them all is large and lasting.

For permission to quote from private papers I am pleased to have this opportunity of thanking Lady Lethem, Mrs. F. de F. Daniel, Mrs. H. S. W. Edwardes, and Mrs. B. H. Garvey.

I must mention separately the extraordinary help given me by Commander J. H. Carrow, Sir Bryan Sharwood Smith, Sir Arthur Weatherhead, and L. C. Giles. In talks and correspondence they chipped away, with uncommon patience and generosity, at the massive block of ignorance I began with. Later they went over the manuscript with meticulous care and retrieved battalions of big and little faults. While they and the others listed above bear no responsibility for the final product, my debts to them are beyond describing.

Contents

Glossary of Terms, Abbreviations, and Notes on Usage

ALKALI (from the Arabic 'Al Kadi'). Moslem judge, i.e. judge in a Native Court using Moslem Law.

BAIT-EL-MAL (Arabic). Native Treasury, i.e. the accounts department of a Native Authority. Written 'Baitulmal' in Hausa. Often spelled 'Beit-el-mal' in British documents.

BATURE (plural: turawa). White man.

HABE (plural). Fulani word meaning 'pagans'. Used by the Fulani to refer contemptuously to the Hausa. Used especially by the Fulani to describe the Hausa dynasties and states conquered by them in the Holy War of the early 1800s.

JANGALI. Cattle tax.

JIHAD (English form of the Arabic word). War to propagate Islam, 'Holy War'. In Nigeria this normally refers to the Fulani conquest of the Hausa states in the early 1800s. Written 'jihadi' or 'jahadi' in Hausa.

MALAM (Hausa plural: malamai). Literate person. Islamic teacher or scholar. Northern clerk or scribe. Literate member of a Native Authority department, e.g. 'Agricultural malam'. Spelled 'mallam' in Sokoto.

RUGA (plural: rugage). A cattle camp of the nomad Fulani. Made up of temporary 'beehive' huts and temporary enclosures for each owner's herd.

SABON GARI. Literally 'New Town'. Refers to the southern quarter of a Northern Nigerian community, i.e. that part where people from southern areas live. Typical inhabitants were government employees, drivers, shopkeepers, *et al.* Sabon garis grew up under British rule, outside such Northern towns as Zaria and Kano. They were laid out with straight, wide streets which contrasted with the wandering alleyways of older parts of the towns.

SARKI (usual plural: sarakuna). Chief or emir. Also sultan, king, head of any group or area, e.g. Sarkin Kajuru. Also refers to a function or job, e.g. sarkin bariki, meaning a man whose job it is to keep a rest house in good order and to admit guests. The possessive singular, 'sarkin', is the form most often used in the following pages.

TALAKAWA (singular: talaka). Commoners, the common people, those who hold no office, are not employed by Native Authorities or Government Offices, are not wealthy, of high birth, etc.

ABBREVIATIONS

D.O.—District Officer

A.D.O.—Assistant District Officer

D.H.—District Head

N.A.—Native Authority (see note 1, p. 49)

S.N.P.—Secretary Northern Provinces, the officer ranking second after the Lieutenant Governor or Chief Commissioner

S.N.A.—Secretary for Native Affairs, a Lagos post carrying responsibility for native administration affairs throughout Nigeria

C.R.P.—The Colonial Records Project of Oxford University

K.—The National Archives, Kaduna

P.—Materials privately held or not to be ascribed as to source

USAGE

Residents in charge of provinces are referred to as in official documents, e.g. 'Resident Kano', meaning the Resident in charge of Kano Province. So too with District Officers, e.g. 'D.O. Gwandu', and Assistant District Officers, e.g. 'A.D.O. Rijau'. This type of description may also be functional, e.g. 'A.D.O. Judicial'.

The phrase 'Anglo-African Government', used frequently in this book, is employed because it is thought more descriptive of government in Northern Nigeria during the colonial period than are such phrases as 'indirect rule' or 'colonial government'. The phrase was not of course used officially, nor is it common in the literature.

The word 'pagan' appears frequently in the following pages just as it does in official documents of the period. There is no pejorative inference here. 'Pagan' meant non-Moslem originally and later meant non-Christian as well.

Footnotes referring to interviews and correspondence with officers will give the officer's last name and the date of the letter or interview. More details, including biographical information, may be found in the Acknowledgements and, in many cases, in the List of Officers.

List of Officers

The following is a list of some of the officers mentioned in the text and notes. It will be seen that biographical facts are incomplete in many cases; the list doubtless contains inaccuracies. When two or more printed sources were consulted, sometimes accompanied by verbal testimony, there emerged a number of conflicting versions of such details as postings and dates. The list is included nevertheless because it does provide some idea of the personality of the Northern Service. It may be noted too that the difficulty of gathering simple biographical information of this kind is itself symptomatic of the British colonial system. Colonies enjoyed such autonomy that London had little knowledge of their internal personnel activities after officers were recruited and sent out for the first time. Staff Lists, Gazettes, etc., issued within colonies were often incomplete as to domestic British information and they were not always accurate about postings because of last-minute changes, illness, and other factors. In any case, information sought for this list was not available in any one place, in Britain or in Nigeria.

CAPT. GEORGE HOWARD ABADIE, C.M.G. Manchester Regiment. A.D.C. to the High Commissioner. Served as Resident in Zaria and Kano, 1902–4 and on Sokoto Expedition, 1903. Died in Kano, 1904.

SIR THEODORE (SAMUEL) ADAMS, C.M.G. Born 1885. Educated at King's School, Canterbury, and All Souls College, Oxford. Served in the Federated Malay States, 1908–36. Chief Commissioner, Northern Nigeria, 1937–43. Died 1961.

CYRIL WILSON ALEXANDER, C.M.G. Born 1879. Educated at Shrewsbury and Trinity College, Cambridge. LL.B. Served in Southern Nigeria and Lagos, 1906–16. Military service, Northern Nigeria, 1917–18. Southern Provinces, 1919–24. Acting S.N.P., 1924. Resident Kano, 1925–7. Acting Lieutenant Governor, Northern Provinces, 1927. Resident Kano, 1927–8. Lieutenant Governor, Southern Provinces, 1929–30. Lieutenant Governor, Northern Provinces, 1930–2. Retired 1932. Died 1947.

EDWARD JOHN ARNETT, C.M.G. Born 1876. Educated at St. Paul's School and St. Catherine's College, Cambridge. Middle Temple. Served in the Crown Agents' office, 1901–3. Provincial and Secretariat service, Northern Nigeria, 1903–8. Acting

Resident and Resident Zaria, Kano, and Sokoto, 1908–20. Acting Lieutenant Governor, Northern Provinces, 1920–1 and 1923. Resident Cameroons, 1925–8. Acting Lieutenant Governor, Southern Provinces, 1929–32. Retired 1932. Died 1940.

HENRY FLEMING BACKWELL. Born 1884. Educated at Charterhouse and King's College, Cambridge. Served in Bauchi, Sokoto, and in the Secretariat, 1909–25. Resident Adamawa, Sokoto, Niger, and Zaria, 1926–38. Retired 1939. Deceased.

SIR FRANK BADDELEY, C.M.G. Born 1874. Educated at Magdalene College, Cambridge. Inner Temple. Served in the Malayan Civil Service, 1897–1924. Chief Secretary, Nigeria, and occasionally Officer Administering the Government, 1924–31. Died 1965.

DAVID MACDONALD HERBERT BECK, M.C. Born 1891. Educated at Weymouth College and Exeter College, Oxford. Served in the London and Kano Trading Company, Kano, 1913–14. Lieutenant, West African Frontier Force, First World War. Served in Nupe, Zaria, Abeokuta, Nassarawa, and Sokoto, 1919–33. Resident Plateau, Zaria, and Benue. Retired 1945.

SIR (HENRY) HESKETH (JOUJOU) BELL, K.C.M.G. Born 1865. Educated in Paris. Colonial Service in the West Indies, the Gold Coast, the Bahamas, and again in the West Indies, 1882–1906. Governor of Uganda, 1906–9. Governor of Northern Nigeria, 1909–12. Governor of the Leeward Islands, 1912–15. Governor of Mauritius, 1915–24. Died 1952.

SIR BERNARD (HENRY) BOURDILLON, G.C.M.G., K.B.E. Born 1883. Educated at Tonbridge School and St. John's College, Oxford. Served in the Indian Civil Service, 1908–14. Seconded to Mesopotamia, 1914–19, and on political duty in Iraq until 1929. Chief Secretary, Ceylon, 1929–32. Governor of Uganda, 1932–5. Governor of Nigeria, 1935–43. Died 1948.

HUGH MIDDLETON BRICE-SMITH. Born 1884. Educated at Pocklington School and Queens' College, Cambridge. Served in Kabba, Muri, and Kano, 1909–17. Niger and Zaria, 1919–31. Southern Provinces, 1931–4. Died 1967.

GEORGE SINCLAIR BROWNE, C.M.G. Born 1880. Educated at Malvern College and Hertford College, Oxford. Served in provincial and Secretariat posts, Northern Nigeria, 1906–16. Acting Private Secretary to the Governor-General, 1917–18. Resident Yola and Zaria, with service as Secretary Northern Provinces and Secretary Native Affairs (Lagos), 1919–30. Resident Cameroons, 1931–2. Chief Commissioner, Northern Nigeria, 1933–6. Died 1946.

MAJ. SIR JOHN (ALDER) BURDON, K.B.E., C.M.G. Born 1866. Educated at King Edward VI School, Norwich, and Corpus Christi College, Cambridge. Served in the Cameron Highlanders. Niger Sudan Campaign 1897. Commandant, Royal Niger Constabulary, 1898–9. Resident Bida and Sokoto, 1900–10, with Secretariat duty. Colonial Secretary, Barbados, 1910–15. Administrator, St. Kitts, 1915–25. Governor of British Honduras, 1925–31. Died 1933.

PERCY GEORGE BUTCHER. Born 1890. Educated at Perse School and Exeter College, Oxford. Lieutenant in France, 1915–19. Served in Lokoja, Bida, and Bornu, 1919–28, with service in education during the 1930s. Served in Bornu, Zaria, and Kano. Retired 1940. Deceased.

FELIX W. BYNG-HALL. Born 1870. Captain, Suffolk Regiment. South African War. West African Frontier Force, 1900–3, including Kano Expedition. Resident Bassa, Zaria, and Kabba, 1903–24.

SIR DONALD (CHARLES) CAMERON, G.C.M.G., K.B.E., LL.D. (Cantab.). Born 1872. Educated in the West Indies and at Rathmines School, Dublin. Colonial Service, British Guiana, Newfoundland, Mauritius, 1890–1907. Secretariat, Lagos, 1908–14, with tours as provincial commissioner and in various departments and as Governor's deputy. Central Secretary, then Chief Secretary, Nigeria, 1914–24. Governor of Tanganyika, 1925–31. Governor of Nigeria, 1931–5. Died 1948.

DR. FEATHERSTONE CARGILL, C.M.G. Born 1870. Educated at Fettes College and Edinburgh University. Served in the Royal Niger Company. Resident Kano and Lokoja, 1903–6. Retired 1906. Died 1959.

JOHN HINTON CARROW, C.M.G., D.S.C. Born 1890. Educated at Clifton College. Served in the Royal Navy, 1905–19 (Commander on the Retired List). Served in Kano, 1919–33, with brief Secretariat service. Resident Sokoto and Kano, 1933–46, with brief service in the Admiralty during the Second World War. Acting Chief Commissioner, 1944 and 1945–6. In charge of groundnut production in Northern Nigeria during the Second World War. Retired 1946.

(ARTHUR) JOYCE (LUNEL) CARY. Born 1888. Educated at Clifton and Trinity College, Oxford. Served in the British Red Cross, Montenegrin Battalion, during the Balkan War, 1912–13. Cameroons Campaign, 1915–16. Bauchi and Borgu, 1914–19. Retired 1920. Died 1957.

SIR HUGH CLIFFORD, G.C.M.G., G.B.E. Born 1866. Educated at Woburn Park under the 13th Lord Petre. Appointed to the Malayan Civil Service, 1883. Commissioner of the Cocos and Keeling Islands, 1894. Colonial Secretary, Trinidad, 1903–7. Chief Secretary, Ceylon, 1907–12. Governor of the Gold Coast, 1912–19. Governor of Nigeria, 1919–25. Governor of Ceylon, 1925–7. Governor of the Straits Settlements, 1927–9. Died 1941.

FRANCIS DE FOREST DANIEL. Born 1886. Educated at Marlborough College. Nigerian Railways and Customs services, 1912–14. Served in the Administration from 1914, in Kano, Sokoto, Bauchi, and Kaduna. Resident Zaria and Ilorin. Retired 1939. Died 1965.

PIERRE DE PUTRON. Born 1886. Educated at Eton and University College, Oxford. Served in Borgu, Sokoto, Abuja, and Bornu, 1909–25. Resident Bornu, 1925–33. Retired 1934. Deceased.

HAROLD STANLEY WHITFIELD EDWARDES. Born 1879. Served in the South African War. Served in Nupe, Zaria, Ilorin, Bauchi, and Sokoto, 1905–20. Resident Sokoto, Kontagora, Kabba, and Munshi. Retired 1925. Died 1963.

HUGH PERCIVAL ELLIOTT. Born 1911. Educated at St. Lawrence College, Ramsgate, and at Hertford College, Oxford. Served in Benue, Kano, and Zaria, 1935–45, and as Private Secretary to the Chief Commissioner. Seconded to the Colonial Office, 1946. Supervisor of the Colonial Services Course, Oxford, from 1948. Later returned to Nigeria and served in the Eastern Region.

MAJ. ARTHUR HOSKYNS FESTING, C.M.G., D.S.O. Born 1870. Served in the Royal Niger Company, in the South African War, and in the Sudan. West African Frontier Force, 1901–2. Resident Kano, 1906–7. Retired 1912. Killed in action, Gallipoli, 1915.

MAJ. JOHN MORTON FREMANTLE, C.M.G., M.B.E., D.C.M. Born 1876. Educated at Eton and Hertford College, Oxford. Served in the South African War. Private Secretary to the Secretary of State for War, 1903, and to the Governor-General of Canada, 1910–11. Resident Katsina, Kano, Zaria, Kabba, Bassa, Borgu, Yola, Muri, Bauchi, and Nupe, 1904–24. Acting Lieutenant Governor, 1925. Acting S.N.P., 1928. Retired 1929. Died 1936.

LAWRENCE CRANMER GILES, M.B.E. Born 1909. Educated at King Edward's School, Birmingham, and Queen's College, Oxford. Served in Zaria, Katsina, Kano, Sokoto, Bauchi, and Lokoja, 1933–55. Supervisor of the Colonial Services Course, Oxford. Retired 1955.

COL. SIR (EDWARD) PERCY GIROUARD, K.C.M.G., D.S.O. Born 1867. Served in the Royal Engineers, Sudan. Director of Railways, Egypt and South Africa. High Commissioner, then Governor, Northern Nigeria, 1907–9. Governor of the East African Protectorate, 1909–12. Died 1932.

HERBERT SYMONDS GOLDSMITH, C.M.G. Born 1873. Educated at Eastbourne College. Officer of the Legion of Honour. Served in the Marine Department, Lagos, 1899–1901. Served in the Administration, Lower Benue, Bida, and Sokoto, 1901–9. Resident Niger. Chief Secretary to the Government of Northern Nigeria, 1911, and Acting Governor, 1912. Acting Lieutenant Governor, 1915. Lieutenant Governor, 1917–21. Died 1945.

SIR WILLIAM (FREDERICK) GOWERS, K.C.M.G. Born 1875. Educated at Rugby and Trinity College, Cambridge. Served in the British South African Company, Southern Rhodesia, 1899–1902. Resident Yola, Muri, Sokoto, Bauchi, and Kano, 1903–12. Acting Chief Secretary, 1912. Served in the Cameroons, 1914–16. Lieutenant Governor, 1921–5. Governor of Uganda, 1925–32. Senior Crown Agent, 1932–8. Died 1954.

SIR SELWYN (MACGREGOR) GRIER, K.C.M.G. Born 1878. Educated at Marlborough and Pembroke College, Cambridge. Barrister. Lieutenant, Nigerian Land Contingent, 1914–17. Resident Zaria, Bauchi, and Ibadan, 1906–13. Served in the Secretariats at Kaduna and Lagos and as Director of Education, Southern Provinces. Colonial Secretary, Trinidad, 1929–35. Governor of the Windward Islands, 1935–7. Died 1945.

PERCY GRAHAM HARRIS. Born 1894. Educated at St. Bees School. Solicitor and book-keeper. Lieutenant, Nigeria Regiment. France, 1916. Served in the Secretariat and in Kano, Sokoto, Kabba, and Niger, 1919–34. S.N.P., 1935. Consul-General, Duala, 1940–2. Resident Cameroons, 1944. Died 1945.

ARCHIBALD CHARLES GARDINER HASTINGS. Born 1878. Educated at Charterhouse. Military service, 1900–1. Served in H.B.M. Consulate at Fez, 1901–5. Served in Bauchi, Kano, Bornu, and Sokoto, 1906–20. Resident Kano and Nupe, 1921–4.

HON. HARRY BALDWIN HERMAN-HODGE. Born 1886. Educated at Winchester and Magdalen College, Oxford. Served in Bauchi, Bornu, Yola, and Ilorin, 1909–15. Cameroons, 1914 and 1916. Acting Resident and Resident Ilorin, 1920–33.

FRANCIS HUMPHREYS, O.B.E. Born 1905. Educated at Charterhouse and Cambridge. Served in Zaria and Katsina, 1928–39. Private Secretary to the Governor, 1939–40. Military Service,

B

1940–4. Resident Niger and Bornu, 1945–55, with Secretariat service. Secretary to the Commissioner for Nigeria in the United Kingdom, 1955–6. Died 1967.

MAJ. HENRY DOUGLAS LARYMORE, C.M.G. Born 1867. Educated at Westminster. Served in India, Jamaica, and the Gold Coast. Seconded to the War Office during the First World War and worked briefly in the United States on munitions. Resident Kabba, Borgu, Nupe, and Yola, 1902–20. Retired 1921. Died 1946.

THOMAS EDWIN LETCHWORTH, C.M.G. Born 1906. Educated at Downside and Christ's College, Cambridge. Served in Bornu, Benue, Zaria, and Katsina, 1928–43. Seconded to the Gambia, 1943–5. Acting Resident and Resident Bornu, Kabba, and Niger, 1948–1958. Retired 1959.

SIR GORDON (JAMES) LETHEM, K.C.M.G. Born 1886. Educated at Mill Hill School and Edinburgh University. Served in Ilorin and Bornu, 1911–24, with war service in the Cameroons. Served at various times as S.N.P., S.N.A., and Acting Lieutenant Governor. Resident Sokoto, 1933. Governor of the Seychelles, 1933–5. Governor of the Leeward Islands, 1936–41, and of British Guiana, 1941–6. Died 1962.

HAROLD OFFLEY LINDSELL. Born 1884. Educated at Bradfield College and at All Souls College, Oxford. Served in Niger, Sokoto, Kano, and briefly in the Southern Provinces, 1909–25. Resident Sokoto and Kano, 1925–38. Deceased.

SIR FREDERICK (DEALTRY) LUGARD, G.C.M.G., C.B., D.S.O. (later Lord Lugard, of Abinger, P.C.). Born 1858. Educated at Rossall School and briefly at Sandhurst. Served in Afghanistan, Burma, Nyasaland, and in the Imperial British East African Company. Raised the West African Frontier Force and commanded expeditions on the Niger. High Commissioner of Northern Nigeria, 1900–6. Governor of Hong Kong, 1907–12. Governor of Northern and Southern Nigeria, 1912–14, and Governor-General of Nigeria, 1914–18. Afterwards British Member of the Permanent Mandates Commission, League of Nations. Died 1945.

MAJ. AUGUSTUS McCLINTOCK, D.S.O. Born 1866. Served in the Seaforth Highlanders and in the West African Frontier Force. Resident in Bauchi and, notably, in Bornu, from 1901 until his death in 1912.

HENRY HALE MIDDLETON. Born 1885. Educated at Warwick School and Hertford College, Oxford. Served in Zaria, Bauchi, and Kano, with brief Secretariat service, 1910–23. Acting S.N.P.,

1926 and 1928. Resident Bauchi and Plateau. Retired 1935. Deceased.

WALTER MORGAN, C.M.G. Born 1886. Educated at Merchant Taylors' School and Jesus College, Oxford. Served in Nassarawa, Kano, and Bauchi, 1910–25. Acting S.N.A., 1928, and Acting Chief Commissioner, 1934–5. Resident Bauchi, Benue, and Zaria. Retired 1937. Died 1960.

FREDERICK MITCHELL NOAD. Born 1895. Lieutenant, West African Frontier Force, 1915–20. Served in Kano, Plateau, and Sokoto, 1920–36. Resident Kano, Zaria, and Plateau. Retired 1947. Died 1966.

MAJ. SIR CHARLES (WILLIAM JAMES) ORR, K.C.M.G. Born 1870. Educated at Bath College and at Woolwich. Served in India, South Africa, and China. Resident Northern Nigeria, including Bauchi and Zaria, 1903–11, with Secretariat service. Chief Secretary, Cyprus, 1911–19. Colonial Secretary, Gibraltar, 1919–26. Governor of the Bahamas, 1926–31. Died 1945.

SIR (HERBERT) RICHMOND PALMER, K.C.M.G., C.B.E. Born 1877. Educated at Oundle and Trinity College, Cambridge. LL.B. Served in Kano and Katsina, with Secretariat service, 1904–17. Visited Egypt, Sudan, etc., studying law and taxation, 1911 and 1918. Resident Bornu, Kano, and Sokoto. Acting Lieutenant Governor, 1921 and 1924. Lieutenant Governor, 1925–30. Governor of the Gambia, 1930–3. Governor of Cyprus, 1933–9. Died 1958.

SIR JOHN (ROBERT) PATTERSON, K.B.E., C.M.G. Born 1892. Educated at Haileybury and Pembroke College, Cambridge. Served in Bornu and briefly in the Secretariat, 1915–37. Resident Kano, 1938. Chief Commissioner, 1943–7.

D. A. POTT, O.B.E. Born 1913. Educated at Charterhouse and Oxford. Served from 1936 in Ilorin, Niger, Adamawa, Katsina, Kano, and Sokoto, with military service and with Secretariat duties. Permanent Secretary, Ministry for Local Government. Retired 1962.

HORACE ARTHUR PRANKERD. Born 1883. Educated at Ipswich School and Queens' College, Cambridge. Barrister. Served in Nupe, Bassa, Nassarawa, and Kano, 1910–28. Resident Sokoto, 1928.

MAJ. UPTON FITZHERBERT RUXTON, C.M.G. Born 1873. Worcestershire Regiment. Served in the South African War and in the Niger Company. Assistant Resident and Resident Lower Benue, Yola, Gwandu, and Bornu, 1901–14. Admiralty, 1915–18.

On Foreign Office duties in Constantinople, 1919. Resident Buea, 1921. Acting Lieutenant Governor and Lieutenant Governor, Southern Provinces, 1925–9. Died 1954.

JOHN CARMELO CAMILLO PIO SCIORTINO. Born 1875. Educated at the Malta Lyceum. Served in Ilorin, Kabba, Yola, Bornu, and Benue, 1903–21, with Secretariat duties. Resident Nassarawa, Zaria, Nupe, Munshi, and Kabba. Retired 1929.

SIR BRYAN (EVERS) SHARWOOD SMITH, K.C.M.G., K.C.V.O., K.B.E., E.D. Born 1899. Educated at Aldenham School. Served in the Royal Flying Corps in the First World War and in Germany and India. Served in the Cameroons, 1921–7, and in Sokoto, Kano, Zaria, and Niger, 1927–43. Military intelligence duties, 1940–2. Resident Niger, Sokoto, and Kano, 1943–52, and Acting Chief Commissioner, 1950. Lieutenant Governor and later Governor of Northern Nigeria, 1952–7.

ANDERSON COLIN TALBOT-EDWARDS. Born 1908. Educated at Rossall School and St. John's College, Cambridge. Served in Zaria and elsewhere in the North, 1931–9. Seconded to the Colonial Office, 1939, to the office of the Resident Minister for West Africa, 1942, and to the West African Council, 1945. Assistant Chief Secretary, Nyasaland, 1946, and Deputy Chief Secretary, 1948.

PHILIP ANTHONY TEGETMEIER, O.B.E. Born 1897. Military service in India and Mesopotamia, 1915–18. Political service, Iraq, 1920–2. Served in Bornu, 1922–9. Acting Resident and Resident Bornu and Niger, with Secretariat duties. Transferred to Zanzibar, then seconded to Colonial Office, 1940s.

CHARLES LINDSAY TEMPLE, C.M.G. Born 1871. Foreign Office duties in Paraguay and Brazil. Resident Bauchi, Sokoto, and Kano, 1901–13, with Secretariat duties. Chief Secretary, 1910–13. Lieutenant Governor, 1914–17. Died 1929.

SIR ERIC (WESTBURY) THOMPSTONE, K.B.E., C.M.G., M.C. Born 1897. Educated at Shrewsbury. Military service during the First World War in France and Italy. Served in Bauchi, Benue, and Sokoto, 1919–40, with Secretariat service. S.N.P., 1940. Resident Adamawa, Bornu, and Kano. Chief Commissioner, 1947–51. Lieutenant Governor, 1951–2.

SIR GEORGE (JOHN FREDERICK) TOMLINSON, K.C.M.G., C.B.E. Born 1876. Educated at Charterhouse and University College, Oxford. Served in the Transvaal Education Service and on the staff of Sir Percy Girouard, Sokoto, 1907. Director of Educ-

ation in the Gold Coast, 1909. Served in Sokoto, Kano, and
Bornu, 1911–18. Acting S.N.P., 1919, and Acting S.N.A., 1921.
Transferred to the Colonial Office, 1928. Assistant Under-
Secretary of State, 1930–9. Died 1963.

HUMPHREY DARRELL TUPPER-CAREY. Born 1893. Educated
at Eton. Served in East Africa, 1914–18. Administrative service in
Kenya, 1919–21. Served in Sokoto, Kabba, and Bornu, 1922–50.
Served in the Forestry Department after retirement, 1950.

SIR WILLIAM WALLACE, K.C.M.G. Born 1856. Served in the
Royal Niger Company from 1878. Resident General, Northern
Nigeria, 1900. Deputy High Commissioner, 1900–10, often serving
as Officer Administering the Government. Died 1916.

ALGERNON EDWARD WALWYN (VERE-WALWYN), C.M.G.
Born 1888. Educated at Bath and at Peterhouse, Cambridge.
Served in Kano and Niger, 1915–31, with Secretariat service.
Resident Bornu. S.N.P., 1934 and 1938. Retired 1943.

SIR ARTHUR (TRENHAM) WEATHERHEAD, C.M.G. Born 1905.
Educated at St. Bees School and Queen's College, Oxford. Served
in the Sudan Plantations Syndicate from 1927. Served in Kano,
Bornu, Niger, Zaria, and Sokoto, 1930–50, with Secretariat
service. Resident Sokoto, Kano, and Plateau. Deputy Governor,
1958–60.

GUSTAVUS WILLIAM WEBSTER, M.B.E. Born 1876. Served in
Nassarawa, Yola, Kano, Bauchi, and Munshi, 1901–19, with
Secretariat service. Resident Sokoto and Yola, 1920–30. Deputy
Colonial Secretary, Lagos, 1931. Retired 1932.

STANHOPE WHITE. Born 1913. Educated at Harrogate Grammar
School and Emmanuel College, Cambridge. Served from 1936 in
Bornu, Zaria, Benue, Kano, and Sokoto, with military service and
with Secretariat duties. Acting Director, Groundnut Scheme,
1949. Resigned 1954.

CLAUDE WIGHTWICK. Born 1881. Served in Bauchi, Kano, and
Bornu, 1906–19. Acting Resident and Resident Bauchi and Kano.
Retired 1927.

CHARLES ASHBEE WOODHOUSE. Born 1884. Educated at Marl-
borough and Brasenose College, Oxford. Served in Kabba, Bassa,
Bauchi, and Sokoto, 1908–22, with Secretariat service. Resident
Zaria, Bauchi, Niger, and Sokoto. Retired 1932. Died 1965.

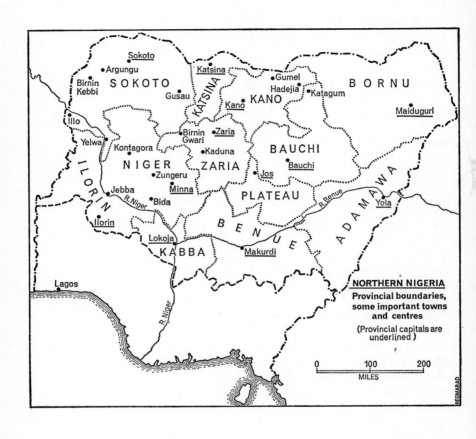

NORTHERN NIGERIA
Provincial boundaries,
some important towns
and centres

(Provincial capitals are
underlined)

0   100   200
MILES

I

Introduction

THROUGHOUT the first sixty years of this century there took place in Northern Nigeria an extraordinary demonstration of co-operative government between two quite different breeds of men. Together they gave that large, heavily populated, and heterogeneous country a blend of order and healthy forward movement that compares favourably with any it had known before. Their record is eminently worthy of study in a time such as ours when the physical barriers between races are everywhere lowered but when those against understanding and trust are as high as ever.

To take the measure of British rule in Northern Nigeria we must look at its origins and trace the pattern of its development down to the 1950s when it became aware that its days were numbered. Why did Britain become interested in this part of Africa during the last years of the nineteenth century and how was it that she decided to establish a formal administration there? What were the political circumstances of African society at the time? What relationship was worked out between the two races and how and in what way was it done? What were the views of the British as to immediate desiderata, possibilities, obstacles, and ultimate aims? What was the apparent outlook of the Africans and how was it taken into account? As time went on, what changes occurred and how did the parties seem to be influencing and adjusting to one another? When all was said and done, how do we appraise the British contribution; that is to say, what difference did it make to the Africans that they had the British among them for half a century rather than going their own way as they had done before 1900?

As these are obvious questions we may ask why they have not been dealt with more satisfactorily in the literature of imperialism and of African studies. And if the picture of Africa's recent past that does emerge from available sources could stand improvement, what explanations suggest themselves?

There is, in the first place, the scholar's ageless and universal problem of trying to get his thinking tuned to a place and an era other than his own. Many students of European activity in lands outside Europe have approached their subjects still carrying a heavy burden of domestic values. While there is no such thing as a *tabula rasa*, it is possible to be aware of subjectivity's dangers and to keep the problem in mind as one treads an unmarked trail for the first time. There are risks enough for people who study esoteric areas today in an attempt to learn about their present economies or societies. For historians the path is yet more treacherous in that they deal with subjects that are both unfamiliar and out of time. 'What may have been admirable and even altruistic fifty years ago,' writes a former Northern Nigerian officer, 'is now probably impertinent and grossly offensive. There are too many x's in the formula. Not only do the conditions change but also the eye through which they are viewed.'[1]

In the case of alien rule, moreover, we note a curious and persistent bias, in modern times at any rate. The merits of particular circumstances need not be looked at, for the possession of political power by a man of one race over people of another is silently assumed to be *ipso facto* wrong. Overseas dominion is not judged by the same standards as are used to assay municipal rule, although it will be plain that human beings are involved in both types and that therefore good, bad, and indifferent results will obtain variously in each. Speaking of European politics on the eve of the First World War, an eminent scholar discusses machinations and attitudes on the home continent; then, turning to Europe's doings in Africa, he says that 'even colonial' territories and activities were affected by the same ideas he mentions with reference to Europe itself.[2] Why *even*?

In African studies one or two tendencies may be noted that are unlikely to result in sound views on and descriptions of colonial rule. African specialists who have done excellent and

---

[1] Letchworth, 29 March 1965.
[2] E. H. Carr, *The Twenty Years' Crisis, 1919–1939*, London, 1949 (2nd ed.), p. 112.

valuable work on societies within that continent have understandably protested that in the past there has not been enough
work on Africa itself and, comparatively, too much on Europe
in Africa or on Africa viewed simplistically through European
eyes. It is quite to be expected that these scholars would insist
on the importance of their subject, and no one who values new
research in hitherto under-attended fields will fail to welcome
their products. But in their zeal to assert the rights of Africa
and to scold Europe for its past blindness they appear to go too
far and to end by saying that the colonial years were completely
unimportant or that no good was done then or that everything
bad in contemporary Africa is Europe's fault. Sometimes they
will have it all three ways at once. The over-reaction is understandable but it can do a disservice to history. One Africanist
deals matter-of-factly with the general barbarity and specific
misdeeds of African rulers; but when treating the activities of
Europeans in the same areas and time spans he pulls his reader
up short with highly pejorative, even ferocious, passages, con-
trasting sharply with the objectivity that went before.[1] It is as
though savagery of the most bestial kind is reckoned to be quite
unexceptionable when displayed by indigenous folk—on whose
behalf, incidentally, the claim is frequently put forward that
they possessed a higher civilization than Europeans realized—
whereas misconduct by outsiders is culpable in the extreme.

Dealing specifically with European administration in Africa,
the specialist occasionally makes the same sort of mistake that
he delights in catching non-Africanists at. He too can fall into
the trap of accepting myths at face value and of failing to
distinguish between theory and fact. From an oral historian of
Hausaland we learn that Lugard's Political Memoranda were
a fixed standard against which the subsequent British performance in Northern Nigeria can be adequately judged.[2] This
would be like saying that all we have to know about nineteenth-
century Fulani units may be found in the writings of Mohammed
Bello, Commander of the Faithful, who, like Lugard, had the
job of building an administration and exhorting his followers

---

[1] J. Vansina, *Kingdoms of the Savanna*, Madison, 1966, especially pp. 135–244.
[2] M. G. Smith, 'Historical and Cultural Conditions of Political Corruption
Among the Hausa', *Comparative Studies in Society and History*, VI, 2 (January 1964),
p. 184.

with written statements about the aims of government. 'Few British administrators', continues the historian, 'thought to ask in what way the Fulani administration deviated from Muslim norms.'[1] We shall see that this is not accurate. Getting things wrong is hardly exceptional—we all do it. But the cavalier attitude of some Africanists requires to be mentioned. The picture of British rule emerging from their work permits us to doubt that students of one aspect of African life are necessarily competent to judge other aspects without first doing their share of sweated labour along with the rest.[2]

Testimony from the British themselves is not lacking. On the contrary, there is a vast literature and one that continues to grow. Much of this, however, is pitched at a rather high level and is concerned with policy and the London–Government House axis. The apologia of an ex-governor, in any case, is apt to be received with suspicion, especially if it seems to adopt a defensive posture or to offer shrill defiance to all critics. At the next level down, civil servants have tended to a fatalistic or properly subordinate silence, doubting that they would be believed if they told the unwashed truth about institutions that the modern world convicts without trial. Why, asks one, should they bother to defend colonial government in an age when it is everywhere believed to be '. . . an out-of-date, inefficient and slightly unsuccessful form of tyranny'.[3]

In passing we may also mention the problem of contributions to African topics by area specialists and by social scientists respectively, whether these relate to the past or to the present, and we may ask why there has not been greater fulfilment of

[1] Ibid., p. 186.

[2] In an introduction to a new edition of C. L. Temple's *Native Races and Their Rulers* (originally published in Cape Town, 1918; edition reprinted by Cass, London, 1968), M. Hiskett begins by noting that 'an adequate account' of Temple's background and career may be found in Margery Perham's biography of Lugard and in David Muffett's book on the campaigns of the British Occupation, *Concerning Brave Captains* (London, 1964). This is certainly not the case, as both of those authors themselves insist. The editor goes on to say that Temple was not a scholar—a puzzling irrelevance, to say the very least. In the remainder of his introduction the editor gives us many things of interest to Africanists. What he does not provide is precisely what one looks for in an essay meant to precede Temple's work: something of Temple as a man, set in the context of what the early Residents really faced in Northern Nigeria as opposed to the mainly theoretical and abstract version of reality found in sources cited in the editor's footnotes.

[3] J. Thrupp, administrative officer, writing from Buea, 4 June 1961.

hopes for complementary work by the two groups in recent years. Colonialism and nationalism are organically joined. The latter grew out of the former and cannot be understood without reference to it, any more than a final evaluation of colonialism is possible without reference to the nationalisms it has spawned. There was expectation after the Second World War that area studies programmes would marry traditional scholarship on particular cultures to the new insights into human nature and society that social scientists were gaining. As sub-Sahara Africa was still under colonial rule at that point, it was hoped that the new studies would reveal much about European government in Africa as well as about the local societies themselves. From the 1940s onwards, in fact, a good deal of interest has been shown in colonial and nationalist Africa by scholars who trace their lineage from Comte and Weber, by anthropologists, political scientists, and sociologists interested in how societies are structured and how they work—an ideally complementary interest to the compiling and synthesizing concerns of historians, linguists, musicologists, and specialists on literature, ethnography, and folklore.[1] What was not fully appreciated at first by area specialists who welcomed social scientists to their field was that the newcomers were primarily, if not exclusively, interested in experiments in new settings and not in learning about and adding to knowledge of the areas themselves. They looked, as they did at home, for laws and regularities which could be used to support theories of political and social behaviour, treating African communities as case studies rather than subjects on which knowledge was to be got for its own sake.[2] They were fond of comparisons, and the wider the international scope the better. Whereas traditional students of the area had been gatherers of facts and had seen theory as an essence rising

[1] Cf. Sir Hamilton Gibb, *Area Studies Reconsidered*, School of Oriental and African Studies, London, 1963, p. 14. It may be noted, in this regard, that scholars who begin to specialize in African studies or who have a peripheral interest in them have not enjoyed the advantages of a rich and massive literature such as has been available to Sinologists, Islamists, and others whose work may be grounded in high cultures of the past.

[2] Cf. F. A. Olafson, 'Some Observations on Area Study Programs', *The American Behavioral Scientist*, VIII, 1 (September 1964), pp. 11–14, and Hugh Tinker, *Ballot Box and Bayonet*, London, 1964, p. 2. The Lugard Memorial Lecture of 1967, as reported in *West Africa*, 1 July 1967, p. 845, and given by Professor Daryll Forde, contained comments on African studies which are relevant here.

off the warm body of reality, latter-day social scientists seemed
to be reversing the process: they came already supplied with
theory, or at least with well-developed hypothetical constructs,
into the various openings of which they would place factual
data selected for their apparent appropriateness to the pre-
conceived mould. Not all have been as unempirical as this.
But too many have lacked that vital sense of the past that would
serve as a warning against the dangers of arbitrary eclecticism.[1]
Too few have stayed long enough to acquire the linguistic and
other situational skills without which basic appreciation of the
atmosphere is difficult.[2]

The present work is an attempt to address the questions
posed above by undertaking a detailed study of a single, important territory in colonial Africa during the era immediately
preceding independence. Northern Nigeria commends itself for
special attention, being the most populous British-ruled unit in
sub-Sahara Africa.[3] The greater part of it had shared the experience of Fulani rule, yet there was great ethnic, topographic,
economic, and cultural diversity. It was the scene of a famous
experiment in native administration which was to be widely
imitated.

The time span—roughly the first half of the present century—
covers the years when European rule was first established and
continues through all the core period, or 'Golden Age', of

---

[1] Cf. Charles Tilly, 'New Ways in History', *History and Theory*, vi, 2 (1967), pp.
247–52.

[2] People on both sides, i.e. in area studies and in social science theory, continue to call for complementary work, as Gibb does in his remarks cited in note 1,
p. 5, above. Several years ago I heard a discussion between a historian specializing
in Latin America and a sociologist whose recent work had been almost exclusively
theoretical. The latter said that people in his position were helpless *vis-à-vis* unfamiliar areas of the world until provided with factual data and also their context and that such provision was the function of the area specialist. Some months
later, however, I heard a political scientist put the matter differently. Having
worked on Africa and being at the time about to turn his attention to Latin
America, he remarked that social science theorists were the 'shock troops' whose
job it was to enter unmapped territory first, ahead of everyone. They would then
provide the theoretical framework within which the infantryman area specialist
would classify his data. In recent years there has been a certain amount of sound
and fury inside each camp. But the issues have not been joined in any major way.

[3] Northern Nigeria was a separate protectorate at first, and until 1914 it dealt
with London direct. In the 1950s it became again virtually separate. In the interim
it enjoyed a large measure of autonomy (see ch. 3 below), even though it was
legally and financially under Lagos.

settled administration. As we look at what was done in these years we are not bothered, as are students of the later, transition era, by the self-consciousness, artificiality, and protesting of a regime whose sands are running out and whose work goes forward in the glare of international publicity. An administrator who is constantly looking over his shoulder and worrying about being misunderstood may not actually conduct his affairs in a very different way from one who does not have this problem. But the air of unreality surrounding his daily stint may assume the proportions of a smokescreen which students must penetrate if they are to see the essentials of everyday work. As regards the later period, moreover, it is arguable if we are even now in a position to do more than guess at the important decisions and actions, both British and African, of colonial government's last decade. British documentation on the transfer of power is not readily available. The African side will perhaps never be adequately covered.

The focus in these pages is on the British. While it is not possible in the nature of things to speak of British activity without giving detailed attention also to Africans with whom they worked, one must nevertheless abjure any expertise on the vital subject of how the Africans felt. That topic is eminently researchable. We may hope that Africans and Africanists will increasingly delve into such materials as Hausa and Arabic papers in the Archives at Kaduna and in the files of Native Authorities throughout the Region. It is especially to be hoped that extensive oral history will be pursued in these times when African graduates of the Anglo-African system are available in large numbers, many of them still holding office.

Within British cadres we are concerned primarily with the Administration as opposed to other services, such as Education and Agriculture. Commercial and religious bodies lie yet further out towards the periphery. The work of all of them is touched on, sometimes in detail, for the Administration was central to everything. The District Officer's perspective was broad; perhaps no one else was in so good a position to take a locality's pulse. And few general practitioners in human history were as active and powerful in the whole sweep of community life as D.O.s were.

Official papers on the British period offer an embarrassment of riches. Some years ago most divisions and provinces in Northern Nigeria gave up their non-current files to a central archive where, at the time of one's work, there was no limitation of access like the old fifty-year rule in Chancery Lane. Other evidence is still found in administrative offices, touring diaries being the most valuable, followed closely by confidential files on such matters as the conduct of chiefs and members of their councils. Private papers, such as letters and diaries, are available in great quantity, thanks to the Colonial Records Project of Oxford University and to the generosity of retired administrators and their families. Students may also consult the memories of dozens of men who lived and worked in Northern Nigeria during the period covered, most of them now retired and living in England. Personal testimony made use of here starts in 1908 and comes down to 1967.

There are advantages to be gained through the balancing and blending of evidence drawn from all these sources. The value of official files is in the incomparably current and authoritative view they provide on what the Government was doing, when, how, and for what official reasons. An official letter or memorandum, however, will be disadvantageous in that it was originally addressed to knowledgeable participants, to members of a small society of experts, and it is therefore just as remarkable for what it does not say as for what it does. Without being able to read between the lines the student is certain to misunderstand a very great deal, for he will lack the necessary social and psychological context. Unless he knows something of the personalities of particular correspondents and their relationship he may well miss the spirit of what they say to one another.

This is one reason why private papers are so helpful. With the bars of officialdom lowered men speak more openly. Comparing the private letter with what is said in an official file, one finds missing links, plain truths, the warts without which no portrait is very convincing. But there are difficulties here as well. Given the luxury and licence of a confidential backroom, it is only human to indulge in forms of self-congratulation and rationalizing that one would not exercise in so public a place as an office letter. The secret man is an important ingredient, but he is not the whole man. So too with letters to parents and other relatives living far away in the England of one's fast-receding youth.

Depending on the writer's relationship with his family, such letters can be wonderfully revealing of what was going on in Africa; or they can be couched in the special language that dutiful sons use with mothers who must be protected by a film of mythology from the real world's harshness.

Conversations with men who took part in the events being studied are uniquely valuable and are a source which, after all, is denied to most students of history. In talks and subsequent correspondence a normally silent service speaks up and at great length. Points not elucidated in documents can be gone over and questions asked. Extenuating circumstances may be looked into so that the student is able, to an extent, to break through the document's flat and arid surface. Furthermore, one man's verbal account can be checked against another's and still another's. This can mitigate somewhat the inevitable hazards of bad memory, of pride, and of that indefinable combination of nostalgia and time-cushioning that makes it hard for anyone to transport himself back to the spirit of former days. It is all too easy to give ourselves the second chance that real life denies us.

Using such sources in combination, one aims at a dialogue between written and spoken testimony on the one hand, and on the other a series of flexible hypotheses as to what it all means. At first, before extensive research has begun, hypotheses so predominate that they can be mistaken for reality itself. Then follows a rather disconcerting process of immersing oneself in masses of material and of trying to differentiate between the essential and the trivial. Like old friends who prove faithless, lesser notions fade into insignificance, while others, perhaps not perceived at first, assume the proportions of major themes. One ends with ideas that have stood the test of research and with evidence that has been looked at from more than one side. If the final result is more impressionistic than photographic there will be those who think that it is just as well. When the subject is human beings the work will, yet awhile, owe more to art than to science.[1]

---

[1] The impressionistic nature of the work is reflected, for example, in the fact that I have concentrated on typically 'Northern' provinces—Sokoto, Zaria, Kano—rather than on the Middle Belt, and have not aimed at a comprehensive survey, as a definitive history would do.

If this book adds to our knowledge of an important region in West Africa and of Britain, that will be justification enough. However—and even if one has undertaken the work for reasons of personal interest and nothing more—it may be permissible to speculate on possible uses to which studies of this kind might be put.

One thinks first of the need that any people has to know about its past as a means of increasing its total self-knowledge. Throughout that nationalist era that gathered momentum in Asia and the Caribbean in the 1930s and reached a crescendo in Africa in the fifties and sixties there has been a steadily mounting worldwide sympathy for colonial peoples, a feeling that their aspirations were a matter of right, and a readiness to help them. There has also been a good deal of effort to win their approval, some of it motivated by a guilty conscience about what is conceived to be European misconduct in the past and some of it having to do with leading nations' age-old need to find allies. One result of both the sympathy and the Big Power self-interest has been a shielding of Africans from awareness of their own shortcomings. They have been given a crutch. What they need, however, is not flattery but the self-esteem that comes from independent accomplishment. The longer they go on telling themselves that their troubles may be laid at the door of their departed alien masters, the longer they will have deferred the day of necessary disillusion. 'The ignorance of the recent past is incredible,' writes a friend of Northern Nigeria, '. . . no one has read any of the standard works on the British acquisition or [on] . . . the development of the country.'[1]

Other nations, especially powerful ones, ought to know more about Africa too. The subject of how Africans might be expected to react in various situations today can be illuminated by information on how they reached their present state and what about them has changed and not changed. There are sameness and change also in the ground rules whereby economically powerful states deal with the rest. Victorian Britain dealt with Peru on a relatively straightforward, take-it-or-leave-it basis involving little intimate knowledge or participation by Europeans internally. Raw materials were picked up and finished

[1] The letter from which this quotation comes was written in Northern Nigeria during 1966. The writer cannot be identified here.

products put down. For the most part the country was otherwise ignored, as befits a ward unit that is irrelevant to world politics. Today's major powers seem to be stumbling towards a similar political ordering of the world. The United States, Russia, and China have become educated rather soon on the facts of life in places like Africa. Disheartening as it must be to Africans, there is greater distance between them and the international leaders now than there was between South America and Europe a hundred years ago. But economic relations have altered. Research on investment opportunities must be done more carefully these days and it requires close knowledge of social and political factors. Aliens are found inside new countries in considerable numbers, working for indigenous governments and educational institutions or representing international organizations and foreign business firms. Communications have become so efficient and easy that Africa, for all its weakness, will not remain a sleepy backwater as Latin America did. Today's foreign visitor has to know Africa better than Victorian traders knew their ports of call.

The Northern Nigerian experience with bi-racial government can be suggestive also for people whose present-day responsibilities are reminiscent of what the British faced not so long ago. Former District Officers would find the following statement so familiar that they might assume it came from Lugard or Cameron: '[The Government's aim is] . . . to develop the peoples of the . . . Territory so that they can assume the responsibilities of self-government, to stimulate them to become . . . economically self-sufficient . . . and to encourage them to foster respect for their cultures while affording them an opportunity to take on those aspects of western [civilization] which will enable them to lead richer lives.'[1] Yet it refers to a United Nations Trust Territory administered at this moment by the United States. In the area of practical administration old D.O.s would also recognize the benchmarks of their own former work in a description of duties put out by a governmental recruiter as recently as 1966. In that year the newsletter sent to retired U.S. Air Force officers advertised openings in Vietnam

[1] *General Information for Prospective Employees,* United States Department of Interior, Personnel Office, Trust Territory of the Pacific, Saipan, November 1965, p. 2.

C

that sounded much the same as positions filled by Englishmen all over the world in times past and still held at that point by a residual handful in Northern Nigeria. The advertisement made clear that the essential requirement was for men of Western education and integrity who could hold the ring in a situation of confusion and local incompetence. They would be required to supervise and take responsibility for all manner of community activities and to be the living, objective links between their areas and the central government. Americans now performing these tasks in that tortured land are experiencing many of the same discouragements and satisfactions that British D.O.s came to take in their stride. Some things under the sun are new, but others are not very new at all, and the world is a pretty small place.

2

Founding Anglo-African Government

IN 1900, when she assumed formal responsibility for Northern Nigeria, Britain's knowledge and experience of the area were remarkably slight. A handful of British nationals had had extensive trading experience in the new Protectorate's southerly regions along the Niger and the Benue and a few had made brief excursions into the northern parts on various missions, commercial, religious, scholarly, and political. Far and away the greater part of the dependency was unknown territory, a land whose inhabitants were as oblivious of the power now raising its flag in their midst as the new rulers were ignorant of them and of their country.

In Britain over the last decade and a half of the nineteenth century this part of Africa had figured more and more in public discussion and in the concerns of groups whose disparate interests in the region and views on its future were no less lively and persistent in their expression for being grounded in little or no concrete knowledge. To some the region, perhaps unimportant in and of itself, was one which rival nations must be kept out of. The thoughts of others turned to moral obligations of one kind or another, duties that men and women in Britain thought their country ought to recognize and act upon in Africa. And still others, doubtless the best-informed about actual conditions there, saw Northern Nigeria as a place that could be valuable. Each of these viewpoints is relevant to the meandering courses by which Britain came to acquire yet another overseas territory and to the compelling question of what she would do in and with the country once her responsibility for it was established.

It is an axiom of the last important phase of overseas expansion on the part of the major European powers that their technological superiority and their concern with foreign dominion drew them forward continuously, if fitfully, into Asia and Africa until, by the close of the period, they had effectively divided up all areas of interest to them. It is equally axiomatic that most territories were merely pawns in the game of international competition, that there was usually no correlation between the economic value of a territory and the desire of one or more powers to acquire it, and that a clear distinction must be drawn between the hasty occupation of lands for reasons of international prestige and the later rationalizations of imperial presences that have come to occupy so prominent a place in the literature of imperialism and colonialism. To this it must be added that in the case of Britain there tended to be more distance between the various interested groups operating on the home scene than was true of her two main competitors, and that scepticism and reluctance characterized the attitude of all British governments down to and including the final Scramble.

London's view of West Africa generally from the 1870s onwards was that it was not an area of large strategic concern— a trivial place compared with India, for example—that the public purse should certainly not be drawn on for political activity in such places, and that those British who went there for one reason or another ought to pay their own way.[1] Coupled with this, however, was an instinct so basic as gradually to assume the force of constant policy: that one's nationals must not be so inconvenienced by the nationals of other powers that the prestige of the home country could suffer. In the absence of weighty economic or strategic factors it is hard to see any motive that compared in importance with that of nationalistic sentiment. Northern Nigeria became British because London did not much care for the idea of its becoming French or German.

---

[1] Cf. David Fieldhouse, 'Imperialism—An Historiographical Revision', *Economic History Review*, XIV, 2 (1961); R. Robinson, J. Gallagher, and A. Denny, *Africa and the Victorians*, London, 1961; R. Robinson and J. Gallagher, 'The Partition of Africa', in F. H. Hinsley (ed.), *The New Cambridge Modern History*, vol. XI, Cambridge, 1962; J. Gallagher and R. Robinson, 'Imperialism of Free Trade', *Economic History Review*, VI, 1 (1953); J. E. Flint, introduction to Mary Kingsley, *West African Studies*, London, Cass, 1964; C. W. Newbury, 'Victorians, Republicans and the Partition of West Africa', *Journal of African History*, III, 3 (1962); and in *The Cambridge History of the British Empire*, vol. III, Cambridge, 1959: 'International Rivalry in the Colonial Sphere', by F. H. Hinsley; 'International Rivalry, 1885–1895', by F. H. Hinsley; 'British Foreign Policy and Colonial Questions', by F. H. Hinsley; 'The Opening of Tropical Africa', by J. Simmons; 'Imperial Problems in British Politics, 1880–1895', by R. Robinson; 'Finance, Trade and Communications', by E. A. Benians; and 'Changing Attitudes and Widening Responsibilities, 1895–1914', by A. F. Madden.

Before the 1890s 'British' meant simply that the regions of the Niger coast and its delta and ill-defined hinterlands to the north were looked on by all concerned as ones in which the interests of various British groups would predominate. Where Northern Nigeria itself was concerned, as opposed to the better-known southern areas, London and Berlin were in agreement as to spheres of influence in the regions of the upper Benue and northwards, and London and Paris by 1890 had agreed that the territories of 'The Kingdom of Sokoto' and eastwards to Lake Chad would be British. The British Government would have preferred to leave it at that. Such administering as there was—precious little as we shall see—would be left to the Royal Niger Company, given a charter in 1886, because London saw that in this way it could have the best of two worlds: Paris and Berlin could be told that British interests were represented on the ground; yet the arrangement would cost nothing and ultimate discretion would remain with the Government. But so minimum and informal a solution was not to prove satisfactory for long. Granting rights to a trading company without commensurate responsibilities aggravated pressures within African societies and among British commercial groups that London found more and more difficult to ignore. A more serious problem from Britain's viewpoint was the forward movement of French military expeditions, which was urged on by a general weakness, if not vacuity of power, throughout the Western Sudan and which at times outpaced the wishes of the Government in Paris. In particular there was a danger that France would call the bluff of the Niger Company's treaties with chiefs in northern areas, documents of little or no importance to the chiefs themselves and backed by neither occupation nor exchanges of practical functions such as were in effect farther south.

By the late 1890s Britain and France had become involved in military 'steeplechases' in the Nile Valley as well as in the upper Niger area. Britain went forward because the actions of her rivals made it impossible for her to go on marking time. The purely negative aim of keeping others out was now confronted by a situation in which the old instrumentalities were shown to be inadequate. Paper agreements with one's competitors were enough as long as the parties dealt with spheres of influence on the diplomatic plane only. Now there were garrisons and incipient administrations across boundaries which, being heretofore unmanned, had not had to be demarcated with any precision. A formal administration, however minimal, would henceforth be necessary. It would be wrong to infer, however, that the facing of this by the British Government in 1897–8 reflected any fundamental change in their outlook. West Africa was still a nuisance. The thought of spending money there remained unattractive to most elements in the Government and Civil Service and the great negative—unwillingness to be outdistanced by rivals—was still the prime mover.

Groups outside politics and commerce who were interested in Northern Nigeria before 1900 are important more for the influence they would have on later developments in the region than for a decisive role in bringing about its acquisition. Even so, the manner in which that influence was brought to bear was usually indirect, making it hard to measure. In mentioning it we are noting one of the streams of British outlook and concern that was relevant in late Victorian times rather than tracing lines of specific power or suggestion.[1] At the base of most British humanitarian views on Africa for more than a century lay a determination to abolish slavery and to promote Christianity. Whether or not they were directly involved in early explorations, humanitarian and church bodies were deeply interested in accounts of African conditions brought back by travellers from the late eighteenth century onwards. It has been pointed out often enough that part of such interest was generated by a sense of guilt because of Europe's role in the slave trade. Some felt a genuine religious conviction and a wish to share Christianity's benefits, while with others there was a range of amorphous impulses having to do with the notion that the higher culture that one enjoyed at home ought somehow to be exported to places not yet aware of it. The concept of cultural conceit is not altogether satisfactory, for very often there was nothing patronizing in people's views; these tended to arise spontaneously and unthinkingly from awareness of the wide technological gulf dividing European from African life.

As the nineteenth century wore on and the actual involvement

[1] Cf. Madden, and Flint and Kingsley, op. cit., and Mary Kingsley, *Travels in West Africa*, London, 1897; John E. Flint, *Sir George Goldie and the Making of Nigeria*, London, 1960.

of British missionary and trading groups increased along the West African coasts and inland, attitudes among the various groups naturally tended to harden along lines reflecting their widely different activities. A merchant who makes his living from matching wits with African middlemen in the buying, collection, and transport of palm oil will hardly have the same view of African rights and needs as will a missionary whose business is persuasion or education. Nor will those who manage their respective organizations back home. The demonstrable relationship between increased commerce and prosperity in Africa and a decrease in the need for and incidence of slave trading might have seemed to create a basis for common satisfaction. In practice it had done little to bridge occupational gaps between people who lived out their lives in separate worlds. Nevertheless, conditions were improving on the coasts; Britain was becoming more and more closely involved; and competition from France and Germany pushed old adversaries towards a degree of united Britishness in outlook and action that would have seemed unattainable earlier. By the late 1890s the Aborigines Protection Societies and the Socialists were both in favour of Britain going forward.

There were others who wanted their country to play more of a role in Africa than she had done, but whose conception of that increased role contained reservations about the desirability of haphazard Europeanizing. The most prominent of these was Mary Kingsley, who travelled to West Africa, wrote about it, and tried to influence public policy towards it during the last years before Britain proclaimed a protectorate over Northern Nigeria. One of Miss Kingsley's most essential ideas was that more intercourse between Europe and Africa, particularly trade, could be beneficial to both, but that this should come about without 'bastardizing' the African.[1] His basic nature, so markedly different from the European's, must not be harmed and must remain intact as he developed into a better and stronger human being. Otherwise his contacts with foreigners, now increasing rapidly and uncontrolledly, would leave him confused and defenceless in a world whose values were not his and whose technological superiority he could never hope to resist. Here was a strong contrast with Portuguese and French

[1] See Kingsley, *West African Studies*, ch. xvii and Introduction.

views of assimilation. Neither this particular British viewpoint nor opposing ones on the Continent were entirely new in the. 1890s. The Kingsley view was important because it was destined to continue as one of the mainstreams of official and unofficial thought all through British times and beyond the day of Nigerian independence.

The people whose ideas were to have the most immediate and down-to-earth effect on the composition and work of the new government were the traders who maintained permanent establishments in and above the Niger delta itself.[1] We have observed that the main work of the Royal Niger Company and its predecessors had been carried on well to the south of territories that were to form the core area of the Protectorate; that is to say, lands claimed by the Sultan of Sokoto and the Shehu of Bornu. On the Niger no European agent of the Company had been stationed above Eggan, claimed but seldom controlled by the Nupe Chief, himself only the nominal and indirect vassal of Sokoto. On the Benue the northernmost Europeans were at Ibi, also normally outside the effective range of northern chiefs. Yet the Company's men were at least on the scene; their head had gone to Berlin with the British delegation in 1885 and had drawn the boundary with German Cameroons; a representative of the Company had made treaties with Sokoto and Gwandu in 1885; others had maintained more or less continuous contact with other Moslem political units such as Nupe and Ilorin on the Niger and with Yola far up the Benue; and another was made British Vice-Consul on the Niger in 1884. If the Company did not actually administer Africans, its presence, its experience, its military strength, and its paper pretences made it an invaluable instrument against the time when Britain might decide to move.

Inevitably the Company looked on the northern chiefdoms as potential markets and therefore areas which must be kept British. Their principals in England were naturally prominent in what came to be called the Forward Party, or school. To them the desired objective was full chartered company rule as with earlier enterprises in India and North America, whereas

---

[1] The account of the activities of the traders found in Flint's biography of Goldie (note 1, p. 16 above) is excellent, especially on the interplay of British and African factors.

other elements in the Forward Party favoured one degree or another of supervision by the Government itself. Agreeing with rivals on spheres of influence was enough for some. Minimum representation on the spot satisfied others. And still others agreed with the Macdonald Report of 1890 (on the more southerly areas) that responsible government demanded robust administration *in situ*. When at the end of the nineties the Government decided to go ahead, they used people and ideas from the Forward Party as they saw fit, being impelled to action, however, more by the activities of the French than by the blandishments of any domestic organization or interest.

In the early nineties there had been a standstill, following on the Anglo-French agreement of 1890 on their respective spheres in the Niger area. French military expeditions advanced, however, in 1895 and 1896, the British Government at first giving Paris assurances that they would not be resisted. By 1897 the Niger Company was at war with Nupe and Ilorin. African political units that had come into direct contact with the Europeans, a small minority of the group that would comprise the new territory, had been weakened by the experience, and this weakness acted as the natural counterpart to French initiative in drawing the British forward. By 1897 also, the Colonial Secretary, very much a proponent of Forward politics, was organizing a military force to check France on the Niger. All thought of allowing the Company to go on representing British interests had ceased, and in 1898 compensation was agreed upon and plans made for the Colonial Office to take formal responsibility for administration. A settlement with France was arrived at in 1898. By the latter half of 1899 preparations had been completed for proclaiming the Protectorate of Northern Nigeria on 1 January 1900. International politics had run its course. Yet as the Union Jack went up over the Niger Company station at Lokoja, British knowledge of the North as a whole was still minute. 'Protectorate' at this point represented intention and determination rather than fact. Even as such, it would make more of an impression in London, Paris, and Berlin than in Sokoto, Bornu, Kano, and the other northern states.

If the handful of Europeans who witnessed the flag-raising—their chief most of all—had firm ideas on the question of what lay before them and how they would go about their task, these would now be set against objective determinants powerful enough to daunt all but the most resourceful organizers and innovators. Colonel Lugard and his small staff started out with anything but a clean slate. In the first place there was the *sine qua non* of money. After fighting the Colonial Office for most of 1899 Lugard ended with a budget for the first year of £135,000, £45,000 of which came from Southern Nigeria in the form of customs duties and the rest from London as a grant-in-aid.[1] Britain's attitude towards the degree of administration that would suffice is shown in the figure of £10,000 a year for administrative staff. Until the territory could be occupied and its chiefs brought under control there would be no possibility of collecting taxes locally. The Protectorate would have to make do meanwhile with whatever could be wheedled out of a reluctant Colonial Office, backed as it was by a notoriously tight-fisted Treasury. In the first year there were nine political officers posted in a chain running from Ilorin to Jebba, where headquarters were moved in the early weeks, and thence along the Niger–Benue through Lokoja and Loko to Ibi. There were 104 members of the staff by 1901, but this included all departments such as medical and public works and every staff grade down to clerks and storekeepers. Government could be many things—efficient, honest, imaginative. It could not be strong and far-reaching in the scope of its activities.

Financially limited in this way, the new regime had also to reckon with London's intentions—it would be too much to dignify them with the name of policy—which the first High Commissioner's wife summed up in words of devastating candour:

The exact measure of responsibility accepted by Great Britain in Northern Nigeria, at the moment of the establishment of British administration there, would have been difficult to define. The vague title of suzerain covered the position, and, beyond a general desire that slave-raiding should be suppressed and trade routes thrown open, there was probably no wish in any quarter in England to see a rapid advance towards the assumption of more defined duties, or of responsibilities which would involve expense. The public generally knew nothing of the country. Political necessities had imposed the creation of a military force for the defence, not only of the

[1] See Margery Perham, *Lugard*, London, 1960, vol. ii, ch. 3.

Nigerian, but of all West African frontiers. A small grant-in-aid to meet other administrative expenses was reluctantly added by the Treasury to the sum required for the maintenance of the West African Frontier Force. These concessions were made rather by respect for the judgment and the wishes of Mr. Chamberlain, then occupying the position of Secretary of State for the Colonies, than by any strong conviction on the part of the British Government that Northern Nigeria was likely to prove a very valuable acquisition to the Crown; and in the absence of a clearly expressed interest on the part of the House of Commons in the adoption of a new West African policy, it seemed improbable that funds would be willingly voted for any full development of the Nigerian Protectorate. In these circumstances the wishes of the Government and of the country, if they had to be condensed into one phrase of instruction to the High Commissioner, would perhaps best have been rendered by the words, 'Go slow!'[1]

Behind this statement of an intention to be present so that another power could not be, there lay what might be called the British psyche of the times, a factor whose importance was not conveyed fully in the spoken word. Unlike the Germans to one side of them and more than the French on the other, the British were deeply experienced in the business of living among other races and directing them in the sphere of government. Over the centuries her worldwide experience had relieved Britain of many illusions and had inculcated in thousands of British expatriates an almost instinctive sense of what could be done with and to subject races and what, on the other hand, might better be left unattempted. It is said that the late Victorians were confident, and indeed they were, especially by comparison with their sons and grandsons of the post-1945 era. It was a confidence mixed with the common sense, and in many cases the humility, that comes to those who have fought battles before and know when to lower their sights. Lugard had spent years in India and East Africa. The previous itineraries of his early associates read like an almanac of the tropical world at the turn of the century. Some, like Ruxton, had been in the South African War; Gowers was in Rhodesia; Larymore had seen service in other parts of West Africa and before that in India; Temple had been in India, Paraguay, and Brazil; and Goldsmith was in Nigeria before the Protectorate. Particularly useful were the Niger

[1] Lady Lugard, *A Tropical Dependency*, London, 1905, pp. 418–19.

Company men who stayed on with Lugard—Wallace, Burdon, Hewby, Cargill, Festing, and Ruxton—thus providing continuity of experience and attitude.

Company officials had hardly been stamped out of a common mould. On the contrary, such as Hewby and Burdon were later to take drastically different lines in native administration. But their experience with Moslem-ruled states lying on the northern fringes of the Company's trading sphere had given them all a high opinion of Fulani administrative talent. They saw clearly enough the glaring contrast between the politically primitive southern groups and the better-organized and therefore more dangerous Moslem units. While it made good commercial sense to protect the former from the latter, the hard-bitten Europeans who ran Company posts along the Niger–Benue aimed at friendly relations with Moslem chiefs and could not help feeling respect for their power. Not all the Company's military expeditions had met with easy success. The handful of Europeans who maintained themselves in the midst of African societies came to realize how little could be accomplished in the way of change. Shortly before the Protectorate began, Sir George Goldie, head of the Niger Company, spoke in commonsense terms of the advisability, indeed the necessity, of avoiding impulsive innovation.[1] The familiar shortcomings of their own rulers would be easier for Africans to bear than well-meaning but ignorant action by outsiders. Moreover, such action could be self-defeating in provoking African resentment and perhaps resistance. To the heavy if negative factor of London's parsimony we may add the practicality and moderation of the case-hardened men who were a majority in the first administration. European influence there would surely be. But there was neither the capacity nor the inclination abruptly to alter the basis of indigenous society and government.

The nature of African polities in 1900 is thus a subject of transcending importance, especially by comparison with those in French areas where the new rulers were more inclined to make changes. Society in the average Northern Nigerian chiefdom had a wholeness which Lugard's officers could not miss. Many had already seen that making a change at one level involved the risk of wider effects. Disciplining, restricting, or

[1] Cf. Flint, op. cit., p. 258, and Stanhope White, *Dan Bana*, London, 1966, p. 96.

removing someone in authority without a compensating act designed to fill up the hole or fit a new part as recognizable and efficient as the old might weaken the whole structure at a time when the British were not in a position to make recompense from their own resources. African rulers and people understood and were used to one another. Society was authoritarian. Everyone knew his place and tended to accept it and function adequately within it. European officers continued to observe all through British times that peasants so completely accepted the authority of office-holders that they did not even expect to be spoken to on those rare occasions when there was direct contact between rulers and ruled.[1] Homogeneity throughout the whole area, however, was low, and the binding forces of weather, soil, and religion were stronger than those of language, race, or government. Within each separate or semi-autonomous chiefdom were many occupational, racial, and religious groupings. At one extreme were pagan communities living apart from near-by Moslem centres and resisting by force of arms any attempt to tax or control. At the other were slave villages whose relationship to chiefs was not unlike that of French serfs to feudal overlords in the Early Middle Ages. In between these were communities, including those in which chiefs had their own residences, of traders, artisans, farmers, and herdsmen forming the core of political units with which the British would now come to grips. As seen by these communities the legitimate and expected function of chiefs was taxation. Given the minimum scope of government then prevailing, this function was in practice virtually synonymous with political authority, and if carried out in the proper, traditional way was neither an unreasonable burden nor a source of protest.[2] In return—one speaks of the ideal situation rather than the invariable norm—chiefs and their courtiers and rural representatives gave protection from attacks by other chiefs and mediation and judgement in disputes between individuals and between communities. For those to whom Islam was a living force in everyday life, chiefs were important also as symbols and defenders of the Faith.[3] Many

---

[1] Carrow, 24 September 1965.
[2] Cf. C. K. Meek, *The Northern Tribes of Nigeria*, London, 1925, p. 257; Capt. C. W. J. Orr, *The Making of Northern Nigeria*, London, 1911, p. 157.
[3] East, 18 February 1966.

a sadder and wiser British officer was to find that the religious standing of chiefs occasionally had more substance, to chiefs and people alike, than did their traditional role in various forms of practical administration.

The aspect of chiefs' performance which inevitably caught the European's eye as much as any other was its oppressiveness. Rulers and people were *par excellence* 'the spoilers and the spoiled'.[1] After a decade of British presence in Bornu a farmer would still be stopped by a passing office-holder and relieved of his threepence. Not only would he be surprised if this did not happen but he would deliberately obstruct the course of European justice directed at bringing the abuse to an end. Government and exploitation were the same, and one only stored up future trouble for oneself if one tried to resist. Surrounded by increasing numbers of relatives and retainers and dealing with the general populace through layers of office-holders and representatives from the court outwards to the countryside, the strongest and most benevolent chief was hard put to it to keep extortion down. To the new rulers of the country the situation presented two faces: on the one hand, Fulani capabilities in the area of administration were considerable and were vital assets owing to the authoritarian character of society with its attendant apathy and ignorance on the part of the public; but corruption and oppression if unchecked could leave society demoralized and the economy stagnant. This was possible despite the obvious brakes on misgovernment: peasants could 'vote with their feet', decamping to the territory of neighbouring chiefs or to inaccessible areas; and the most ruthless tax collector could see that there was a limit to what peasants would bear and that moderation was in his own interests over the long haul.

The question whether there had been so much oppression and exploitation, by indigenous standards, over the latter part of the nineteenth century that it had contributed to a general decline in population, agricultural productivity, and trade is one which the literature does not satisfactorily answer.[2] Nor

---

[1] H. B. Herman-Hodge (pseud. 'Langa Langa'), *Up Against It In Nigeria*, London, 1922, p. 102.

[2] Among those who feel that there was such a decline are M. Hiskett, introduction to C. L. Temple, *Native Races and Their Rulers*, London, Cass, 1968, and O. Temple and C. L. Temple, *Notes on the Tribes, Provinces, Emirates and States of the Northern Provinces of Nigeria*, Lagos, 1922, p. 398. East (interview, 9 March 1966)

does anyone maintain that Fulani or Kanuri government in pre-British times was a brilliant success in providing positive, progressive administration as a basis for economic and social health; a basis for society, yes, familiar, workable, and working. Although documentation is grossly inadequate, it is probably true to say that on balance the early nineteenth-century up-heavals that established Fulani hegemony had increased and strengthened Islam as a social cement and had provided more political unity than the area had known before.[1] Even bearing in mind such traumas as the Kano civil war of the 1890s, the banditry of Buhari of Hadejia and Umaru and Ibrahim of Kontagora, and constant slave-raiding and internecine fighting throughout Sokoto's loose-jointed domains, the cultural–political fabric was meliorable. If it could stand improvement it was nonetheless too strong to be ignored or toppled by the small British cadre that confronted it. That same right of conquest that is officially recognized in the traditions of Islam every-where and that the Fulani had availed themselves of almost a century before was now Britain's to exercise in her own way and according to her means. The new government would be Anglo-African, an amalgam of local reality and imported inspiration and action.

Lugard's first task was to achieve a minimum of control over the Protectorate by placing administrative officers in the major political centres and by establishing a system of garrisons to support them in maintaining order. What the real military strength of the northern chiefdoms was and how much resist-ance would be encountered no one knew. From the Niger Company the new regime inherited the rudiments of control over riverain areas in the south which now became provinces under the names Borgu, Ilorin, Nupe, Kabba, Bassa, Nassa-rawa, and Muri. During the interregnum when the Company's hold had relaxed and Lugard's had not yet been established, elements in Nupe rose against the Company's puppet Chief and

---

agrees, while Carrow (12 February 1966) doubts that this can be documented one way or the other. See also M. G. Smith, 'Historical and Cultural Conditions of Political Corruption Among the Hausa', *Comparative Studies in Society and History*, vi, 2 (January 1964).

[1] Cf. Hiskett, loc. cit.; D. M. Last, *Sokoto in the Nineteenth Century With Special Reference to the Vizierate*, Ibadan, 1964.

drove him out. In 1901 Lugard reinstated this Chief and also marched against Kontagora, whose notorious slave-raiding master was captured and temporarily deprived of power. Yola's Chief, long hostile to British enterprises, was driven out and a successor appointed who would agree to the victors' terms. With relative ease and within less than two years Lugard had consolidated the south and placed British Residents in the towns of all its principal chiefs, those who were under British influence from the outset and those who now owed their positions to the new authority. In the summer of 1901 the headquarters of the Protectorate was moved northwards to Zungeru on the Kaduna River where it would remain until the end of the First World War. The northward push continued in 1902 to Zaria, Bauchi, and Bornu. Zaria's Chief had invited the British in with the request that they help him deal with Kontagora, but a year later, as a result of his intrigues with Kano, he was deposed and a successor appointed. Bauchi resisted as Yola had done and with the same result, a new Chief appointed by the British. It was the French who drove out the usurper, Rabeh, from Bornu, the British then occupying in their wake, installing the old Kanemi House and beginning the long work of restoring order in the country's biggest province after decades of war and anarchy. As before, Residents and garrisons were placed in each capital.

Of the major states this left only Kano and Sokoto. By the spring of 1903 both had been assaulted and their chiefs replaced, Lugard taking special care with Sokoto in view of its importance as the religious and political headplace of all the Protectorate's units except Bornu. The military phase of coming to grips was now past, although there would be an aftermath. In 1906 a rising took place near Sokoto, the net effect of which was to prove the loyalty of the major chiefs to the British and, once again, the unanswerable superiority of European technology. In the same year there were small expeditions in pagan areas near the Benue, and the last recalcitrant among the more important northern chiefdoms, Hadejia, was brought to heel. Control had been established bloodlessly over others, such as Gwandu, Katsina, and Argungu. Some chiefs, such as Abuja's, preferred to resist to the end. Others, such as Katsina's, were at first accepted by the victors, largely because scarce resources necessitated the rule 'innocent until proven guilty', but were later found unreliable and were replaced.

The first stage, covering the Protectorate with a network of incipient political headquarters backed by garrisons, was an obvious and necessary one if the British were to go beyond a mere roping off of a sphere of influence and were to begin affecting African government in a positive way.[1] There can be no serious suggestion that the British were present by any right but that of conquest. The moral quality of their rule, and its practical effects, would now be demonstrated and would be judged according to the standards of the onlooker. The great achievement of Lugard, whose high commissionership ended in 1906, was precisely the directing of this vital foundation work without which nothing of lasting importance could be done. In the building of Anglo-African government in Northern Nigeria the first head of the administration should be credited with two accomplishments above all others: conceiving the ground plans and co-ordinating the work of his subordinates in carrying these forward; and persuading London to help rather than interfere. The latter activity necessarily kept him away from Nigeria for long periods. These absences, together with the factor of primitive communications, would give individual officers in outlying posts the opportunity and habit of relying to a remarkable extent on their own initiative.

Once the provincial structure was built there began, almost imperceptibly at first and with great variety from post to post, the processes of accommodation whereby Residents and chiefs came to work in harness. From the outset and continuing throughout the whole of the British period there was a rhythm between tradition and innovation, between Africa and Europe,

---

[1] This view is disputed by D. J. M. Muffett in his book *Concerning Brave Captains*, London, 1964. One agrees with Hastings (A. C. G. Hastings, *Nigerian Days*, London, 1925), who says in another context that, generally speaking, 'Every action of ours was watched . . . and delay would have been disastrous' (p. 35). It was impossible to take over hostile areas gently. Like the Fulani, Lugard came with the sword, and the regime must be judged on its whole performance through to 1960. The campaigns of 1900–3 were relatively humane and bloodless. Speed was a good thing in seeing to this, as delay would have been productive of more pain for the Africans in the long run. It is doubtful that the Sultan would have treated with the British in any case. Until Residents and garrisons were put in places like Sokoto, nothing could be done. Once Britain had decided to invade and take over the country there was no practical alternative to the course taken by Lugard.

D

between a tendency to relapse to the familiar and a sometimes wavering insistence on going forward to the untried. Which tendency prevailed in which situations depended on each separate combination of circumstances: was the African Chief strong, efficient, forward-looking, or was he the prisoner of a slave bureaucracy or a helpless figurehead in a dissolute claque of relatives and hangers-on? Was the British Resident a man of energy, imagination, sympathy, and skill, or a time-serving office-holder preoccupied with rules and reports and the presumed wishes of higher authority? Was the state rich and comparatively homogeneous like Kano or poor and polyglot like Yauri? No two units were alike. They all shared in the ceaseless rhythm of sameness and change. Political officers would go on bemoaning the implacable lethargy of Africa to the day of independence; but their predecessors of Lugard's time would have been astonished at the spectacle of Northern Nigeria's altered face by the 1950s.

In the Moslem-ruled states of the North—the British early began to speak of them as emirates—the chiefs, judges, land-owners, and rural tax collectors were well enough organized and entrenched so that Residents would necessarily bend their first efforts to learning how things worked and gradually to supervising and exerting minimum discipline rather than taking a fully active part themselves. Bornu under Hewby, Thomson, McClintock, and Benton got more European direction at first because its native dynasty had been shattered in the last years of the nineteenth century and administration had to be rebuilt almost *ab ovo*. Some of the minor emirates, such as Gumel, had always been weak and haphazard in organization by comparison with mighty neighbours such as Kano, and they too would therefore receive more British pushing. The force of this would depend on how often an officer could visit them—an administrator in residence was at first impossible in most cases—and what kind of men the administrators were. Elsewhere, particularly south of the Benue, strong central administration was unknown. There was no powerful authority through whom the British could operate. Even such minimum functions as assessments, tax collecting, and protecting lines of communication from slavers and brigands demanded the creation of new instruments that were bound to seem strange and artificial to the local people. As in Southern Nigeria, systems of client chiefs, or entrepreneurs at least, grew up. Bassa and Muri drew on Nupe and Nassarawa for a kind of warrant officer caste. British-trained clerks from the Gold Coast, Sierra Leone, and Lagos were stationed in government offices and, *faute de mieux*, often found themselves exercising more responsibility than either the British or the natives liked. Until the power vacuum could be filled by increased British and more trained locals, pagan areas would be troubled with foreigners whose skills were needed but whose predictable human tendency to exploit was seen as a heavy price to pay for bringing order.

Lugard made the point as strongly as he could that all chiefs, even the Sultan of Sokoto, were henceforth agents of the Government at Zungeru and that the authority of the local Resident was above theirs. Legally this was vassalage and not a treaty relationship such as the one that linked the Hadhrami sultans to the Government of Aden. Like Fulani rule before it, British authority came from conquest and was absolute. 'But yet for all this,' read the proclamations of appointment given to chiefs, 'it is not the intention of the Governor to strip you of all authority, but on the contrary he wishes to rule together with you, to strengthen your authority and that of the law of the land and to perpetuate the customs of the people in so far as this does not stand in the way of what is just, and in that of good government; and [in so far as] it tends to humanity, that is to say the duty of one man to another.'[1] Taxation, appointment of all officials, war, and control of land were reserved to the Government, not to chiefs, and in return there would be protection and no interference with religion except when it conflicted with good government or humanity.[2]

This sounds theoretical and legalistic enough and indeed the reality of administration is not conveyed by it to any great extent. The most important functions of early Residents and their

---

[1] Lugard's title had been High Commissioner while his two successors were styled Governor, as he himself was on returning in 1912. The proclamation quoted here is in the office of the Northern Division, Kano Province (Hadejia), and is dated 3 December 1907.

[2] Paying tax or tribute was of course a traditional acknowledgement of suzerainty on the part of the African and was therefore not considered exceptionable. The British view of tax rates was that they should be high enough to allow development but not so high as to be onerous.

staffs were assessment, pacification of outlying areas that were only nominally under emirate jurisdiction, and the regularizing of finance.

Assessment meant much more than a census. Before anything of practical effect could be done, whether on indigenous or European lines, the British had to have not only the basic demographic, economic, and linguistic facts in each area but a down-to-earth grasp of how society held together, what the values and attitudes of various groups were, and therefore what channels of authority existed and how the flow of power was managed. Temple aimed at nothing less than '. . . a complete knowledge of the daily life of the individual native'.[1] Whether or not one had an anthropological bent, the day was full of learning, gathering facts, sorting out apparent contradictions, and discovering in the course of hard knocks what could and could not be done and at what cost. Headquarters pounded the Residents with requests for information and advice on possible courses of action, and more than one officer hedged his reply with the admission that he just did not know.[2] What were the emirs' sources of income? How were taxes gathered? How was the money spent? What were the various systems of land tenure and in particular what were the peasants' rights in regard to the cultivating of unused tracts? Were the Fulani rulers so corrupt that they should be removed? After taking the Government's share of taxes, fixed in 1904 at one-quarter, should the British interfere with the Emir in the expenditure of his share? Should the British impose more geographical regularization in place of the present arabesque individualism in the organization of fiefs and tax collection? What kind of education should be provided in government schools?[3] Should pagans be ruled separately from Moslems? Was the state of security in the countryside such that political officers needed

[1] The Temples, op. cit., preface.

[2] See *Political Conference Agenda*, 1909. This document is a compilation of correspondence and minutes of meetings between the Residents and officers at Headquarters beginning in Lugard's High Commissionership and extending through the Governorship of Girouard. Pages are numbered separately for each section. Attention is called to the section on Tribute, remarks of Ruxton, p. 1. I am grateful to Dame Margery Perham for allowing me to consult Lugard's personal copy.

[3] By 1908 there were schools at Lokoja, Kontagora, Sokoto, Katsina, Kano, and Bauchi.

military escorts? What kinds of punishments should be permitted for what crimes?

Finance was central to everything. Although subventions from London increased in the first few years, it was clear that the Protectorate's development would be geared in the long run to its own wealth. Moreover, the curbing of native abuses and the starting of administrative improvements would both be tied to financial control. Zungeru's hand was strengthened in 1903 by the imposing of caravan tolls and thereafter by taking fixed percentages of chiefs' taxes and gradually exercising more supervision over their own shares. The overall evolution of increased Europeanizing was in part the result of planning by headquarters and by individual Residents. More profoundly it was a function of the mere presence of the British, their acceptance by the chiefs (albeit sometimes grudgingly), and the contrast between strong, insistent European standards and native weakness. The initial step of the occupation having been taken, the logic of gradually increasing innovation was irresistible, and the rest was largely momentum.

So too with pacifying. In 1906 Hastings was sent by Howard, the Resident Bauchi, to take over Gombe Emirate in the eastern part of the Province.[1] Finding certain pagan communities just as determined to resist the British as they had the Fulani, he subdued them by military action. Lugard's successor, who heard about it afterwards, disapproved strongly. But the men on the spot knew that the alternative, giving in to defiance, would have meant a loss of British prestige in the eyes of the local Emir, not to mention forfeiting revenue and putting up with continued outlawry. Four years later one of Hastings's successors, Herman-Hodge, was engaged on the same sort of work.[2] There were never enough administrators. Supervision was never continuous enough. The same tasks of jacking up and putting right would be repeated over and over with a regularity that could not fail to breed a certain scepticism in the British as to the likelihood of lessons being learned and discipline accepted once and for all.

To the south in Bassa, where the British had to work without benefit of strong political institutions, pacification was still more important. Arriving there in 1911, Woodhouse found

---

[1] Hastings, op. cit., pp. 40 ff. and 77.   [2] Herman-Hodge, op. cit., pp. 43–4.

villagers still resisting assessment and taxation. A government representative would be sent to the area from which no taxes had been received and would demand a pledge of loyalty and immediate payment. If there was resistance the place would be attacked forthwith by government troops from the nearest garrison. A typical engagement described by Woodhouse resulted in the deaths of forty villagers and the razing of their village.[1] Vast areas with weak and alien headmen made guerrilla activity natural. Garrisons were few and widely scattered. Yet it soon became clear to outlaw communities that resistance was not worth while. Their raids on each other also became more risky, with the British determined to stop them. Once the cycle of raid and counter-raid had been broken by government troops or police, communities were left with the habit of violence but without the specific provocations of former times. Isolated outbreaks continued. But by the second decade of British presence tribal fighting had been drastically reduced and most communities throughout the North were paying their taxes without protest.

In some places the Protectorate made very little real difference at first. Larymore and the Emir of Hadejia met each other in 1904 much as two brother potentates would do.[2] As he crossed the river by Hadejia town the Englishman saw ranged on the other side a spectacle of silent, dignified power, the Emir and all his retinue including hundreds of armed cavalry drawn up to receive the visitor. A message had been sent ahead to pull down the town gates, and this had been done. Greetings were exchanged. The Emir accompanied the Englishman seven miles out on his way to Kano. Larymore asked that the mallams pray to Allah for his safe journey. Europe then disappeared over the horizon and Hadejia relapsed again to virtually complete independence. In Borgu it was much the same, a tour of inspection rather than the hand of government reaching out to grip local society.[3] As late as 1921 Lethem could write that

---

[1] Diaries of C. A. Woodhouse, C.R.P., entry of 17 November 1911. The job of finding and recognizing local sarkis, as conducted by early Residents at Zaria, was described over thirty years later to an A.D.O. on tour in the Southern Districts of Zaria Emirate and was well remembered by old men in the area (diaries of L. C. Giles, 2nd Tour, 1935, at Kagarko).

[2] Mrs. C. Larymore, *A Resident's Wife in Nigeria*, London, 1908, pp. 99 ff.

[3] Ibid., pp. 151 ff.

Dikwa had been up to that time administered by its Shehu 'on purely native lines, unchecked and unrevised', with annual visits by an officer from Maiduguri.[1] In some areas with permanent European staffs in residence there was a tendency to let the local Fulani manage things, perhaps aided by the clerks. 'My messengers duly assessed and collected the tax', observed Hopkinson in Biu.[2] Tomlinson, on tour through Sokoto Province in 1907, remarked blandly, '. . . in a country so vast as this we do not pretend to do much in the nature of direct government but, whenever we can, we employ native administration'.[3] In this process some officers knew that they were in the hands of their N.C.O.s. 'One can't get anything except through these damn messengers.'[4]

Yet there was always the other side of the coin. Change, if subtle, was noticeable everywhere. No officer lived at Hadejia until 1917, but visitors from Katagum and Kano made their influence felt. An Assistant Resident, Maynard, chose the new Emir in 1909, a boy of nineteen who was to rule until the mid-1920s.[5] 'Everything I have told him has been carried out with the utmost promptitude', wrote Morgan Owen a few years later.[6] To which Brice-Smith, touring from Baban Mutum, added candidly, 'During the absence of the Political Officer [the young Chief] is rarely visible, but he displays great energy and zeal when visited.'[7] The comments of officers over the years showed their appreciation of limiting factors but also the determination of some of them to overcome these in time. Fremantle thought the Emir 'little more than a child' and felt that touring officers must do more to win his confidence.[8] Hastings considered him fundamentally lacking in qualities necessary to leadership and held out less hope than the others.[9] Palmer

[1] Annual Report, Dikwa, 1921, p. 2. Lethem Papers, C.R.P. Dikwa was of course under German administration until the First World War.

[2] Quoted with raised eyebrows by Herman-Hodge, op. cit., p. 127; see also T. F. Carlyle, writing to Lethem from Yola, 4 September 1921, about the 1921–2 Estimates for Yola having been done by the Chief Clerk there. Lethem Papers, C.R.P. This referred to the provincial section of the Government Estimates.

[3] To his parents, 15 September 1907, C.R.P.

[4] Capt. J. H. de H. Smyth to Lethem, Bornu, 3 July 1917, C.R.P.

[5] Secret File on Emirs, Hadejia, 3 December 1907 ff. (Northern Division Office, Hadejia, Kano Province.)

[6] Confidential Reports on Emirs (book), Hadejia Office, entry of June 1912.

[7] Ibid., November 1915.

[8] Ibid., March 1910.   [9] Ibid., June 1910.

tended to agree, noting that the boy's weakness made him so
much the sport of factions that responsibility probably could
never 'be fastened on him'.[1] It was not the Emir alone who held
up progress. 'Unfortunately there is a lack of free and good men
in Hadejia, or else a strong executive council could be formed
to assist the Emir.'[2] When the post finally got a resident officer,
and an unusually vigorous one at that, the cycle of passivity
and corruption was cut into more effectively. Hale Middleton
found the Emir 'receptive to progressive ideas . . . in court he
displays a sense of justice quite remarkable in a native'.[3]
Hadejia never became a model emirate; but by the late 1920s
the drifting days of minimum British interference seemed
remote indeed.

In Bornu, Residents worked on the Shehu himself and on his
central administration, while touring officers hacked away at
making government better in the countryside. A District Head,
Bello, had that maddening combination that was to be the
despair of forward-looking officers throughout the North—
great ability plus an equally great resourcefulness in milking
the peasants.[4] The District Head told the Resident that town
X should pay 300 saas of grain to the Government, meanwhile
instructing his own subordinates to collect 700. If he removed
the man, Herman-Hodge knew that he could not easily find
an adequate replacement. At least fifteen subordinates would
also have to be disciplined if the abuses were to be stopped, and
as always no peasant could be induced to give testimony. Yet
something had to be done. There was famine and the peasants
were protecting themselves by hiding their grain, while near-by
districts starved. Allowing Bello to continue unchecked would
only support the Shehu's fatalistic view that the district could
not survive without him. Sacking him outright would weaken
the administration without correcting the trouble, for the new
District Head would doubtless behave similarly. Herman-
Hodge's action illustrates the working compromise that was
being put into effect all over the North, a choosing of middle
ground between passive acceptance of corruption and ruthless,

---

[1] Confidential Reports on Emirs (book), Hadejia Office, entry of September
1910.   [2] Liddard, ibid., November 1911.
[3] Ibid., December 1917, and Secret File on Emirs, 31 December 1918.
[4] Herman-Hodge, op. cit., pp. 130 ff.

destructive discipline. Bello was temporarily assigned to duties in the provincial capital and his salary was quietly indented to make up the lost revenue without bringing him to an overly public disgrace. His place in the district was taken for the time being by another. When he later returned it was with a different cadre of assistants. No British officer was so naïve as to think that corruption had been stamped out completely, but action of this kind, repeated again and again, would have its effect. Meanwhile a new generation of office-holders was growing up.

How African government worked in major emirates like Kano and Katsina and what the British could do about it was a subject much discussed among the Residents, especially in the early years when their weakness made more for studying than acting. Palmer, when still in his twenties, was sent to Katsina where he was for some time 'the sole pebble on the beach' and therefore left to his own devices.[1] One emir had been deposed just before Palmer's arrival and he himself saw to the replacing of another in 1906, to the disgruntlement of the Governor.[2] 'The people care far more how they are ruled than who rules them', he wrote to his superior, Cargill, in Kano.[3] Legitimacy was a false issue. The British could and should put in any chief they chose. The trouble in both Katsina and Kano, however, was the power of the household slaves, who outmanœuvred rural representatives and courtiers and had the servants of the British in their pay. 'Nothing would be gained by changing the Emir [again]—but I do think a more direct administration and the destruction of the [household slaves] should be carried out at all costs.'[4] In seeing to this Palmer allied himself with the Emir, the courtiers, and the country chiefs. Slave corruption was of course followed by that of the new native administration. But this was subjected from the first to the continuing challenge and correcting of Palmer, who worked with and through African officials only because

[1] Stanhope White found this remark on Palmer by Temple in the files of Kano Provincial Office and quoted it to me in his letter of 17 August 1966.

[2] See Sir Richmond Palmer, 'Some Observations on Capt. Rattray's Papers', *Journal of the African Society*, xxxiii (January 1934).

[3] 14 March 1907, K.

[4] Confidential Notes on Indirect Rule, 12 August 1908 ff., various officers, K. Included in the same file is some earlier correspondence. This quotation is from Palmer in Katsina to Festing in Kano, 2 September 1907.

there was no alternative. The aim was strong, efficient, and honest government. Until the Africans could achieve this alone the British should interfere wherever and whenever necessary.

Festing, Cargill's successor at Kano, battled against corruption by constantly changing the Emir's underlings as well as the interpreters and his own servants.[1] But he felt that part of the blame was on the British for changing officers frequently and not impressing the Emir's government with British determination or the peasants with the benefits of the new order. Cargill agreed that British weakness and the incomprehensibility of European ways were at the bottom of the difficulty, along with African corruption and general laxity. Particularly disturbing to the Emir was Cargill's action in giving direct supervision to rural representatives, not to mention reports he had heard of the killing of the Emir of Hadejia in the British punitive expedition of 1906 and the deposing of the Emir of Katsina in the same year.

I have never been able to effect reforms after consultation with and with the concurrence of the Emir . . . because he has invariably adopted an attitude of *non possumus* towards all proposals, although always intimating his willingness to accept a direct order . . . it is this frame of mind which Major Festing describes as passive resistance . . . personally I am afraid I have got into the habit of giving him direct orders . . . and it is likely that this has tended to upset his sense of the dignity due to his position.[2]

Deposition Cargill rejected, even though the Emir's well-known drunkenness had made him unpopular with his own people, for such action would damage the office as well as the incumbent. All possible successors interviewed by Cargill were thought to be worse. Smashing the slave power and depriving the Emir of his evil companions at court was therefore the only sensible course; that and educating the young.

Such education was seen as the key to every hope of improvement at Yola, where Barclay struggled with an equally obstructive and reactionary Emir.[3] Extortion by tax collectors was such that Barclay's soldiers and office staff were interfering directly,

[1] Hand-written notes, 'Kano Report No. 35', 29 December 1907, ibid.
[2] Pencilled draft of a note to append to Festing's Report, written by Cargill some time in 1907, at Kano, ibid.
[3] To Secretary, Zungeru, 12 August 1908, ibid.

giving the Emir the same feeling of insecurity felt by his fellow chief in Kano. One result was an attempt by the Emir to keep the British from influencing his sons. This they were doing, however, and the boys seemed promising. At the request of the Colonial Office Barclay wrote a note on the situation at Yola and on alternatives facing the Protectorate Government in dealing with chiefs. This was sent around to other Residents and they commented from their own experience. Barclay saw the uprooting of the indigenous political system as an impossibility and the arbitrary sacking of emirs as 'both unfair and impolitic'.[1] Successors would have to be drawn from the same ruling class and would be no improvement. The British must hang on, applying patience, discipline, and encouragement in the hope that society could be slowly improved. They would not be loved or even understood at first, but time would bring change for the better.

Festing took a generally less sanguine view, judging the Fulani rulers to be hopelessly effete. The only chance was to cut young Fulani off from their home environment. Tutorials by British officers, recommended by Barclay, would be pointless in Kano. 'I have so great a dislike for these erotic and feeble-minded youths that I feel I could do them no good.'[2] Palmer, giving voice again from Katsina, was sure that the emirs all expected the British to leave and were meanwhile only pretending to co-operate. They underrated the intelligence of the Europeans and overrated their power. A 'man-to-man' system whereby the British acted only through the Fulani meant 'our political extermination'.

Whether we wish to be so or not we are the rulers. We must be either above or below the rank and file . . . the Protectorate has its laws and ordinances, and our functions have long been far in excess of mere Residential Advisers . . . a native can no more understand the idea of joint rule by Emirs and Residents than he can understand the doctrine of the Trinity; and where the Resident does exercise a fairly strong influence, he is bound to be recognized as a big [man], if not . . . bigger . . . than the Emir.[3]

Hewby in Bornu wanted a middle course between the extreme man-to-man policy, which left the British in advisory positions

[1] To Secretary, Zungeru, 12 August 1908, ibid.
[2] Ibid., 9 December 1908.   [3] Ibid., 9 November 1908.

only, and one which so exalted the European that an important chief could be made to grovel to a telegraph linesman, something he had seen in Nafada not long before.[1] Like Cargill, Hewby had been in the Niger Company and he was a thoroughgoing empiricist. British behaviour towards the native should depend on the degree of control obtaining in given areas and the bearing of the people towards the Europeans. If the populace was content and African rule was efficient and just, the Europeans could relax. If not, intervention was called for.

It was clear to the Colonial Office that Zungeru, though it might give instructions to Residents as it was undeniably entitled to do, was most often in the position of co-ordinator and asker for information and advice. Lugard, though inclined to concentrate authority in his own hands, proceeded in an experimental way and had the good sense not to make it impossible for his provincial subordinates to react quickly to local happenings. The alternative, compelling Residents to check with headquarters before taking action, would have meant administrative paralysis. Relations between headquarters and the Residents in early years thus evolved naturally, and the burgeoning files of directives, rules, and regulations emanating from Zungeru and later Kaduna are not entirely revealing as to what actually took place.[2]

Lugard put up with the independence of Residents. His successors, Girouard, Governor from 1906 to 1909, and Bell, Governor from then until Lugard's return in 1912, were in an even weaker position to do anything about it.[3] If Lugard knew less about the country than did the Niger Company men among the Residents, at least he was the first Head of the Government and had himself been in Nigeria before, not to mention his achievements and reputation elsewhere. His prestige with his own and later Residents was incomparable. Girouard, a railway engineer brought to the country primarily for that reason, wisely accepted the primacy of the Residents in their own areas. He was heavily engaged in the building of the new railway and

[1] To Secretary, Zungeru, undated note written by Hewby as he was leaving Kano in 1908 to take over Bornu.

[2] Cf. Hastings's remarks about '. . . things not mentioned in the written word', (op. cit., p. 18).

[3] See Mary Bull, 'Indirect Rule in Northern Nigeria, 1906–1911', *Essays in Imperial Government*, K. Robinson and F. Madden (eds.), Oxford, 1963, p. 84.

as a newcomer was at something of a disadvantage, being faced by a phalanx of experienced, entrenched men on whom he had to rely for the maintenance of order throughout the country and for his own education as to its society and government. So too with Bell, described by a contemporary as being 'tied to a tiger' in Northern Nigeria, and well known elsewhere as not the sort of governor who tries to overawe his subordinates.[1] By 1913 Lugard, again in charge of the Northern administration and the rest of Nigeria as well, was writing gloomily that the Residents were carrying all before them and 'the Governor is left out'.[2]

One reason for diversity and individuality in the actions of Residents was that conditions varied so much from place to place that an overall policy would have been exceedingly hard to devise, much less carry out. On the matter of salaries for chiefs, Girouard admitted that Residents were already working out their respective procedures and that this was probably best.[3] He kicked back at them most often on minor or abstract points, lecturing Palmer, for example, on Moslem Law, but not interfering with that officer's own interpretations in Katsina.[4] Ruxton in Muri was no zealot on local discretion as such; indeed, he deplored the practice of leaving senior officers so long in Benue provinces that everything tended to stagnate.[5] Yet he found policy directives from headquarters so vague and general that he produced his own instructions for the guidance of juniors.[6] Young Woodhouse, newly arrived from Oxford in 1908, found Lugard's Political Memoranda 'rather interesting in parts' but hardly pertinent to what he was doing.[7] At Zaria in 1905 Orr and Fremantle discussed 'to what extent systems [of the various officers] should or could dovetail into each other',

---

[1] Cf. Perham, op. cit., II, p. 474, quoting Morel; Lugard, ibid., p. 477, writing to his wife, spoke of 'poor Bell' in this context; see also the comments of an officer who had served under Bell in Uganda: Sir G. Archer, *Personal and Historical Memoirs of an East African Administrator*, Edinburgh, 1963, p. 44.

[2] Perham, op. cit., II, p. 479.

[3] *Political Conference Agenda*, 1909, Salaries for Chiefs, p. 5.

[4] Ibid., Taxation, p. 11.

[5] Ibid., Amalgamation of Provinces, pp. 8 ff.

[6] 'Instructions for the Guidance of Newly Joined Officers', copied in the Muri Provincial Office in 1909 by H. M. Brice-Smith, C.R.P.

[7] Diaries, 2 May 1908, C.R.P. Reading the Memoranda was obviously a chore; he '. . . stuck nobly at it until 2 o'clock', ibid.

as though they were talking of the constitutions of separate and sovereign entities.[1] When Byng-Hall completely reversed Sciortino's policy in Bassa he not only confused his subordinates but got from Girouard, who called in for lunch, 'a freer hand than he had ever dreamt of'.[2]

The classic case, because it established so important a precedent, was the devising of a native treasury system in Katsina. The Emir, who had been appointed by Palmer, suggested to the young officer that a division be made between tax proceeds kept by himself and what was wanted by the Government, and that the British officer help the Emir in budgeting the local portion.[3] Wallace, the Acting Governor, said that Girouard's formal approval would be needed, but he would not interfere if Palmer and the Emir wished to arrange it. Therefore, wrote Palmer later, 'I just did it.'[4] The much copied arrangements became, more than any other factor, the basis of finance in the Native Authority system throughout the North.

The game of telling headquarters what the Residents knew it wanted to hear was almost inevitable in a large country with poor communications. More often than not even Lugard had refrained from giving direct orders and had concentrated on asking questions. In so open-ended a situation the Residents would have been other than human had they not gone ahead on their own, leaving Zungeru in the dark, and later framing reports in such a way as to seem to conform to the stratispheric generalizations that passed for policy.[5] In Benue, where chieftancy was not strong, the pretence of ruling through Africans had to be maintained. 'The Resident was a conscientious and memo-respecting officer, who was careful, when making indents . . . to preface the application with the pious formula:

---

[1] A. F. Fremantle (ed.), *Two African Journals and Other Papers of the Late John Morton Fremantle, C.M.G., M.B.E.*, printed for private circulation, London, 1938, p. 38.

[2] Woodhouse to his sister, from Itobe, 19 April 1909, Letters of C. A. Woodhouse, C.R.P.

[3] Sir Richmond Palmer, 17 December 1949, P.

[4] To Lethem, from the Gambia, November 1932. Lethem Papers, C.R.P.

[5] Under pressure in the Cameron years (see ch. 3 below) Lethem did some research on this in the Kaduna files and found that the early procedures of other offices were like his own in this regard. See his letter to G. S. Browne, 17 August 1933, Lethem Papers, C.R.P. Gowers did not even meet Lugard until 1906, the year of Lugard's departure (Sir William Gowers, 4 September 1950, P.).

"The Emir requests," which is very right and proper, for is it not an earnest of Indirect Rule?"[1]

It was not long before this sort of thing became commonplace. Whiteley wrote to a colleague about the Lieutenant Governor's reaction to something he had sent in during 1919: 'His Honour's comments on my Fika report were very funny . . . he . . . said it was the best Assessment Report he had seen from Bornu so far, which—remembering my eyewash and tongue in cheek method—will tickle you as much as it does me.'[2]

On other occasions officers opposed headquarters openly. Burdon stood up to Lugard on the question whether African office-holders should be allowed to go on receiving the special tribute attaching to their positions, and he won his point.[3] Later, when Wallace, the Acting Governor, ordered one of Burdon's officers to proceed from Sokoto to Argungu with a military escort, Burdon replied that no escort was better than a small one and himself promptly rode off with the junior officer, leaving the escort behind.[4]

It was not illogical that their own subordinates should maintain a similar independence *vis-à-vis* the Residents. If Kano was a long way from Zungeru, Katagum and Hadejia were distant enough from Kano to rule out close, continuous scrutiny of their affairs by the Resident. When a very junior officer from Katagum tentatively selected a successor to the Emir of Hadejia in 1909 the Resident Kano, Temple, replied that he preferred another candidate.[5] But three months later the officer in charge of Katagum, Fremantle, installed the candidate selected earlier and then informed Temple. Such insubordination may not have pleased Temple in practice, although officially he was on record as favouring the maximum latitude for people in out-stations.[6]

The comparatively high degree of discretion thus enjoyed by subordinates put a premium on personality and character as factors determining administrative posture and action. There was not and never has been a British colonial type. The style

[1] Herman-Hodge, op. cit., p. 157.
[2] To Lethem, from Maiduguri, 30 January 1919, Lethem Papers, C.R.P.
[3] *Political Conference Agenda*, 1909, Kurdin Sarauta, pp. 1–2.
[4] Burdon to Wallace, 14 November 1909, K.
[5] Secret File on Emirs of Hadejia, 6 February 1909 and 16 May 1909.
[6] See his Kano Report, 1909, paras. 30–2. Papers of H. M. Brice-Smith, C.R.P.

and effect of government are found rather in collections of attitudes and daily tasks. Some thought a good deal about promotion and would have been, indeed later were, just as happy in Whitehall. Others had more in common with cavaliers who joined Prince Rupert after the cause was lost. Some were really too reflective and sensitive to function well in situations where quick decision and rough justice were the alternatives to failure. And many had that indefinable mixture of horse-sense, energy, and patience that came to be considered the ideal attributes of the good bush D.O.[1]

In a goodly number of early officers one notices traces of that part of the Victorian psyche that seems especially dated in these times of muted idealism. Larymore and his wife were deeply moved at the sight of Clapperton's grave, as they thought of the fortitude and selflessness with which he faced his coming death.[2] Speaking to new recruits, Mrs. Larymore remarked, 'You must start with a firm determination to make the best of everything . . . your unselfishness must be untiring . . . do not lose heart . . . things will be better tomorrow. . . .'[3] Hearing of his brother's death in France, Tomlinson wrote, as who would today, of how splendid it was to die gloriously, 'with a smile on his face'.[4] Victorian too was a kind of subjective certainty about right and wrong which left little room for anthropological doubts based on a realization that perhaps Africans would see things differently. After being in the country only a few months Woodhouse was handing down judgements with confidence. 'They [the defendants whom he was trying] were both to blame and were put in prison for 14 days.'[5]

For the average officer his Englishness was accentuated precisely because he did find himself in strange surroundings, among people whom he could come to know but would never really understand. No matter how much he loved Africa and his work, no one was totally immune to loneliness, which could lead 'to undiscussed and ill-advised action[s]' of many kinds.[6]

---

[1] District Officer (D.O.) became an official rank after the Amalgamation of Nigeria in 1914. The old ranks had been Resident and Assistant Resident in various classes. The new ones were Resident, District Officer, and Assistant District Officer.

[2] Op. cit., pp. 97–8. [3] Ibid., p. 271.

[4] Letters of 1 June 1917 and 2 November 1917, C.R.P.

[5] Diaries, 17 August 1908, C.R.P.

[6] Burdon in Sokoto to Wallace in Zungeru, 14 November 1909, K.

Diaries are full of home thoughts and of countless small bringings of England to Africa. Gardens and food and sport were as English as they could be made to be. Every morning before sunrise Fremantle ran three times around the Katagum town wall in his Hertford colours.[1] Daniel and Woodhouse found unexpected pleasure in meeting other old Marlburians far from home. Books, newspapers, and above all letters, were eagerly awaited.[2]

There were officers who spoke mainly of Africa and who came to feel strangers in their own country when they went there on leave. Something in them responded more to the exotic than to the familiar, and a few tended to shun their own kind.[3] A few married African women and stayed on after their careers were over. But to most, Africa was to be appreciated, not joined. The gulf remained whether one was sympathetic or not, interested or not, deeply involved or rather removed, as some were who held staff positions. Ruxton saw the Benue Africans as children and favoured a relationship with them not unlike that between officers and men in the army. Palmer thought the Fulani ruling classes anything but childish: on the contrary, they were diabolically clever and they assumed that the British could be deceived without difficulty.[4] Tomlinson, who did not stay in Africa for a full career, seemed to have trouble taking the native seriously—'one gets attached to these absurd black people'—and in his early days saw Africans primarily as objects of paternalistic concern and duty.[5] At the back of nearly everyone's mind was the notion, however vaguely formed, that in the course of time it was the Africans who would change. This would happen painlessly and at the Africans' pace. But it was a question of leaders and followers rather than participants in cultural exchange. The logic of Britain's military and administrative position was such that it could hardly be otherwise.

[1] A. F. Fremantle, op. cit., p. 73.

[2] Cf. letters of F. de F. Daniel, 1912 and 1913, C.R.P. Woodhouse, on meeting the famous 'Pa' Benton for the first time, noted only that Benton had been at Corpus Christi College, Oxford, and of a subaltern encountered in Lokoja only that he, like Woodhouse himself, had been at Marlborough: letters of 2 May 1908 and 4 January 1912, C.R.P.

[3] A few early Bornu officers took mistresses from the Shuwa Arabs. See letters of 3 July 1917, 11 September 1919, and 3 February 1924, Lethem Papers, C.R.P.

[4] Palmer notes especially the Arab concept, 'muhaadana', or pretending to go along: Confidential Notes on Indirect Rule, letter from Katsina, 9 November 1908, K.　　　　　　　　　[5] To his parents, 22 August 1908, C.R.P.

E

In 1908 a junior officer told his family how he spent a typical day in Kabba.[1] His boy woke him at 6.00 with cocoa and in his pyjamas he walked for a time in the garden and near the station prison to see what work the prisoners were doing and how the new Government houses were getting on. Breakfast was at 7.30 and he strolled over to the office at 8.00. There, being in a one-man post, he was Justice of the Peace, superintendent of police, public works manager, postmaster, sheriff, medical officer, and overseer of whatever came up. He remanded a man for complicity in a murder (the Resident would hear the case presently), issued a summons in a civil case, lectured rebellious prisoners, inspected their food, and then mounted a formal inspection of the guard. On alternate days he looked down the rifle barrels to see if they were clean, and every Monday there was a thorough inspection of each soldier's kit. He heard the sergeant's report on the guards, prisoners, barracks, and on the safes, and then gave some medicine to a sick prisoner. Office hours were from 8.00 to 2.00. He read files, dealt with letters from provincial headquarters, heard a few complaints, and in between other things studied Hausa. Lunch was at 2.00, followed by rest and perhaps writing a letter or two. He read until 4.00, then took a walk and did a bit of shooting after tea. After a drink and a bath, dinner was at 7.30. He went straight to bed with a book and was asleep by 9.00.

Farther north and on bigger stations there would be polo and tennis and very soon there would be a club to visit in the evening. Most people spent a good deal of time on assessment and tax work, methods varying greatly from place to place. In Muri tax was collected in kind, there being as yet no available coin, and one officer used his gramophone to hurry the local people into bringing in their cloth and guinea corn.[2] He let it be known that unless collections were satisfactory the gramophone would be shut off between tea and dinner. Where railway construction was going on, recruitment of labour was the concern of everyone from the Resident down.[3] Officers stationed near mines or

---

[1] Woodhouse to his mother, 14 June 1908, C.R.P.

[2] Brice-Smith, 28 July 1966.

[3] This, for example, was Goldsmith's main concern at Bida. Carrow, 7 March 1966, suggests that 'recruitment' was a contemporary euphemism for forced labour. See the Edwardes Papers, C.R.P., especially Bauchi, 1914, 'Enlisted Labour for Railways'.

other major European enterprises dealt with labour problems and all the frictions that naturally arose between native authorities and the managers of alien firms. Every province had its special jobs that were shared out *ad hoc*. In Kano Daniel had to look after the estate of a European who died there, and later in Sokoto found himself doing anti-famine work and boundary marking.

For all but a small number of the more senior people the first benchmark of the system was discontinuity in postings. In 1905 Fremantle had three posts in as many months.[1] Edwardes arrived in Numan in 1913, stayed ten days, and was recalled to Bauchi, where he had just come from. He had accomplished nothing in Numan and had wasted thirty-two days on the road.[2] Disruptions caused by illness, home leaves, crises, and conflicting administrative demands would keep continuity an unresolved problem to the end.[3] The related problem of illness was also basically unsolvable. A wide range of physical adjustments had to be made before the European could function adequately in the tropics. Someone was always down with fever. Many were invalided home before their tours had expired. One of Yola's outstations lost two officers in less than a month during 1915, the first leaving to replace a sick colleague in Bauchi and the second coming down with typhoid. Doctors, far too few on the ground in any case, could do little about the persistent headaches that did so much to reduce administrative efficiency in early years.

A more dangerous enemy in the long run was paper. Lugard's passion for accountability in writing helped to defeat the vital aim of keeping officers in close touch with the people and drove some to either defiance or despair.[4] His more easy-going

[1] Fremantle, op. cit., p. 38. [2] Herman-Hodge, op. cit., p. 124.

[3] In the earliest days some Residents were left in the same posts for rather a long time, as Ruxton's complaint shows (*Political Conference Agenda*, 1909, Amalgamation of Provinces, pp. 8 ff.). But this varied, being more true of Benue than of Kano, for example. In the 1920s some senior Residents, such as Webster at Sokoto, stayed so long in their provinces that Sir Donald Cameron made a change on this point an essential of his plans for reform (see ch. 3 below). Junior officers were transferred too often all through the British period.

[4] Cf. Orr to Lugard, Report No. 17 on Zaria, February 1905; in private correspondence Sir William Gowers, Sir Richmond Palmer, and Sir George Tomlinson all stressed this point. In his letter of 26 November 1949, P., Gowers said that, much as they were all devoted to Lugard, the arrival of Sir Percy Girouard came as a relief, from the standpoint of bureaucratic demands.

contemporaries and successors alleviated the situation, but through the years bureaucratic demands rose steadily, giving the practical, down-to-earth officer a permanent distaste for the 'bumf' that blocked his view of the real Africa.

Yet progress was made. Africans and British would see it differently, but for both it meant a tightening of Europe's hold, an unrelenting pressure for change. Africans were no longer permitted to indulge in certain activities that had preoccupied them before 1900. Slave-raiding and fighting among emirates dried up. Lawlessness in the countryside took longer to deal with, but its days were numbered as well, and by the end of the First World War even the back roads were relatively safe for unarmed travellers. Despite the imposition of tolls, trade increased greatly. As Orr points out, the very attempts of caravans to escape payment had the effect of bringing once isolated communities into closer touch with the main centres of commerce and government.[1] No longer concerned about slave-raiders, peasants took up desirable land at greater distances from walled villages and granaries came to be built in the open.[2] The capital of Gwandu Emirate was moved to a site that would have been indefensible against armed attack from neighbouring Argungu but which was infinitely preferable on other counts, such as a better supply of water and fish and of millet for the horses.[3]

In the governmental realm change came gradually and to a remarkable extent spontaneously. Reflected in the process were both the stubborn traditionalism of Africa and a tendency on Britain's part not to force the pace but to put up with any condition of local government that did not violently offend her sense of humanity and efficiency. In retrospect it is the accommodation and adjustment of the two sides that stands out rather than a consistent response to some body of abstract principle. In Zaria, for example, the Emir Aliyu at first appealed to the British as a man of great personal charm and as a ruler of rare ability. His moral lapses and those of his family could therefore

[1] Op. cit., p. 148.

[2] Brice-Smith in his letter of 28 July 1966 comments on the amazement expressed by the party of Africans travelling with him north of Kano in 1913 because of the granaries they saw unattended and far from any village.

[3] For comments on this change and its local effects I am grateful to the Emir of Gwandu, the Waziri, and the Magajin Rafin, interviewed at Birnin Kebbi, 25 August 1965.

be suffered in silence. Orr took the Emir's eldest son, a notorious extortionist, on tour with him in 1909 and tried to influence the young man towards British ideas of justice and honesty.[1] His successors through to 1915 also tried, all of them realizing that the basic fault in emirate administration lay with the Emir himself, who, much as they admired his ability, always gave offices to 'weak characters whom he can easily control and exploit for his own ends'.[2] Through the years officers were less and less able to accept blatant nepotism and oppression. Gentle proddings and attempts at education all failed. Finally the Emir's extortionist son was sacked from his Native Authority post in 1916 and another, a drunkard, in 1917. The Emir's own downfall was delayed until 1920. In the earliest days of the occupation the British were so thin on the ground that they had eagerly sought out able chiefs and local officials and had given full encouragement to those like Aliyu who proved competent. Grier, Resident Zaria in 1906, formed quite a close friendship with the Emir, leaving Aliyu with the impression that in the eyes of the British he could do no wrong. As the railway advanced northwards through Zaria Province the Emir made himself highly useful in the recruitment of labour, and during the First World War he performed equally valuable services. Dr. Miller, the C.M.S. missionary who lived in Zaria, was close to the Emir, and some Residents fell into the habit of using him as a go-between with Aliyu rather than getting information on the Emir's activities at first hand.[3] In these circumstances the Emir came to see himself as both indispensable and privileged. He indulged freely in slaving, in forced labour on his own farms, and in extortion and maltreatment of subordinates, being accused eventually of other crimes as well, including the employment of paid murderers.[4]

What the Emir could not fully appreciate was that his habitual excesses were now taking place in a context of Anglo-African government markedly different from that in which he had come to power. The British were stronger and more experienced. The First World War, with its staff cuts, was over and

[1] Orr to Zungeru, 29 October 1909, K.; and see Fremantle, op. cit., pp. 81 ff.
[2] Resident Zaria to Lieutenant Governor, 30 November 1915, K.
[3] Arnett, Resident Zaria, to Goldsmith, Lieutenant Governor, 23 July 1920, K.
[4] Arnett, Acting Lieutenant Governor, to Byng-Hall, Resident, 10 November 1920 and reply, 11 November 1920, K.

more attention was being given to agricultural and other development, with correspondingly greater demands on local administrations. Following each dismissal of a Native Authority official there was an increase in the number of office-holders, both at court and in the countryside, who could see that it was the British and not the Emir who held ultimate power. Failing to see that he was increasingly surrounded by the dissatisfied and the hostile, the Emir became bolder and more arrogant, gradually placing himself in a position where his past services to the Government would no longer protect him from charges of wrongdoing. Once he realized that a full-scale investigation was under way and that his own African officials were giving evidence against him, Aliyu sought to have the Resident murdered, and he started rumours that his old friend Grier, then an important official in Kaduna, was coming back as Resident.[1] It was too late. Having offended the more pious among his own subjects by taking slave concubines as young as fourteen years of age and having convinced the British that his corruption now overshadowed his efficiency, the Emir was finished.[2]

The aftermath of the case emphasizes why the British were reluctant to move quickly in such matters and why a chief could be very unsatisfactory in other ways and yet survive if only he was an able administrator. Two years after the Emir had been summoned to Kaduna in disgrace the Resident Zaria was only just beginning to make progress in restoring the morale and competence of the local administration.[3] Although a large number of important people in Zaria had testified against Aliyu and had been relieved at his dismissal, one effect was to shatter the machinery of government. This was bound to happen

[1] Byng-Hall to Arnett, 25 October 1920 and 9 November 1920, K. The point of no return and of decision by Kaduna is difficult to identify. Palmer, in his letter of 1 November 1928 to Lethem, says that G. S. Browne was Aliyu's nemesis. This is plausible since Browne, Resident Zaria in 1906, was Secretary Northern Provinces, Kaduna, in 1920 and was no friend to a soft policy (see Lethem Papers, C.R.P.). Grier was Acting S.N.P. during part of 1920.

[2] In July, Arnett, then Resident Zaria, had written, 'Even though the Emir may have placed himself within reach of the law we do not regard a criminal prosecution as at all advisable . . . this . . . will depend . . . upon . . . political expediency' (28 July 1920 to Lieutenant Governor, K.). In short, the way in which the case developed convinced the British that it was no longer expedient to allow Aliyu to continue in office. The whole affair was managed in a most empirical way throughout, and no one mentioned policy. Cf. Arnett Papers, 1922, C.R.P.

[3] Sciortino, Handing-Over Notes, 9 June 1922, K.

in authoritarian regimes where so much depended on the example and initiative of the leading figure. The new Emir lacked confidence. His subordinates did not know what his style of government would be and how the new distribution of authority would be managed. The lesson of disruption had been learned by all, and in the core period of British rule now beginning every attempt would be made to discipline and influence but to avoid drastic surgery.

Meanwhile, throughout the North change was coming in more positive and less dramatic ways. Native Authorities (N.A.s) —the initials originally referred to the chiefs themselves and soon came to mean the whole machine of local administration— were developing into financial and judicial bodies more akin to European institutions and were moving away from traditional forms and activities.[1] We have seen that early Residents in Kano tried to break into the circle of misrule by doing away with the slave bureaucracy as Palmer did in Katsina. When Temple arrived as Resident Kano, however, he found the Emir and his fief-holding courtiers virtually powerless.[2] Everywhere in the countryside village headmen were also helpless and slave tax collectors and court hangers-on were still running the Emirate for their own benefit. The tax map of Kano showed an arabesque mosaic of confusion with no geographical organization by communities and districts and no uniformity of rates. Temple moved to alter the Emir's role from patriarchal figurehead to effective chief. In the place of individualistic chaos and corruption he tried to put a rational and consistent system based on community heads who were representative of the people. If tax payments, equitably assessed, could be made to local officials in the first instance, those who brought the money in could be held to account according to the known facts of personal wealth and land use. If fief-holders were made responsible for actual administration in areas traditionally assigned to them, a balance of central, intermediate, and local power might be arrived at.

[1] On the development of the N.A.s see A. H. M. Kirk-Greene, *The Principles of Native Administration in Nigeria*, London, 1965, p. 30, note 1; Lord Hailey, *An African Survey*, London, 1957, p. 453; there had been a Native Authority Ordinance in 1907 and another in 1910. Cameron in 1933 was to further rationalize the rules. Cf. Margery Perham, *Native Administration in Nigeria*, London, 1937, pp. 383 ff.

[2] Cf. Palmer, Acting Lieutenant Governor, to Wightwick, Acting Resident Kano, 27 June 1921, K. Carrow, 6 July 1966.

The British, as overseers, would then possess a series of levers by which to influence the operation of the whole machine.

Temple first deposed the slave waziri (chief official under the Emir) who had acted as messenger to various Residents and eventually as central co-ordinator of the slave monopoly in tax collections.[1] The Emir was urged to rely instead on groups of prominent men in the Emirate for general purposes as well as for specific matters, such as the administration of justice. The Resident did not deceive himself that this would prevent a new kind of corruption, but he had reason to believe that it would offer some hope of improvement. A Beit-el-mal, or native treasury, was started, the country having gradually abandoned cowrie shells for British coinage, and this, being a central fund, could be audited by the British.[2] Most important, the Emirate was divided up into fixed administrative units and sub-units, with officials from the bottom up having the function of representing the people and being responsible for taxation and public order in their areas. Ideally, officials at the lowest level, hamlets and villages, would be literally of the people. Those charged with management of districts would reside there rather than remain at court and leave their affairs to slaves. This would contribute to greater stability and security in communities and would lead to higher agricultural productivity.

Temple was able to report well on some district heads and not badly on others. Rent collectors, many of whom were slaves or ex-slaves, were made to live in their areas. They were still too numerous in Kano—around 1,000 in all—and their standard of honesty was low. What consoled Temple was that it had been possible to make a start, to affect the system without major disruption. Few experienced British officers were perfectionists in these matters. Any improvement was cause for joy. Encouraged by Temple's support, the Emir sacked two officials who had deliberately held back taxes in the hope of getting larger shares for themselves. This was an example to others who would trim their sails in the realization that traditional abuses would henceforth be subject to increasing challenge. As their power

---

[1] Kano Report, 1909, para. 45.
[2] The changeover was piecemeal, area by area. Cf. Hastings, op. cit., p. 29; Herman-Hodge, op. cit., p. 32; Temple's Kano Report, 1909, paras. 221 ff. 20,000 cowries equalled 10*s.* at the Kano Beit-el-mal in 1909.

grew, men like Temple would try to strike a balance between two extremes: if they interfered not at all the indigenous system would function undisturbed and there would be little or no improvement in society or government; if there was drastic interference, a virtual takeover by the British, conditions would improve but without a corresponding rise in the competence of native officials; society would have been supplied with a crutch, which, when removed, would leave it unable to advance on its own.

There was still a long way to go. By 1909 only some 3,000 square miles out of a total of 13,000 in the Emirate had been assessed. Slavery had been officially abolished, but everyone knew that it continued to flourish. There were still too few British officers, although the end of the First World War would swell their numbers and at last give Residents the junior staff they needed to bring outlying areas under administration and to man headquarter offices more adequately. N.A.s, undoubtedly more unchanged than changed, especially in outlook, nevertheless found themselves doing different things and doing familiar things in different ways. Young office-holders, many of them graduates of Mr. Vischer's school in Kano, could read and write Hausa in Roman characters instead of Arabic script, which was less suited to the kind of communication that government offices and commercial firms needed. In their attempts to reorganize Kano and the other emirates the British discovered what could be changed and what could not. If they could never stop corruption and inefficiency they could at least realign their context, spend the Emirate's wealth differently, punish and reward differently, and supervise a social order in which new generations would find conditions subtly altered from those their parents had known.

As the 1920s began, the ingredients of Anglo-African government were well established. No more questions would be raised as to whether or not the chiefs should be retained. For their part British officers were built into the system. The development of each province, division, and emirate would depend on working relationships between officers and chiefs and between their respective subordinates. Patterns of life would vary greatly over the face of the Region and through the passing years, but the characteristic themes would remain constant: a rhythm of tradition and change, governed in each case by its own particular balance of native and alien forces. As always in human affairs, the weight of precedent would be heavy and the pull of momentum strong. With the framework of administration firmly and empirically built and strengthened by two decades of experience and progress, it is not to be wondered at that London and Lagos, and even Kaduna, would have difficulty in remodelling the structure or abruptly altering the direction of movement. Like the Fulani–Hausa genre before it, Anglo-African government was racy of the soil. Therein lay its particular genius.

3
Policy

I N the literature of all governmental systems the word policy is common and the imprecision with which it is used invites confusion. Students of colonial government come across the word so often that they may be forgiven for feeling at times that it is almost a question of every man his own policy. The word may refer to a pious dictum having little or no connection with reality. It may be a rationalization after the fact, or a general statement made *ab initio* which either does or does not prove relevant later on. Policies sometimes cover a hard and fast body of rules, empirically arrived at or not, effective or not. There is sometimes more than one policy or more than one conception or interpretation of the same policy. This last has always been characteristic in the British colonial system with its multitude of autonomous units scattered across the earth and not linked until recently by especially efficient communications. Lack of central control from London and a wide variety of governmental forms within the whole imperial group made for pluralism and flexibility in the policy realm. This was the case within Nigeria as well and even within the regions into which the Protectorate was divided.

Here we are concerned with policy, or official intent, as one of the factors bearing on administrative situations. Generally speaking, it tended to be more substantial at the point when the administration was being planned and brought into being and at the other end of the British period, the years when her departure was known to be imminent, than in the intervening years. From the late 1890s until the end of the First World War Britain's policy of being present, keeping costs down, and maintaining order—there are those who would call these an absence of policy—was an important but by no means exclusive or overweening factor on an administrative horizon that included other weighty determinants as well. In the 1950s it was

Britain's policy to leave the country in a planned and orderly fashion with power being handed over to certain people in a certain way. No one would hold that the factor of intention was unimportant at this stage. In the interim, during the twenties, thirties, and forties, there was little money for financing large-scale innovation and the prospects were therefore not bright for any plan that looked too far beyond present reality. An administrative officer with imagination and drive—anyone from a Governor to the District Officer in charge of a division—could devise plans and take action. The most famous case, which will presently be examined, took place in the governorship of Sir Donald Cameron. For the most part such attempts were not too successful if they found themselves competing with precedent and the momentum of daily administrative action. This being so, it is necessary to focus ultimately on Residents and their subordinates in order to gauge accurately the nature and effectiveness of British rule. The work of the Provincial Administration is emphasized, however, not because London, Lagos, and Kaduna are thought to be unimportant but because Residents and District Officers were the cutting edge of government. Here we must ask what influence higher authority had on their work.

It has long been a commonplace that the nineteenth-century Colonial Office knew very little of Crown Colonies, that the general public knew still less, and that Parliamentary interest and knowledge were low enough to constitute a serious problem for that rare Secretary of State who was concerned with the colonies in a major way and who stayed in office long enough to do anything about them.[1] The expansionist ideas of Herbert and Lucas and other civil servants, especially as used by Chamberlain, were important in ultimately bringing Britain to Nigeria, even if they were not as much so as were the actions of French steeplechasers. Thereafter the Office acted as a governor on the engine of colonial administration 'and not the boiler'.[2] The C.O. was more important as a withholder of funds and co-operation, a reviewer and schoolmaster with regard to requests from the field, than as a creator and director.

[1] Cf. R. B. Pugh, 'The Colonial Office, 1801–1925', *The Cambridge History of the British Empire*, Cambridge, 1959; Sir Charles Jeffries, *The Colonial Office*, London, 1956, p. 43.   [2] Sir George Goldie, quoted in Flint, op. cit., p. 275.

Understanding this full well, an astute Governor like Girouard was diplomatic enough to make it appear to London that he considered himself its agent, meanwhile going his own way.[1] Lugard wanted not only a reasonably free hand locally but at the very least a tacit acceptance by London that 'the local Governors are responsible, and . . . Downing Street does not govern directly'.[2] Whether or not the Office realized or admitted the extent of its own passivity relative to Lagos, governors were not in fact subjected to close, continuous supervision.[3] What London could and did do was appoint governors, recruit subordinate staff, and extend or withhold rewards— promotions, knighthoods—and the approval or disapproval of schemes submitted to it. Until the implementation of the Colonial Development and Welfare Act in 1945 virtually all else was left to the men on the spot.

If, therefore, governors could in effect frame their own policies it might have been expected that they would have little difficulty commanding the obedience of subordinates in carrying these into effect. Before the era of nationalism colonial governments were autocracies, governors had sweeping powers, and, legally, subordinates could not resist or oppose them. In practice the position was complicated. The financial limitation was of the first importance, leaving even the most forceful and popular governor in no position to do anything very costly. His financial authority could be a negative factor, as London's could, for he did hold the purse strings of the Protectorate. The N.A. Treasury system in the North, however, left considerable discretion with officers in charge of divisions and provinces. So too with the technical departments. As head of the central organization in Lagos, the Governor might have been expected to wield great influence over such competitors of the Provincial Administration as Education, Agricultural, and Public Works officers. In fact there would be a running fight throughout the inter-war years over the question whether such officers would follow the direction of their own depart-

[1] See Bull, op. cit., p. 61, note 2.

[2] Perham, *Lugard*, ii, p. 267.

[3] Northern Nigeria was a separate dependency from 1900 to 1914, being governed from 1912 to 1914 by the same officer who ran the rest of Nigeria. From 1914 onwards the North was under the Governor in Lagos, Lugard having the title Governor-General from then until 1918.

ment heads or of local administrators. On balance the pre-eminence of the Administrative Service was maintained despite the wishes of more than one governor. Constitutionally the Governor's hand was strong also in the Executive and Legislative Councils which sat in Lagos and had authority throughout the Protectorate. In Lugard's time the Northern chiefs, along with those from other parts of the country, had *ex officio* membership in the Legislative Council but did not in fact attend its meetings.[1] Considering this situation anomalous, Clifford abolished the chiefs' membership and the North was represented in Lagos by the Lieutenant Governor and, legally, by four or five of the senior Residents. In addition to holding up one form of inter-communication and political progress among Africans throughout the whole Protectorate, the new arrangement increased the power of Northern officers *vis-à-vis* the Governor.

Their Excellencies could ill afford this. Already lieutenant governors exercised authority that verged on the autonomous. They were appointed by the Crown, as were governors, and they dealt with the Colonial Office directly on most matters.[2] For the strong-minded Lugard, who had presided over the creation of the North, this was an agony, particularly as the lieutenant governor during half of Lugard's time in Lagos was Charles Temple, an experienced officer of brilliance and determination. Lugard's successor, Clifford, is said to have been determined to reduce the authority of lieutenant governors, having tried to eliminate the position outright and been frustrated in this by the Colonial Secretary, Lord Milner.[3] All through the 1920s there was bad blood between Lagos and Kaduna, each side intriguing avidly against the other in London. Northerners were sure that an elaborate scheme to undermine them had been hatched, that the post of Secretary

---

[1] I am grateful to Commander Carrow (6 January 1966) for a detailed exposition of this matter.

[2] Lord Passfield told Palmer, then Lieutenant Governor, that the C.O. would do nothing to diminish the autonomy of lieutenant governors unless the Governor complained (Palmer to Lethem, 28 June 1930, Lethem Papers, C.R.P.). Cf. Leonard Woolf, *Downhill All the Way*, London, 1967, p. 238.

[3] Lethem Papers, 1 November 1928. The writers of the letters are of course Northern partisans and their opinions must be carefully weighed in the scales with other evidence, such as is found in the Kaduna Archives and in the Cameron–Lugard correspondence.

for Native Affairs had been created primarily to undercut Kaduna, and that Lagos sought to use the Kaduna post of Secretary Northern Provinces for the same purpose.[1] On his visits to the North and in correspondence Clifford handled the then Lieutenant Governor, Gowers, with kid gloves, addressing him not as a subordinate but as a brother sovereign.[2] One of the Governor's major policy statements is careful to stress that no criticism and no direct orders are implied, that he, the Governor, knows that His Honour, the Lieutenant Governor, agrees with him, and that the delicately proffered suggestions in the statement are meant for junior officers who require guidance in matters which are of course old hat to His Honour.[3] By the 1930s the lieutenant governorship had given way to a chief commissionership, incumbents holding office on the appointment of the Secretary of State, not the Crown. Yet Kaduna's subordination was more apparent than real, and suspicion and mistrust had not abated. Even though the Chief Commissioner in 1937, Adams, was certainly no opponent of the Governor, Bourdillon, and had previously served in Malaya, not in the North, the two officers found themselves disagreeing on many of the same issues that had divided their respective predecessors. When Bourdillon asked Adams to sound the Sultan of Sokoto on his attitude to sitting in the Legislative Council (the Governor hoping that the Sultan would agree), Adams tried to have the Resident Sokoto present the question in such a way as to produce the opposite result.[4] Moreover, Bourdillon was just as careful as his predecessors had been to defer to Northern sensibilities. He remarked to the Northern Residents in conclave: 'The policy of Government must be founded not only upon the experience of its senior officers but upon their own interpretation of that experience.'[5] This may

---

[1] Lethem Papers. Palmer says that the plot was Cameron's mainly, that Browne was put in Kaduna as S.N.P. to spy on Cameron's foes there, and that Cameron deliberately visited Kaduna twice when Palmer, then Acting Lieutenant Governor, was on tour. Again, the bias necessitates great care. But the fact that Browne later became Cameron's chief commissioner in Kaduna would seem to lend weight to Palmer's assertions.

[2] Cf. Clifford to Gowers, 25 February 1922, K., on the Sokoto crisis of 1921–2.

[3] Cf. Kirk-Greene, op. cit., pp. 174 ff., especially paragraphs 1, 3, 5, 9, and 24.

[4] Carrow (6 January 1966), who was Resident Sokoto at the time. See Nigeria, 'Conference of Residents, Northern Provinces', November 1937, Summary of Proceedings (mimeo). [5] Residents' Conference Summary, ibid.

have seemed to be mere politeness on the part of a governor who, as it happens, was popular in the North. In fact it was an accurate description. Kaduna's autonomy, although threatened more than once, held fast throughout the inter-war period. Governors in Lagos might propound at will; enforcement would be another matter.

Had Lagos and Kaduna got on well together it would still have been true that governors, as birds of passage, would be at a disadvantage when faced with the local knowledge and tenure of the permanent staff. The average governor stayed about six years. Governors were responsible for the whole Protectorate and for relations with London. By contrast the typical senior officer in the North had been there continuously for at least twenty years before the arrival of a governor whom he might find himself opposed to on a question of policy. Many Residents would outlast that governor, as they had his predecessors. 'I would not worry in the least about [the Governor],' wrote one lieutenant governor to a junior colleague; 'if he does come back [from sick leave] it won't be for long.'[1] Governors were older men, not a few of them being unwell, and were nearing the end of their careers.[2] At Government House and in the higher posts of the Secretariat there tended to be a posture of conservatism, a desire to avoid rocking the boat. Governors were naturally jealous of their records, while their seconds-in-command, looking to promotion, were understandably even more anxious to steer clear of any action, positive or negative, that might raise eyebrows in London. The Colonial Service has had its high-ranking stormy petrels. The average governor and chief secretary wanted things to remain quiet, and this inevitably played into the hands of provincial subordinates who soon learned how much they could get away with.

Nevertheless, each governor had an opportunity to impress his style on the Administration. In the period 1912–18 Lugard had little direct day-to-day influence, but most officers were intensely loyal to him and wanted his approval.[3] There was a

[1] Palmer to Lethem, 16 October 1928.

[2] Clifford was well known to have had both physical and psychological problems. Thomson was seriously ill during most of his time in Nigeria and he died a few years later while on the way home from Ceylon, where he went as Governor after leaving Nigeria.

[3] 'We all looked up to him and liked him and had confidence in his judgement,

general inclination to rationalize what one was doing by reference to policies identified with the Governor-General. Hesketh Bell's light hand and Thomson's illness were influences of sorts, if only by default. Cameron put people's backs up, and in some fields this meant less achievement for his governorship than was the case with Bourdillon, whose habit of asking for advice naturally found favour in the provinces.

Governors with a theoretical bent inevitably thought of making their contributions in the form of written statements on the nature and aims of the Government for which they were responsible. In tracing the development of these dicta we may note that their relationship to actual practice presents in the aggregate a complex picture: there was sometimes so tenuous a relationship that policy fades into irrelevance; in other cases policy followed fact at a respectable distance but did give a reasonably accurate picture of it; occasionally there was conflict between the two. Perhaps the most valid generalization is that the two were usually distinct and that policy was most generally a kind of Bible. As such it is no better or worse a guide for the student of Northern Nigerian history than it was for the administrative officer of the time.

The Book of Genesis, Lugard's Political Memoranda, bears a close relation to reality for an unanswerable reason: it was essentially a compilation, with editorializing, of Residents' reports.[1] Its most important contributors were Burdon and Temple. In so far as the Memoranda deal with what should be done in the future, it is seen immediately that they cannot have had much practical effect: Burdon was such a friend to the notion of leaving Africa undisturbed that he wanted to put Kano's Emir under the Sultan of Sokoto, supposing that this was the way it had been at the height of Fulani power after the Jihad. Temple, as we have seen, cut deeply into the authority of both the Sultan and the Emir. Any policy based on their respective recommendations would therefore have to be pitched at such a high level of generalization as to leave practical discretion to the Residents, which is precisely what the Memo-

---

the more so that in detail he relied on us' (Sir Richmond Palmer, undated letter posted in 1949, P.).

[1] See Sir Frederick D. Lugard, *The Dual Mandate in British Tropical Africa*, London, 1922, pp. 103–4; see also note 1, p. 222.

F

randa—or Zungeru at any rate—actually did. Palmer barely glanced at the Memoranda when he was running Katsina.[1] They were neither law nor conscious policy and were soon out of date.[2] Tomlinson recalls that the Memoranda were later 'regarded with something approaching to veneration', but he does not disagree with Gowers's description of them as not having made 'much difference one way or another'.[3] In the time of Girouard, writes Palmer, the Residents became aware that their work was seen by some, mainly in headquarters and in England, as being subsumed under the principle of Indirect Rule. The Governor himself, having had previous service in Moslem lands, was interested in Islam and in land tenure, but, lacking first-hand experience of Northern Nigerian units, he was in no position to work out the specifics of an overall policy.[4] The working hypotheses of Indirect Rule at this point were largely the work of Temple, whom Palmer describes as 'Girouard's political chief of staff'.[5] Doubtless Temple would have contributed the next major statement on the rationale of rule, both because he was an extraordinarily reflective and experienced officer and because, as Lieutenant Governor from 1914 to 1917, he was thought to be approaching the heights from which such statements are made. But his career was cut short prematurely and his musings on the subject, although many consider them the most interesting of all and the most relevant in view of his close familiarity with actual administration, are therefore in the category of opinions expressed by a private citizen.[6] The same must be said of the later writings of Lugard. His Memoranda were revised and reissued in 1918 as his colonial career came to an end, and his second major work on the subject did not appear until 1922, by which time he

[1] 'I don't remember myself doing more than glancing at them . . . from curiosity' (Sir Richmond Palmer, 17 December 1949, P.). Carrow, who arrived in the country in 1919, writes: 'I do not remember being advised or urged to study the Political Memoranda . . . and I did not do so' (6 January 1966).

[2] Note 3, p. 58, above, and see Sir Richmond Palmer, 'Some Observations on Capt. Rattray's Papers', *Journal of the African Society*, XXXIII (January 1934), p. 46.

[3] Sir George Tomlinson, 19 January 1950, P.; Sir William Gowers, 26 November 1949, P. Again, Gowers's remark is relevant: 'I never saw Lugard till 1906' (4 September 1950, P.).

[4] Sir Richmond Palmer, 17 December 1949, P.

[5] Ibid.

[6] In so far, that is, as influence on subsequent action is concerned. See Temple's *Native Races and Their Rulers*, Cape Town, 1918.

could neither speak for nor directly influence actual administration in the North.[1]

It fell to Clifford, Governor from 1919 to 1925, to make the
next important verbalization of official policy. This he did in a
series of minutes which went out to officers in the provinces and
in speeches to the Legislative Council. Whereas, in his Amalgamation Report, Lugard had disapproved the idea of administrative officers taking too direct a hand in Moslem emirates,
Clifford stressed the other desideratum: the need to jolly the
emirates forward into the twentieth century.[2] Actually both
Lugard and Clifford dealt with each side of the coin and with
the dangers inherent in each of the extremes—too much or too
little European intervention. Once again the effect was to toss
the ball to the practitioners, who were thus given latitude to
interpret as they saw fit. All through the 1920s and beyond, the
game of interpreting Clifford's statements continued. The
Governor's ambivalence played into the hands of the
northerners. If Lagos emphasized the role of chiefs as mere
agents of government, Kaduna reminded them that Clifford,
when visiting an emirate, had made a point of receiving the
Chief first and the British officer second.[3] Kaduna remembered,
and would not let Lagos forget, what Clifford had done in
actual circumstances, policy aside. In 1920, when the Resident
Zaria was collecting evidence on the Emir's misconduct and
the Emir was attempting to have the Resident murdered,
Clifford wrote: 'I regard it as improper and inexpedient that
the Government should attempt, in the absence of any complaint by persons believing themselves to have suffered injury,
to press inquisitorial investigations into the personnel of the
harem of a Muhammadan Chief.'[4]

The peasantry must be protected from child raiding, the
Governor went on, 'but I do not consider that the initiative in
such matters can be taken by the Government'.[5] In the following year an officer was so rash as to take one of the Governor's
policy pronouncements literally and to use it as moral and

---

[1] *The Dual Mandate.* See also Cmd. 468, 1920 (The Amalgamation Report).
[2] Cf. Lugard's Amalgamation Report, para. 24, and Clifford's minute of 29 June
1920, S.N.P. to Residents, 16 July 1920, K., as amended variously thereafter.
See also Kirk-Greene, op. cit., pp. 174 ff.
[3] S.N.P. to C. S., Lagos, 23 November 1929, K.
[4] To the Lieutenant Governor, 16 October 1920, K.   [5] Ibid.

official sanction for rooting out corruption in Sokoto N.A.[1] In the course of looking into charges brought by this officer, Clifford himself visited Sokoto, and he took part personally in the correspondence. The result was to cover up a bad situation which then had to be dealt with a decade later, and to uphold the policy of another officer who symbolized the antithesis of His Excellency's stated aims.[2] Clifford is said to have come to Nigeria ill-disposed to Indirect Rule and eager to bury Lugard, its supposed prophet, and not to praise him.[3] In the Zaria and Sokoto cases his actions conflicted head-on with his own policy. During and after his governorship Clifford's statements were either ignored by the northerners or bent to suit their various purposes. As the Governor went off to his next colony Northern autonomy was entering its golden phase and the degree of interference by Europeans was still determined in each emirate by the inclinations and capacity of the officer in charge far more than by anything Lagos said.

During the Thomson governorship, 1925–31, the policy field was dominated by two facts that conspired to bring the North to an apogee of real power *vis-à-vis* Lagos: the Governor was often ill and was in any case not disposed as Clifford had been to take a strong line; and the lieutenant governorship was held for all but Thomson's last year by Palmer, the strongest northerner of them all. Palmer claimed that Thomson ignored him on the boat coming out in 1925 and that he later admitted to him that Lugard had urged this.[4] 'He did not propose to rule through Lieutenant Governors.'[5] Whether this was true or not,

[1] File N.A. Confidential Reports, Sokoto Province, 26 October 1921 ff., K. The circular cited by the officer in question is dated 9 February 1921.

[2] This case will be dealt with in the following two chapters.

[3] Palmer, note 3, p. 58, above. Carrow (6 January 1966) writes: 'Inside the front cover [of Goldsmith's reprint of Lugard's Political Memoranda] was pasted a printed notice which read something like this: "His Excellency the Governor has agreed that this reprint of the Political Memoranda written by Sir Frederick Lugard may be distributed to all offices in the Northern Provinces. His Excellency however directed that the following note should be pasted inside each copy: 'It must be remembered that a number of controversial subjects are included in these memoranda and are dealt with in a dogmatic manner. Those who read these political memoranda should remember that the views expressed therein are not necessarily accepted by the present Government.' " '

[4] To Lethem, 1 November 1928, C.R.P.

[5] Ibid. Reporting to Palmer on a conversation he had had with Thomson, however, Lethem had written earlier, 'He [Thomson] insisted over and over again that

Thomson, like Bourdillon, was not an *a priori* theorist. Unlike Clifford before him and Cameron afterwards, he did not arrive with strong predispositions. After his first tour of the North he remarked, modestly enough, 'Even the sketchiest acquaintance with the districts one has to deal with on paper always seems to me a great help.'[1] Constitutions, he thought, could not be made 'by a stroke of the pen', and must reflect true native opinion; haste was to be avoided, for the gauging of this was difficult and time-consuming.[2] Thomson alone of the inter-war governors issued no major policy statement, refusing, according to Palmer, even to put his name to the latest revision of the Political Memoranda.[3] In the circumstances it is not surprising that a recently published collection of Nigerian policy documents includes the work of only one serving lieutenant governor, Palmer, and excludes only one inter-war governor, Thomson.[4] It was a naked power struggle that raged throughout the Thomson years, not a fight on issues of policy. So strong was Palmer that the efforts of Baddeley, Chief Secretary and Acting Governor in Thomson's absence, to make the North subordinate were a failure. When Lagos tried to use amendments of Clifford's earlier statements to prove that the Lieutenant Governor was merely the Governor's legate in the North and not the 'principal executive authority', Kaduna calmly pointed out that the particular steps which Lagos wanted to take violated the spirit of various Clifford statements as printed in the Gazette and endorsed by London. Kaduna then slyly invited Lagos to verify that it was now repudiating official policy.[5] Northerners serving at Lagos in the post of Secretary

---

he wanted the L.G.s to take the power and that he would back them up' (25 September 1926).

[1] To Lugard, 1 March 1926, P.   [2] To Lord Passfield, 23 June 1930, K.

[3] To Lethem, 24 July 1929, C.R.P.

[4] Kirk-Greene, op. cit.

[5] Chief Secretary to S.N.P., 30 October 1929 (Baddeley to Lethem), and reply, 23 November 1929, K. In the last months of 1925, Thomson having just become Governor and Palmer having just become Lieutenant Governor in the North, there was an exchange between Lagos and Kaduna that shows vividly what the power relationship was. The issue was whether department heads in Lagos should control their own provincial officers or whether these should in effect be under administrative officers in the various provincial posts. Baddeley wrote to Kaduna complaining that medical officers in Kano were being denied entry to Moslem dwellings because administrative officers considered such entry an affront to Islam (Telegram 3612/1925/4). Palmer had a junior officer reply, saying that there

for Native Affairs, Lethem and Morgan in particular, kept Palmer fully informed of developments so that every move by the Secretariat or Government House was anticipated in Kaduna.[1]

Such was the situation when Sir Donald Cameron arrived as Governor in 1931. The new Governor was in many ways Thomson's opposite. Whereas Thomson had been a newcomer, Cameron had had sixteen years of previous Nigerian experience, from 1908 until his departure for Tanganyika in 1924. Cameron's health was not a problem. His vigour was complemented by strength of mind and by unusually well-developed resources in home-based contacts, a vital advantage if Kaduna was to be disciplined. Among colonial governors in the inter-war period he was the theorist *par excellence*, and it would not be too much to say that no incoming governor ever arrived with such detailed plans or with a greater determination to see them put into effect. Cameron's was to be the fullest restatement of policy and the most powerful challenge to regional autonomy. His attempt to bring change from above is thus the classic case showing what a governor could and could not accomplish and what part policy played, at its fullest stretch, in the amalgam of colonial government.

Cameron's basically theoretical and abstract view of administrative problems is understandable. He became a bureaucrat at the age of eighteen and remained so until his retirement at sixty-three.[2] The realities of day-to-day administration in the countryside were things he could read about in stilted official reports or glance at fleetingly during the course of the highly stylized tours of inspection that were arranged for governors. Some governors were able to offset these deficiencies

---

was no plague in Kano, contrary to what Baddeley had heard, that the administrative–medical trouble was in fact confined to one officer in each service ('personal friction'), and that if Lagos thinks a technical department head can compel the L.G. to do what he does not wish to do, it is mistaken: 'This, without His Excellency's specific direction, His Honour declines to do' (Wright to Baddeley, Confidential, 31 December 1925).

[1] See, for example, Morgan, Acting S.N.A., to Lethem, Acting S.N.P., 11 November 1928, on Baddeley's handling of a dispatch from London, C.R.P.

[2] He served in the provincial administration of Southern Nigeria from April 1910 to March 1911, but as Acting Provincial Commissioner, a desk post, not as a touring officer. Also he had two separate posts during this eleven-month period and therefore did not have time to come to know either post well.

by pumping district officers for information whenever they could, and Cameron was famous for having done so, especially in Dar es Salaam. But these interviews were like tutorials in which the instructor, having hastily briefed himself beforehand, seeks to impress the student with the extent of his own knowledge.[1] Cameron was capable of great kindness, generosity, and humour.[2] His contemporaries, however, thought they saw in him some trace of social insecurity, perhaps reflecting his modest background as the son of a West Indian planter. He struck many as being cold, autarchic, and intellectually severe. Resentment bordering on paranoia may have undergirded his testiness towards colleagues in Nigeria, for he is said to have harboured feelings of persecution from his early days under Lugard and a suspicion that he was not fully appreciated. Under Clifford, however, he was given his head, and from then on there was ample scope for his strong organizational abilities and for the well-developed ideas on colonial administration which he had acquired in the West Indies, South America, Mauritius, Nigeria, and eventually Tanganyika. Knighted in 1923, he governed his own colony, Tanganyika, from 1924 to 1931, when the Nigerian governorship, one of the two or three plums of the Colonial Empire, came to him.[3]

Though he claimed to be original in working out his policy in Tanganyika, Cameron obviously drew on Nigerian experience, and he used the word 'plagiarism', albeit humorously, in admitting this to Lugard.[4] The essential ideas are similar from Kingsley and Goldie through Temple, Lugard, and Palmer to Cameron: Europeanize via British tuition, but not so fast as to

[1] A number of Cameron's Tanganyika officers have described this experience to me, notably F. H. Page-Jones, C.M.G., 7 and 8 January 1965.

[2] Again I depend on the testimony of ex-Tanganyika officers, e.g. Dr. A. Sillery, who served in Dar es Salaam during Cameron's first year there, and Sir Rex Surridge, who was in Dar es Salaam for most of Cameron's governorship. See also the sketch of Cameron written by Sir Alan Burns, *Dictionary of National Biography*, London, 1959, pp. 131–2.

[3] Ceylon and Malaya were its only competitors, Thomson going on from Nigeria to the former and Clifford to both. Legally Tanganyika was a League of Nations Mandated Territory, not a British Colony.

[4] 29 July 1926, P. In his book *My Tanganyika Service and Some Nigeria*, London, 1939, Cameron presents the matter rather differently, however; see pp. 33–4. Lugard was aware of a competition on this score and wanted Nigeria to remain the model in the eyes of the world; cf. his letter to Lethem, 13 December 1932, P.

confuse the native, who must ultimately stand on his own feet, backed by his own culture and fortified with enough European-ism to face the challenges of the modern world. Cameron was not satisfied that the North was following this general line. Both his experience in Nigeria up to 1924 and his years in Tanganyika exerted strong influence on the views of Nigerian realities and needs which Cameron had formed well in ad-vance of his arrival as Governor. He drew on Lagos-based assumptions about the North, on comparisons in his own mind between native administration in these two widely different parts of Africa, and on exchanges he had had with Lugard and others about what should be done in the North. Cameron was among those who thought there was great divergence be-tween the theory of Indirect Rule and Northern practice, a situation, in his own words, of 'make-believe', in which admini-strators did as they liked, regardless of policy.[1] Northern emirates and their N.A.s, he thought, were British creatures, artificially founded and zealously protected from outside in-fluence by officers who looked on their Region as 'the Sacred North', a land apart, suspended in place and time.[2] Northerners were trying to make emirates into native states on the Indian pattern, self-sufficient units rather than mere agencies of local government under central direction from Lagos.[3] The neces-sary infusion of European influence was being resisted by excessive concern for supposed African devotion to Islam and to tradition generally. This held up development in the Region and kept it an exotic backwater, attractive to its British pro-tectors but administratively ineffective, corrupt and insensitive to the needs of its own peoples, especially the non-Moslems and non-northerners. The pagans of Northern Nigeria were in danger of permanent victimizing by Moslem rulers, just as were the indigenous populations of East Africa at the hands of white settlers.[4] Most of all—and here, of course, Cameron had reference to his own experience as head of the Secretariat in Lagos—Northern officers were determined to preserve their

[1] Cameron, op. cit., p. 14.

[2] This picture of the North, presented by Cameron in an address at Chatham House, 24 November 1932, was especially resented by the northerners. See Lethem to Lugard, 23 December 1932, C.R.P. Lethem was present and heard the address, 'Indirect Administration in Tropical Countries'.

[3] Cameron to Lugard, 29 June 1928, P.   [4] Ibid., 31 January 1927.

personal power and independence of higher authority. The way to cure all this was to kill Northern separatism, bring the emirs to heel, free pagans from alien domination, and push development in the Region by increasing the power of technical departments in Lagos at the expense of Northern administrators.

Cameron was not at pains to conceal either his views of the North or his plans for bringing about its subordination to Lagos and correcting its mistaken politics. On his way out in 1931 he met on shipboard a Northern officer of middle rank to whom he gave chapter and verse on the subject and on whom he made a powerful, if at first negative, impression.[1] Kaduna itself waited almost as though behind a barricade, knowing Cameron of old and expecting the worst. For several years before Cameron's appointment over-confidence had reigned in the North. Thomson's weakness and Palmer's strength had bred a feeling among northerners that they were masters in their own house, that Lagos barked but did not bite, and that their personal contacts in England would protect them from any resurgence of Clifford–Cameron truculence in Lagos. Palmer, Lethem, and more junior officers called on Lugard regularly and on the major figures in the Colonial Office.[2] The bureaucrats in Lagos dealt in paper, not in people, and they had passed the high-water mark of their power in the Clifford years. The next governor, i.e. after Thomson, would be chosen for devotion to the true principles of Indirect Rule. 'There will be a swing back to Lugardism.'[3] So relaxed and benign was Palmer that he thought of rehabilitating the unfortunate G. S. Browne, who had been Cameron's willing agent in Kaduna, according to the northerners, in the Clifford years, and whom Palmer had therefore exiled to Yola.[4]

Cameron notwithstanding, the northerners were not just intransigent and self-serving. Unlike him, they knew what Anglo-African government was at first hand, for it was they who had created it and operated it from the start. If they had given Bornu a comparatively direct form of rule in the

[1] Carrow, 22 April 1965.
[2] 'I can't believe that the C.O. can be such idiots as to agree [to centralization under Lagos]' (Palmer to Lethem, 14 November 1928, C.R.P.).
[3] Palmer to Lethem, 15 August 1928, C.R.P.
[4] Ibid., 11 February 1928.

beginning it was because Rabeh's devastation had left them
no alternative. If they encouraged the Emir of Kano to take a
firm hand in his emirate and, later on, the Shehu of Bornu in
his, it was because this was a step forward from the bad old days
of slave power, corruption, and ineffectiveness, and from peasant
fear of raiding which kept agriculture back and made government a scourge. What did Cameron know of Temple's problems in Sokoto, Palmer's in Bornu, Hale Middleton's in Kano?
To the Governor Indirect Rule was typewriters, legislation,
and directives from headquarters. To the northerners it was a
handful of Britishers and Africans, the blood and air and soil
of real life. It was real people doing real things year in year out,
gaining confidence and making progress from the chaos of
early times when Cameron was far away in British Guiana and
Mauritius.

To the northerners the crux of the matter was helping the
Region to develop on its own lines. Contrary to Cameron's
assumptions, Palmer had taken a strong stand against traditionalism many times, sacking a hopeless chief in Katsina in the
early years and removing a senior Resident in 1928 for being
too lax. He was against trying to unify the Regions of Nigeria
prematurely because local customs were strong, differences
were real, and a paper unity could lead to the enslavement of
the Moslem North by the semi-Europeanized South.[1] This, in
Palmer's view, would hand the North over to commercial
profiteers in the South and only lead to trouble. Protecting the
North meant recognizing its educational and social weakness by
comparison with the South, especially as regards the trappings
of modern commercialism and bureaucracy. It did not mean
guarding its traditions for their own sake. To their enemies the
northerners were museum curators. They saw themselves as
realistic guides to a better future that would be solidly based
on the stubborn facts of social attitudes and organization.
Cameron they regarded as a theorist who could never appreciate moral issues.[2] Thirty years later a spokesman of theirs still

---

[1] 'The important thing is to persuade Wilson [the Under-Secretary of State]
that one cannot "unify" Nigeria' (Palmer to Lethem, 7 August 1928, C.R.P.).

[2] Commenting on both Cameron and Browne, Morgan distinguished between
those who could appreciate such issues and those who took a legal view of everything—'the legal mind again' (to Lethem, 10 October 1932, C.R.P.).

saw the Sacred North controversy of Cameron's time as a battle between 'doers and thinkers'.[1]

Initial over-confidence gave way on Cameron's arrival to uncertainty and apprehension. Palmer had left the year before, his place as lieutenant governor being taken by Alexander, who, although he had spent his first eighteen years in the South, had the loyalty of the northerners and considered himself one of them.[2] Alexander was an intelligent, sensitive, and reasonable man, not given to the fiery outbursts of Palmer and quite prepared to receive the new Governor in an accommodating way. Had Cameron approached the North in a conciliatory mood it is possible that compromises could have been worked out and co-operation achieved. Instead he went over to the attack from the outset. Staying in Government House Kaduna as Alexander's guest, he remarked that 'there could be only one Government House in Nigeria', and he lectured the Lieutenant Governor on policy.[3] He would write his own political memoranda. He had saved Tanganyika from white settlers and he would save Northern Nigeria from 'N.A. sham'.[4] He addressed the Northern chiefs in an aggressive mood, his interpreter, by coincidence, being the same officer whom he had lectured on shipboard earlier that year. Introducing His Excellency, the officer spoke of him in Hausa as 'the Governor from Lagos', a distinction that was always made on such occasions so that the chiefs, who had little experience of these things, would understand which of the important British officers was meant. Instantly Cameron interrupted, beckoning the officer to his side like an errant schoolboy and commanding, so that all could hear, 'You will kindly introduce me to the Chiefs as the Governor of Nigeria.'[5] All over the North Cameron's previous reputation for haughtiness and arrogance was now confirmed by personal experience of him.[6] Even junior officers, prepared to believe that their superiors had exaggerated, could all produce stories of the Governor's rudeness

---

[1] Sharwood Smith, 17 April 1966.   [2] Except war service in the North, 1917–18.
[3] Alexander to Lethem, June 1931, C.R.P.   [4] Ibid.
[5] The interpreter was Carrow (interview, Weymouth, 22 April 1965).
[6] Woodhouse, going home on retirement leave in 1932, was amazed to find on meeting Cameron in Lagos that the Governor had a human side and was not the full-fledged ogre of whom everyone spoke. (Letters of 19 July 1931, 22 November 1931, and 17 January 1932, C.R.P.)

and implacable bias. Cameron made the Lieutenant Governor accompany him on tour and treated him like any other subordinate rather than, according to previous custom, as the head of the administration in a Region where he himself was a visitor and guest. The nadir was reached at Katsina. Alexander, in his new guise as a mere hanger-on in the Governor's wake, wandered into the local club. At the tennis courts he took his place among the spectators in an unobtrusive way and was not recognized at first. When it was finally realized how their own superior was being treated the local British officials made a point of calling at the Residency to sign the Lieutenant Governor's book as a mark of loyalty to him and disapproval of the Governor.[1]

There soon developed a situation not unlike a state of seige, with both sides adopting positions more extreme than those they normally held. Alexander, who had never been hidebound in such matters, found himself heatedly maintaining to the Governor that if chains were removed from prisoners in the Kano gaol it would be impossible to preserve discipline in the emirate.[2] The fact was overlooked that there was more agreement than disagreement on the basic principles of rule, and an air of unreality came to surround discussion of policy within as well as between the two sides. In Cameron's mind there grew up an impression of the Northern outlook which still persists in the literature of Nigeria but which was inaccurate from the start. The Governor assumed he was fighting the northerners on three main issues and that they were diametrically opposed to him: Westernization versus a doctrinaire form of Indirect Rule that accented blind protection of native custom; economic development versus *laissez-faire*; and control from Lagos versus Regional autonomy. In fact the issues were not distinct one from another, nor were the positions of the combatants clearly drawn. The constant intermingling of the three, in administrative practice, added confusion and made it still more difficult for Lagos and the northerners to understand each other.

[1] I am grateful to Mr. A. A. Shillingford, who was present in Katsina at the time, for sending this account to me.

[2] That this view was not necessarily unrealistic is known in the fact that the Emir of Hadejia made the same point, and vehemently, to the D.O. Hadejia several years later (Emir's Interview Book, 19 November 1934).

On the first issue Cameron himself was not entirely consistent. He would sometimes accuse northerners of ruling too directly, thereby weakening the self-confidence and capacity of N.A.s. At other times he spoke of the British officer as a mere adviser, standing behind the Chief and not interfering enough to correct abuses and bring progress. In fact, as we have seen, the views and actions of officers were a function first of conditions in emirates to which they were assigned and secondly of their own outlook and capacity. Palmer and others had been trying for a balance of discipline and encouragement. The aim was a strong local administration, one which was not so Western as to be incomprehensible to its own people and not so reactionary, incompetent, or corrupt as to offend British standards. When he spoke of Indian states—in fact he did not do so often nor did he elaborate the analogy greatly—Palmer was thinking of making emirates stronger and more capable than he found them.[1] An independent unit, free of British local control and headed singly or jointly for full statehood among the nations of the international community, was not what he had in mind.[2] Neither Cameron nor Palmer saw Northern Nigeria out of the British Empire. Negatively Palmer was against that suffocating form of centralization that leaves everything to distant bureaucrats, British or Southern Nigerian, and robs emirates of the initiative they need to function happily and efficiently.

The Governor was convinced that N.A.s, being under autocratic and Moslem rulers, were not representative either of their own Moslem villagers or of non-Moslem peoples living within their boundaries. To him the weak point in village administration was that those who paid the bulk of the tax had no say in its expenditure.[3] As he had done in Tanganyika, he directed that officers study local peoples to discover what their institutions of government had been traditionally. The aim was to reconstitute local administrations so that no community would have to accept rule by outsiders. All would be represented in councils, some of which would be removed from

---

[1] Sharwood Smith (17 April 1966) does not recall ever hearing the analogy referred to, by Palmer or anyone else.

[2] The fullest exposition of the Palmer view in this regard was set out by his S.N.P., Lethem, for the benefit of a party of visiting M.P.s in 1928 (24 January 1928, K.).

[3] S.N.P. to Residents, putting H.E.'s views, 16 November 1933, K.

the jurisdiction of N.A.s under which they had been placed. To illustrate the abuses he aimed to correct, Cameron circulated to Residents an article on problems of Indirect Rule by Margery Perham. Miss Perham had made a study of native administration in Tanganyika and was about to do the same in Nigeria. British rule was not going as well as it might, the article held, because officers were building emirs up for administrative convenience, an understandable tactic in early years but no longer defensible. The interests of the masses were being ignored. Chiefs were being exalted and isolated. Officers were using them as agents for rapid, Europeanized government, in ignorance of or disregard for the fact that, traditionally, many chiefs had been merely constitutional monarchs. Emirs' councils must be strengthened and broadened to represent the whole community and there should be a return to the village democracy of pre-Fulani times.[1]

Some northerners were appalled at the irrelevance of the Governor's views in the light of known facts, and they reacted with scorn. To the suggestion that D.O.s liked despotic chiefs, one officer replied, 'Who says so?'[2] The notion that chiefs were being puffed up and cut off from their people brought the rejoinder from another, 'What an idea!'[3] A third summed up his reaction with the phrase *'per ardua ad astra'*, and pointed out that emirates had never had conciliar control and decentralization.[4] The D.O. who looked after pagan areas in the southern part of Zaria Emirate drew attention to the fact that some district headmen were in fact representative of their people, for example in Kauru and Kajuru, and he spoke for pragmatic touring officers throughout the North in commenting, 'What matters is his [the District Headman's] functions, not his name.'[5] In many pagan districts where village democracy in the past had meant internecine warfare and chaos, Moslem headmen represented progress, especially when combined with British supervision, and the people did not want to go back to

---

[1] Ibid. Miss Perham's article appeared in *The Journal of the Royal Society of Arts*, 18 May 1934, pp. 689–701.

[2] Comments from officers in Kano Province, on the Resident's Memo of 28 March 1934, K.

[3] Ibid.   [4] Ibid.

[5] Comments of officers in Zaria Province on Memo from the Chief Commissioner, Browne, 2 January 1934, K.

the mismanagement of their own squabbling elders. Islam was increasing among Katsina pagans.[1] In some emirates, where Fulani chiefs ruled almost completely pagan populations, the idea of removing the Chief, even when, as in the case of Jema'a, he was hopelessly inefficient and corrupt, was opposed by the people. There was agreement with the Governor in theory; but, wrote the head of the Region, by now a Cameron appointee, 'the difficulty in practice is that the people themselves do not want councils but prefer chiefs since they have been taught the Moslem system of District Heads by Administrative Officers'.[2] In any case it was too late to go back.[3]

In the economic field Cameron naturally wished to see the whole Protectorate prosper. It is quite unexceptional that he would have noticed a contrast between the eager commercialism of Lagos and the South by comparison with the relatively sleepy and unmaterialistic North. It was natural too that his department heads in Lagos would have given him up-to-date confirmation of his own early impression that Northern sluggishness was due to its hidebound N.A.s backed by reactionary British officers. As late as 1965 one heard the same line from engineers, road builders, and foresters in such places as Zaria, Sokoto, and Kano. A specialist in material things is almost instinctively impatient with the dealer in human beings who is always explaining why it is necessary to go slow. Northerners were perfectly sure that unless African local administrators understood the process of development and learned to manage this themselves economic advances would have no grounding in local cultures. Prosperity would redound to the benefit of people from other parts of Nigeria and the gulf between the Regions would widen still further. Lethem explained to a party of visiting M.P.s in 1928 that the objective was to decentralize 'technical assistance' by having British specialists

---

[1] D.O. Katsina, Lewis, to Resident Zaria, 13 March 1934, K.

[2] Sent by S.N.P. to Resident Zaria, 11 May 1934, K.

[3] The idea of intensive anthropology, much talked of by Cameron, was generally deprecated by senior officers because trained anthropologists would be too few and would lack detailed local knowledge. This was necessary to understand the subject matter in relation to the possibility of making changes. Having ethnography done by seconded administrative officers with anthropological training *and* the needed local knowledge was impracticable owing to the scarcity of staff. (Cf. D.O. Zaria to Resident, 25 January 1935, K.)

operate through the N.A.s rather than independently.[1] This would reduce friction and would give training to Africans. Owing to the small number of British technical and administrative officers and the scarcity of money, it would be impossible in any case to set up separate organizations for economic development in each of the ethnic and linguistic communities into which emirates were divided. N.A.s would have to have powers, for example, over those parts of Hausa towns (*sabon garis*) where people from other parts of the country lived. This of course ran directly counter to Cameron's notion of ethnic autonomy. Once again, however, the main conflict was not on aims but on ways and means. Palmer and the other northerners who had struggled for a generation to bring about various forms of economic improvement in the emirates were hardly against development as such. They felt that 'big departments mean the annihilation of the N.A.s', which in turn meant the disappearance of law and order in the North.[2]

If northerners reacted too quickly, instinctively, and negatively to any and all criticism from Lagos, it was equally true that Cameron and his people failed through inexperience to appreciate precisely why N.A.s were as they were and why therefore economic development was slow. Bornu, for example, they considered blacker than night. In a North that was sacred overall, Bornu was the *sanctum sanctorum* where the power of a small clique of officers was as great as their ideas were reactionary. Zungeru had had only paper control over the early giants—Hewby, Thomson, McClintock, and Benton.[3] It was they who founded the treasury, built the rural administration, got courts going, and created an entirely new headquarters town where none had existed before. They ruled with a firm hand because they had started with a shambles. Indirect Rule was only an abstraction at first, and Hewby, who noted laconically, 'I never appoint a District Head without having consulted the Shehu', was genuinely surprised to get back a rocket from headquarters.[4] Anarchy is normally followed by

[1] This was circulated as a memo from the S.N.P. to Residents, 24 January 1928, K.   [2] Palmer to Lethem, 26 January 1927, C.R.P.

[3] The Bornu Thomson was W. B., who died at sea in 1918, not the Governor of the same name.

[4] T. E. Letchworth, who saw this remark in a file in Provincial Headquarters Maiduguri, was good enough to pass it on to me (4 May 1966).

autocracy in all systems. By 1920 the Bornu N.A. was of course autocratic; it was also as benign as the British could make it. The method, which continued from the founders through Palmer, de Putron, Lethem, and Patterson to Butcher and Tegetmeier, was twofold: 'On no account stir mud' (de Putron), and 'It is good for the people that one District Head should bite the dust each year' (Butcher).[1] In short, the Africans would be allowed to get on with it—how else could they gain the self-confidence that comes only from experience? —but the chopper would be used regularly to remind everyone that there was a limit to abuse of power. Lagos saw only the first of these two inseparable guidelines.

The power of the Bornu team was great in their own province and outside it as well. Palmer went on from there to become Lieutenant Governor and then Governor of the Gambia and later Cyprus. Lethem was Secretary for Native Affairs, Secretary Northern Provinces, and later Governor of the Seychelles and of British Guiana. Patterson became Chief Commissioner later on. All received knighthoods. Lagos can hardly be blamed for its suspicion and even envy of Bornu, both as a fortress of power and as a backward place (by comparison with Kano, for example), where officers seemed to be protecting reaction at the same time as they beat off threats to their own authority. Cameron's third major criticism of the North—that its power was autonomous—was undeniable, even if the use the northerners made of their power be considered justified. That the Governor did not consider it so, he makes clear in his own book.[2] Lugard had had similar doubts about the northerners, and Thomson talked of reducing the rank of lieutenant governor to a chief commissionership, far more subordinate to the Governor than lieutenant governors were.[3] If anything was to be done to get Indirect Rule back on the right track as defined by Cameron and to develop the North economically, it would be necessary to break the northerners' power.

The principal actions of the Governor took place in 1933 and

[1] Ibid.

[2] Op. cit., pp. 14–16, 78–9, 104, 276.

[3] Cf. Perham, *Lugard*, II, p. 476; Commander Carrow to Margery Perham, 5 February 1961; and Lethem to Palmer, 9 October 1928, C.R.P., after a talk which the writer had had with Thomson.

G

1934. Two new ordinances were enacted by the Legislative Council in 1933, one on native courts and another on N.A.s. In 1934 Cameron published his version of the Political Memoranda. There were also the usual speeches to the Legislative Council, notably one delivered in March 1933 that dealt with N.A.s in terms of feudal stagnation versus progress. There was far more reiteration, reminding of long-established desiderata, and placing of special emphasis in all of this than there was actual innovation, although one or two objective changes should be noted.[1] A new court system came into being, replacing the former provincial courts, and native treasuries would now be subject to audit by the central department in Lagos. In response to the Governor's urging, there was an increase in anthropological investigations by administrative officers, as part of their regular duties and in a small number of cases as a special assignment for which one was seconded. Cameron gave much welcomed support also to those officers who had long been working to increase the influence within N.A.s of Africans who had received European education, especially at Katsina College. The Governor believed that he had curtailed the power of D.O.s over technical officers in the provinces by giving each man substantial discretion in his own sphere and having Residents in charge of provinces do the necessary co-ordination.[2] There was no real change in local N.A. supervision in such matters as control of *sabon garis*, although legal safeguards were set up with a view to preventing abuses.[3]

As regards trimming Kaduna's power, Cameron proceeded with care. He knew that London would not smile on proposals for major changes that might involve expense, a possibility if new alignments and organizations were suggested. With the northerners still in direct touch with the Colonial Office, he was aware of the need to make a good case for any change. In the meantime it was important not to give London the notion that he could not control his colony and keep the loyalty of his principal subordinates.[4] In 1932, however, there was an oppor-

[1] Lethem said that Cameron had told him there would be nothing in the new laws that would be contrary to what the northerners had always wanted (Lethem to Alexander, 7 June 1932, C.R.P.).   [2] Cameron, op. cit., p. 276.

[3] Cf. Margery Perham, *Native Administration in Nigeria*, London, 1937, ch. xx.

[4] After calling at the Colonial Office Alexander wrote on this point to Lethem: 15 June 1932 and 21 July 1932, C.R.P.

tunity to bring change through a perfectly normal procedure, at least in the first instance. The Lieutenant Governor, Alexander, retired prematurely for health reasons. Rejecting Morgan and Hale Middleton, either of whom would have continued the Temple–Palmer–Alexander approach in the North, Cameron saw to the appointment of G. S. Browne as Acting Lieutenant Governor.[1] Browne had been in Lagos with Cameron in 1917 and, while serving as Secretary Northern Provinces in the early twenties, he was looked on by Palmer as the spy and agent of Clifford and Cameron. In 1928 this impression of Browne as Lagos's man was strengthened when Thomson rescued Browne from his Yola obscurity and brought him to the capital as Secretary for Native Affairs. By 1931, with Cameron in the governorship, Browne was again Secretary Northern Provinces. From his letters it is clear that Browne expected to become substantive Lieutenant Governor in the autumn of 1933.[2] Instead he became the North's first Chief Commissioner. Government House in Kaduna became Government Lodge.[3] Lethem, the last of the ranking northerners still occupying a key post, ceased to be Secretary Northern Provinces and was temporarily sent to Sokoto as Resident, leaving the Protectorate altogether a few months later to become Governor of the Seychelles. Daniel saw Alexander's departure as 'a terrible loss to the country, especially at this juncture', and there was no response when Morgan asked plaintively, 'Can no one make a stand?'[4] Continuity would be impossible, for Cameron laid it down that no one would serve more than three consecutive tours in the same province. The N.A.s would wither when the chiefs saw that centralization was increasing

[1] Goldsmith and Gowers were not out of step with this approach but were not as important as Temple and Palmer, nor were they faced with the challenges that Alexander was.

[2] To Lethem, 11 October 1932 and 1 January 1933, C.R.P.

[3] An old ramshackle wooden building called Government House dated from Lugard's time. A more modern structure called Government Lodge was built for Sir Graeme Thomson, who never occupied it, as a Northern residence. Heads of the Northern administration occupied the wooden Government House, whose name was changed to 'The Chief Commissioner's Residence' when the title changed in 1933. After 1935 the Chief Commissioners moved to Government Lodge, the wooden building being used thereafter as a rest house (Sharwood Smith, 4 December 1966).

[4] Daniel's letter to his family, from Sokoto, 30 July 1932, C.R.P.; Morgan to Lethem, from Katsina, 10 October 1932, C.R.P.

and the British were no longer relying as much on them and their officials.[1] It seemed to the northerners that Cameron's victory was complete.

Yet as they reflected on the meaning of the changes and as they surveyed their actual situation, provincial officers came to feel that time was on their side. The worldwide Depression made it impossible for technical departments even to maintain their past level of activity, let alone increase it. Retrenchment of staff weakened them more than it did the administrative cadres. On the judicial side the change was more apparent than real. The D.O. was now a junior magistrate in a new court. When he dealt with professionals coming to his province on circuit he had an opportunity to educate them in the ways of African local government so that the problems and potentialities of N.A.s would in future be more real to a bench that had heretofore been preoccupied with English concepts of justice. The D.O. might complain that the Cameronian changes meant 'more law for officers and less justice for the African', but he had to admit that his initial fears were not borne out.[2] Auditing of N.A. accounts by headquarters turned out to be an advantage. It was apparent to all that professional accountants could only say whether the two sides of the ledger were in balance, which they did, but it was still up to administrative officers to discover whether or not N.A.s were managing their accounts properly and to take disciplinary action if needed. In countless small instances northerners saw that it was one thing to proclaim a new policy or pass a new ordinance and quite another to effect it. When the Governor chided the North because no officer in Benue Province could speak Munshi, a northerner reminded him of his order restricting the time that officers could remain in one province, and Cameron admitted the inconsistency.[3]

Downgrading Kaduna's chief post was more of a personal tragedy for Browne than a long-term victory for Lagos. Caught between the Governor and his erstwhile brother

[1] Lethem to Alexander, 14 April 1932, C.R.P.

[2] Sharwood Smith, 17 April 1966. Two of the new circuit judges were former Northern administrators.

[3] Lethem to Browne, 2 August 1933, C.R.P. Lethem was the officer who had this exchange with the Governor. 'Munshi', the unflattering Hausa name for the Tiv, was dropped shortly after this time.

officers, that fundamentally honest and capable administrator spent his final years in disillusionment and ineffectiveness, unable to provide the leadership that the northerners had become accustomed to.[1] Like his Southern predecessor and his Malayan successor, Browne was 'as northern as anyone' on the vital points of Anglo-African government.[2] He did not protest when Lethem wrote him a long, detailed critique of the Governor's programme, including imputation of motives.[3] And, fearing Cameron's disapproval, the Chief Commissioner 'would not even put forward reasonable advice' for the guidance of Residents.[4] When, because of his wife's health, Cameron ended the shortest governorship from Lugard's time to independence, Kaduna found itself almost as strong as before.

In the countryside the interpretation of policy rested as always in the hands of the D.O. Early in the Cameron governorship ranking northerners told each other that, legislation notwithstanding, they would be the ones who implemented, and they rightly assumed that Cameron's Memoranda would be as elastic as others had been. More forward-looking officers knew that they could use the Governor's ideas, abstract as they were, to further various longstanding plans of their own. One junior officer who spent the Cameron years touring rural areas observed that action sometimes did and sometimes did not conform to policy and at other times seemed to have no relation to it at all.[5] The Kamuku of Niger Province were given their own N.A., separate from Moslem emirates, while those of Zaria Province remained under the Chief of Birnin Gwari because the D.O. Zaria felt that on balance this would be a better arrangement for all concerned. The Igbirra stayed under the Atta until 1954. Most of the Gwari of Niger Province were grouped together in their own N.A., but dozens of Gwari communities stayed in Zaria Province, some of them continuing under officials of Zaria Emirate, others under the Chief of Birnin Gwari. The Emir of Jema'a lost some of his pagans, including Jabas in his area, but the Zaria Jabas were not affected. Some pagans got their own courts and councils;

---

[1] Carrow, 2 April 1965.
[2] Sharwood Smith, 6 May 1966.
[3] Lethem to Browne, 8 October 1933, C.R.P.
[4] Carrow, 22 April 1965.
[5] L. C. Giles, Notes, 5 June 1966.

some did not. Some areas received the 'intense anthropology' mentioned by the Governor but remained unchanged. Morgan did his 'research' at Zangon Katab in a single day, and the resulting regrouping of atomized hamlets and villages under a dozen or so selected leaders worked well. Since Cameron had spoken mainly of pagans, the more important Moslem areas in such provinces as Kano were not touched, although hard-pressed D.O.s had for years wished to rationalize their administration. The result of moving three tiny districts out from under the control of the Emir of Jema'a and into an independent Zaria district not subject to its Emir was that the near-by D.O. in Plateau Province could no longer protect them, the Zaria touring officers got to them less often, and they were henceforth bullied by their own clan leaders. A D.O. who worked with the Tiv observed that resuscitated councils were too atrophied to hold the imagination of the community, whose younger generation later opted for a supreme chief.[1] 'Facts are stubborn things in Africa', wrote another. 'How sensible was it of Cameron to try to turn the clock back thirty years? He knew so little of men . . . [and actually thought] that a governor can be advised on N.A.s as he [could] be . . . on public works or post offices.'[2]

Well may it be asked whether the 'Sacred North' controversy was only a tempest in a teapot.[3] In fact, it was more than that, because things were done in Cameron's time that would not have been done under a more easygoing governor. The same D.O. who did not take the Governor's advice about the Zaria Kamuku nonetheless felt that Cameron did the North a service in attacking its complacency.[4] The Kano D.O. who listened with horror to Cameron's shipboard diatribe against the North was equally put off by his own superior's exaggerated defence a few months later.[5] The northerners were more aware of the shortcomings of their system than any governor could have been, and pressure exerted during the Cameron years helped to bring improvement faster than it

---

[1] Stanhope White, op. cit., pp. 138–9.

[2] Giles, note 5, p. 79, above.

[3] A cadet in Cameron's time described it as 'much ado about nothing' (W. R. Crocker, *Nigeria*, London, 1936, p. 222).

[4] Sharwood Smith, 17 April 1966.

[5] Carrow, 22 April 1965.

would have come otherwise. The Governor's very ignorance was helpful, for his shots were often wide of the mark and the northerners found it possible to admit real shortcomings to one another while defending themselves from Lagos's inaccuracy and unfairness. In bestirring themselves they were moved by righteous indignation mingled with awareness that future challenges might be more dangerous.

Some of Cameron's changes brought mixed blessings. A few of the old Bornu bucksticks lingered on in the Province and others edged their way back later on. They were never a team again. Discontinuity in British staff made it easier for N.A. permanent officials to cover up their own malpractices. But the stagnation of which many a buckstick had himself complained was less after Cameron.[1] There were similar patterns in other provinces.

When, however, the Cameron pronouncements and ordinances are set in the context of continuing administration throughout the inter-war period, they do not appear to have been of major importance. In retrospect the oddest thing about the whole affair is the fact that there was so little real disagreement in the policy realm. Cameron's assumptions about native administration present in the aggregate a picture of very considerable confusion. But his revision of the Political Memoranda offers no startling contrast with earlier ones.[2] After having railed against Cameron for a decade, Palmer had no compunction about copying the Cameron Memoranda for use in the Gambia.[3] Ordinary district officers naturally developed a certain cynicism about this. How relevant to bedrock reality is a Bible that can be recommended without reference to the authors of particular scriptures and when those who do the

---

[1] Cf. Patterson's letter to Lethem, 10 August 1923, C.R.P., complaining of de Putron's almost exclusive interest in public works.

[2] Students of actual administration in the two territories governed by Cameron will have noticed the wide discrepancy between bush facts and the Governor's views. When Cameron's confused version of the facts becomes the basis for comparison of the two territories, as happens in his book, it is not surprising that the text often enters spheres of complete unreality.

[3] 'He [Cameron] really knows nothing about Natives and N.A.s and has been masquerading in borrowed plumes. Still, he has his uses and I have been able to introduce indirect methods here by using Cameron's Tanganyika formulae and as a humble follower in his footsteps. It is amusing. How Temple would have said Ha! Ha!' (Palmer to Lethem, from Bathurst, 1 January 1933, C.R.P.).

recommending are not Bible readers themselves and have always proceeded by empirical means?

The Cameron governorship showed once again that the enunciation of policy is a small thing by comparison with administrative momentum and economic penury.[1] The Depression hobbled the North and forced the new Governor to preside over staff retrenchments that slowed the pace of progress throughout the 1930s by comparison with the twenties. Added to this misfortune, lamented by both Cameron and the northerners, there was a drop in morale as a result of widespread suspicion that Lagos was withholding information and otherwise treating the North unfairly. When the smoke had cleared one realized that little had changed and that life in the emirates went on pretty much as before. The factors determining whether there was progress or stagnation and whether relations between officers and chiefs were good or bad were the same as they had always been. The small number of senior British officers and N.A. officials who managed the Region's administrative life were carried along by precedent and the basically unaltered rhythm of daily tasks. Here was the mainstream of everyday existence. Next to its steady rushing power the trickle of suggestion or admonition from the colonial capital hundreds of miles away to the south was intermittent and weak.

[1] Bourdillon's 'Memorandum on the Future Political Development of Nigeria', 1939, should also be mentioned as an interesting further statement of gubernatorial opinion on policy.

4

Colonial Government as a System of Power

EVERY arrangement whereby men exercise power over their fellows has a character and interest of its own and also a wider relevance. When tens of millions of people are involved and when the arrangement remains in force for more than half a century the study of it is bound to be pertinent, in however special a way, to our unending inquiries into the nature of man and society.

We are concerned here with a colonial power system and specifically with its European superstructure. This might seem on the surface to be a mere dinosaur, especially in an anti-colonial age when new nations are at pains to forget or possibly to deny the earlier species. Yet the legacy of the purely British administrative complex that overlay the grass-roots machinery of Anglo-African government is important and will remain so for many generations. No matter how much of its paraphernalia is discarded by African rulers, many things will go on being done in Northern Nigeria, consciously or not, simply because the British did them that way.[1] Several provinces in the North were still in fact being run by British officers as late as 1966 and a number of important offices in Kaduna as well. Habits were deeply ingrained. The changeover to independence had been gradual and peaceful, and the new Regional Government after 1960 had neither the inclination nor the staff and money to sweep the table clean. Nowhere in Africa south of the Sahara is the European administrative imprint plainer and more durable than in Northern Nigeria.

[1] It is impossible to visit or work in Northern Nigerian government offices today without being aware of this in countless small ways, from the arrangement and and use of furniture to the office ritual. J. H. Smith, who had ten years' experience as a District Officer in the British period and at this writing (1967) is still employed by the Government in Kaduna, cites a number of instances, such as the insistence on punctuality at public functions which was imbibed by the late Sir Ahmadu Bello from the practice of Sir Bryan Sharwood Smith, in charge of the North 1952–7, first as Lieutenant Governor, then as Governor.

The system's most outstanding single characteristic was the substantial degree of scope it allowed to individual initiative at the Resident and District Officer levels. Structurally and constitutionally simple to describe, the system was, because of this factor, infinitely various in actual operation. Its officers were in effect members of an élite corps rather than of a civil service in the European sense, for they were not responsible to a legislature. Nor, as we have seen, did they have to respond from day to day to an all-powerful central executive. The official ranking is describable, but the actual exercise of authority made nonsense of this as often as not. The tracing of particular *loci* of power and of the lines connecting them is therefore a matter that involves personalities and inter-personal relationships first and foremost. Moreover, the sands were constantly shifting and the whole pattern must be retraced when major figures move about within it or leave it entirely.

In Lugard's time the North was divided administratively into seventeen provinces. By the time of Cameron these had been reduced to eleven, the total being subdivided into just under forty divisions. Each division was further divided into districts, usually on tribal lines. In some of the more homogeneous areas districts were set up on geographical lines, the headships of some of them being hereditary. Some divisions were coterminous with emirates (Argungu, or Sokoto after the amputation of Dabai-Zuru), but more often they included more than one emirate (the Northern Division of Kano Province or Katsina Division) or a mixture including one or more emirates and one or more pagan areas (Bauchi or Zaria or Gwandu). From the standpoint of the posting of British officers the division was the basic unit, most being in the charge of a man of medium seniority or slightly higher. Depending on the size and importance of the division, he would be alone or aided by one to three assistant district officers or cadets. In practice, certain provinces and divisions had more prestige than others and it was possible to tell by a glance at the list of postings over a period of years which Residents were looked on by Kaduna as being capable of assuming major responsibility and which district officers appeared to be headed for greater things. At a given moment the lion's share of power in the North was thus concentrated in the hands of a couple of dozen men, including the Lieutenant

Governor (Chief Commissioner after 1933), the Secretary
Northern Provinces, the more important Residents, and the
up-and-coming district officers. Depending on local circumstances the concentration could be narrower than this or wider.
Palmer was so forceful and experienced that he gave close
supervision even to the Residents of major provinces such as
Bornu and Kano if he had a special interest in them. Alexander
was not inclined to interfere and did not have as much knowledge of the provinces as Palmer had. Browne's uncomfortable
situation affected his posture with the Residents, as did Adams's
unfamiliarity with local conditions. Each head of the Region
had his own style, there being a world of difference, for example,
between Gowers and Patterson or between Thompstone and
Sharwood Smith. On balance it would be right to say that the
Government was directed by a series of cliques and that few
major cultural areas in the tropical world, not to mention the
more industrialized one, were under the political control of so
small and indispensable an oligarchy as that which managed
the public affairs of Northern Nigeria in the colonial period.[1]
Remove the Governor in Lagos and the system does not miss a
beat. Remove the Northern élite and its government grinds
quickly to a halt.

It should be noted in passing that the reality of the power
structure is not conveyed in most official documents, which,
indeed, tend rather to obscure and confuse it. In the papers of
administration, especially annual reports, gazettes, and minutes
of official conferences, one finds exaggerated deference, for
example, to His Honour the head of the Regional Government,
and this is repeated all the way down through the hierarchy,
allowing an impression of strict adherence to the wishes of higher
authority. From the start the very regularity and official character of reports made them stereotyped and pretentious. Some
officers disliked writing them so much that the task was left to
clerks.[2] One of the reasons for the popularity of Wallace, who

---

[1] This is meant as a descriptive and not a moralistic statement. I emphasize my
intent because of reactions to previous statements of this kind in earlier work of
mine. 'Élite' is not a pejorative word in my opinion. During the colonial period
Northern Nigeria needed nothing so much as what she got from the British, i.e.
responsible autocracy. Nor was there an alternative short of anarchy.
[2] One such, who need not be named, made the second-class clerk draft the
annual report for his division (interview, D. A. Pott, London, 23 March 1965).

acted as Governor during several of Girouard's absences, was
that he cut down the incidence of reports.[1] Palmer observed
frankly that 'there are a great many things which can be said
in conversation and in private letters which do not look well in
an official file', while Carrow later remarked that the univer-
sality of 'window-dressing' made for a picture that was 'rosy and
a little deceptive'.[2] By the same token the testimony of officers
as contained in minutes of Residents' Conferences is not much
of a guide to anything, for 'no one would speak out . . . [there
was always] a dreary agenda' and important issues were scrupu-
lously avoided if they were controversial.[3] Some officers carried
over their distaste for paper into day-to-day administration as
well, one Resident instructing his juniors to save important
matters for personal discussion. 'The D.O. must not become
submerged in local correspondence.'[4] But the volume of paper
work mounted steadily. To the end there was a yawning chasm
between the reality of daily tasks and the version found in
official papers. In response to a plea from Kaduna during the
Second World War that he supplement his annual report by
sending a memorandum on what was really happening in his
N.A., the D.O. Zaria reluctantly provided some details on an
important addition to the Emir's council, admitting by the way
that 'there's not much in writing about it . . . it started in my
fertile imagination'.[5]

Inevitably there was a marked difference in outlook between
the Secretariat on the one hand and the general run of provincial officers on the other. The daily stint of desk men in
Kaduna contrasted sharply with D.O. chores. Each situation
had its own ethos, and the cleavage between them was a challenge to all heads of the Northern administration. Essentially
it was a question of how one spent the working day; the A.D.O.
touring on horseback was certain to see things differently from

---

[1] *Political Conference Agenda*, 1909, Reports, p. 3. Adams wanted reports to be
interesting, and some were (Weatherhead, 25 June 1967).

[2] Palmer to Lethem, 12 October 1918, C.R.P.; Carrow, 11 January 1966,
22 February 1966, 7 March 1966.

[3] Carrow, 11 January 1966. Palmer himself (to Lethem, 7 August 1928, C.R.P.),
who had to preside at many, said that they were uninteresting.

[4] 'Don't write.' (Resident Sokoto, Carrow, to D.O. Gwandu, 9 January 1936,
K.) Quote in text: ibid., 17 December 1934.

[5] D.O. Zaria, 1 September 1943, replying to H. P. W. Murray, S.N.P., 14 April
1943, K.

his opposite number in Kaduna. Over a fifteen-year period beginning in the mid-twenties there was constant correspondence between Kaduna and Sokoto Province, and within the Province, regarding the status of Dabai-Zuru, a pagan area lying some 150 miles south of Sokoto. In 1924 the area was transferred from Kontagora to Sokoto N.A.; in 1927 it became a separate division under Sokoto; in 1930 it was attached to Gwandu, but as a separate N.A.; in 1931 it was part of the new Southern Division of Sokoto Province; in 1933, on the abolition of this division, it was attached again to Sokoto Division; in 1934 it was transferred once more to Gwandu; and in 1939 it returned to Kontagora, but as a separate N.A. Throughout the correspondence on these changes Kaduna's main concerns, not unnaturally, were with lines of authority and with the traditions of the area, viewed historically. A.D.O.s, on the other hand, talked of the feelings of the Zuru Chief and his council members, of the actual amounts of work there were in the various rural offices involved, of distances between these offices and of differences in the talents of chiefs.[1] Some D.O.s regarded the Secretariat as the natural enemy, sure to oppose anything good that one wanted to do.[2] Others saw it as an irrelevance that could become a nuisance if not fed at regular intervals with the kind of paper it seemed to thrive on.[3] Yet in private letters of officers who began with a heavy dose of provincial experience and then went on to headquarters we find a pronounced ambivalence. On the one hand the D.O. situation is seen as the ultimate reality and purity—'I should have been prepared to stay . . . in Bornu till I had earned a decent pension, but I am not too happy at the thought of some years of low-down intrigue and dog-fighting with a possible chance of becoming Lieutenant

---

[1] See correspondence between Kaduna and Resident Sokoto, 18 July 1931 ff., K., on this point. In a more famous case, to be dealt with in detail in the following chapter, a tremendous change in the efficiency and morale of Sokoto N.A. was brought about by changes in the offices of Resident and of Sultan. These changes were a mystery to the Acting Lieutenant Governor, who wrote: 'I have not yet . . . fathomed the apparent volte-face in Sokoto from the evil regime of waziris and sorcerers to the present apparently enlightened and progressive one, with the Sarkin Musulmi all smiles and affability . . .' (Lethem to Browne, 5 July 1933, C.R.P.).

[2] E.g. Edwardes to Cary, quoted in Mahood, op. cit., p. 11.

[3] When Palmer sent Carrow to Kaduna for a stint 'to broaden your mind', Carrow felt that the experience had the opposite effect (11 January 1966).

Governor'; and again, 'I shall be very glad to get back to Bornu
—I am tired of this [the job of acting lieutenant governor]
already.'[1] Yet no one could deny that the road to the top lay
through headquarters and the best D.O. was often as ambitious
as he was devoted to Africa. One future chief commissioner paid
the usual tribute to D.O. life, but noting that the Governor had
sounded him on the possibility of becoming his private secretary,
he added, 'Heaven knows one wants something of that kind in
our job.'[2] As things worked out, the high command in Kaduna
usually consisted of experienced provincial officers. Despite
being engaged in different work from colleagues in the bush,
they shared a common background with them. If they were
legally superior and were given deference accordingly, it was
as senior members of the same club and not as an alien breed.

The power relationship between Kaduna and the Residents
was therefore quite different from the Lagos–Kaduna one. It
did have its institutional aspect, but an understanding of the
system depends on balancing this against personal factors.
Some of Kaduna's functions, such as postings, appear to be
objective and to belong in the category of normal institutional
procedure. An officer returning from leave had to be sent some-
where, as did a cadet arriving in the Protectorate for the first
time. There were always openings. In the course of time it
would seem that everyone would have occasion to serve in good,
bad, and indifferent posts and in different kinds of posts, such
as Moslem or pagan, urban or rural, mountainous or low-lying,
advanced or backward. In fact there was a hierarchy of posts,
and officers soon came to be rated by their superiors so as to
qualify or not qualify in relation to the ranking of possible
assignments. Up until 1930 Bornu was the recognized cradle of
successful men. Afterwards it was Sokoto and Kano, the former
being incomparable in prestige, the latter offering the greatest
challenge to one's organizational and administrative ability.
Occasionally there was a special circumstance: Tegetmeier
went to Bornu because he had served previously in Iraq and
his knowledge of Arabic and of Moslem ways was thought
relevant. Preferences came in if one's reputation was good and

[1] Lethem to Palmer, 9 October 1928; Palmer to Lethem, 21 October 1921,
C.R.P.
[2] Patterson to Lethem, 11 September 1919, C.R.P.

if there was more than one vacancy. Some preferred the social and other amenities of a major place like Zaria, whereas others wanted bush. Kontagora's prestige was certainly not of the highest, yet a former D.O. speaks of it as a 'heaven' of sorts.[1] In his longing to get back to Bornu after serving in Benue, Letchworth was not thinking of promotion so much as of that indefinable fascination that bucksticks felt for the sandy domain of the Kanuri and the Shuwa Arab. Few appeared to rhapsodize over Bida. In any case everyone knew that there were plum postings and punishment posts and a large grey area in between. When, after more than fifteen years in Bornu, de Putron found himself assigned to Benue where polo ponies could not live, he resigned. Hale Middleton also disappeared early, finding Plateau's charms rather limited after Kano's weighty tasks and the glories of Kaduna.

On the institutional side there was also a tendency—not confined to the British as a people but characteristic of them more than of those who incline to an egalitarian style in government—to assign so much integrity of position to a particular office as virtually to depersonalize its human occupant. After years of intimate correspondence with Palmer and later with Alexander, Lethem suddenly adopted the formal salutation 'Mr.' when they reached the office of lieutenant governor. Coming out to Nigeria on a not very large Elder Dempster liner in 1935, the Resident Zaria managed to address not a single word to one of his own junior officers, to whom he was most pleasant just before the young A.D.O. went on tour a few months later.[2] The formal drill surrounding the comings and goings of higher-ups was considerable. Lieutenant governors got gun salutes and a private coach on the railway. Their number twos and sometimes others sent messages of adieu and welcome as they left or re-entered the Protectorate. Their tours in the provinces were royal tours in miniature. A British ambassador who later served as a colonial governor could never quite get used to the rigid formality of the Colonial Service by comparison with the more easy-going ways of embassies.[3] In a

[1] Sharwood Smith, 1 May 1966.
[2] Giles, diary, 1935–6. The voyage lasted about a fortnight. The first-class passengers, then as now, were not all that numerous and it is most improbable that the Resident was unaware of the presence of one of his juniors.
[3] Sir Charles Johnston, *The View From Steamer Point*, London, 1964, ch. 21.

word, the fact that the Lieutenant Governor was a big man in the Region and the Resident in his Province was underscored by the extent to which their offices were encased in protocol and hung about with trappings that no one could miss.

The strength of institutional propriety is shown in the fate of an officer who ran foul of it in Sokoto during 1921. Edwardes, the officer in question, had been in the Province off and on since 1917 and at the time was Acting Resident in the absence on leave of Webster, the substantive Resident. For some time Edwardes had watched with disapproval certain illicit and damaging activities of the Sultan which were bringing the Emirate to a low state of corruption and oppression of the people. Encouraged by a liberal and vigorous policy statement from the Governor, he urged that the Sultan be deposed and he left no doubt in the minds of his superiors that in his opinion the trouble was all due to the laxity of the substantive Resident.[1] Had he confined himself to discussing specific abuses on which evidence could be produced and had he been careful to proceed through the Resident, Edwardes might or might not have made his point; in either case he probably would have caused himself no harm. As it was, he had officially questioned a superior. This, as the Lieutenant Governor was quick to point out, 'constitute[d] a very definite attack on Mr. Webster's administration and capacity'.[2] Swiftly the higher-ups closed ranks. Realizing his mistake, Edwardes backtracked but never regained his balance. The ensuing investigation glossed over the real issue and gave the guilty parties time to cover their tracks. Palmer, who had been Acting Lieutenant Governor in the early stages of the case, was given the unenviable job of writing a report that whitewashed both the Sultan and Webster. On returning to the Province Webster officially repudiated Edwardes's charges against the Sultan.[3] These were eventually borne out with compound interest. But this did nothing to save the unfortunate Edwardes, who was abruptly transferred. His final years were spent in the dustbin posts of Kabba and Munshi and he retired in the mid-1920s, well short of his fiftieth birthday. He had

[1] Edwardes to the Lieutenant Governor, 26 October 1921 ff., K. And see Edwardes Papers, C.R.P., 1921–2.

[2] Gowers, Lieutenant Governor, to Clifford, Governor, 21 January 1922, K.

[3] To S.N.P., 16 May 1922, K.

committed not one but two sins, either of which would have
been enough to ruin him: he had dared to criticize his superior
in an official document; and he had violated a cardinal rule of
these years: 'Do not become known as a friend of the peasants.'[1]

Yet in the long run it was the other side of the coin, the
personal side, that explains most about the Kaduna–Resident
power relationship. Very little can be said about a particular
Resident's position in relation to headquarters unless one knows
what sort of man he was and what Kaduna thought of him.
The catalogue of Kano Residents in the 1920s is a case in point.
Since Goldsmith was probably the weakest of the early lieutenant governors and knew nothing of Kano, Gowers, when
Resident there, did as he liked.[2] If the Province received rather
light-handed government in Gowers's time, the explanation is
not to be found in Kaduna. When Gowers in turn became Lieutenant Governor the same was true of Arnett's power in Kano,
not because Gowers was especially weak in Kaduna but because
his relationship with Arnett was normal and he saw no reason
to interfere with so senior an officer. In fact, during these years
a more junior officer, Hale Middleton, ran Kano Emirate
pretty much on his own, without reference to either the Resident
or the Lieutenant Governor, and was confirmed in his virtual
autonomy by receiving the rank of Resident, a rank that continued to be associated with the job of D.O. Emirate in Kano
Province for some time thereafter. The key to this seemingly
anomalous situation was the respect that both Gowers and
Arnett had for this extraordinary officer, of whom more will be
heard.[3] When in 1925 Palmer, who was junior to Arnett and
not on good terms with him, became Lieutenant Governor, it
was necessary for that reason to move Arnett elsewhere.[4] The
situation now changed completely. Because of his own previous
service in Kano and his exceptionally well-developed ideas
about the need for reforming its administration, Palmer exerted

---

[1] The meaning of this rule was not of course that one should be against the
peasants—on the contrary, everyone from Lugard onwards stressed that a primary
duty was to protect them—but that they should be helped only through their own
rulers.

[2] For most valuable supplementary information on Kano in these years I am
indebted to the best-known Kano man of them all: Carrow (Notes, 6 July 1966).

[3] It will be recalled that Hale Middleton had earlier established a reputation
for firm, independent, and capable rule in Hadejia (ch. 2 above).

[4] Cf. Arnett Papers, 1925, C.R.P.

H

direct influence in the affairs of the Province while at the same time discharging his duties as Lieutenant Governor. The substantive Resident most of the time was Alexander, with Wightwick acting as Resident once or twice and Lindsell a good deal. Unable to speak Hausa, inexperienced in the ways of Northern emirates, and occupied often with special bureaucratic duties under Palmer's direction, Alexander was not in a position to be a strong, much less an independent, Resident. More often than not the day-to-day routine fell on Lindsell and on his junior officers, particularly Carrow, all of them responding ultimately to the lead of the Lieutenant Governor himself in Kaduna. This was the power situation until Palmer left Nigeria in 1930, after which Kano again had several Residents with more independent authority.

The qualities Palmer liked—and when he found them in the Residents of other provinces than Kano and Bornu he was capable of leaving the men alone—were toughness, soundness on policy, and a reputation for being 'solid'.[1] Taken as a whole this meant promoting precisely that balance which has been referred to earlier: coaxing the N.A. forward to efficiency and honesty, but not going over its head or pushing it so hard that it failed to acquire experience and self-confidence. With a senior Resident who was, by his standards, too much of a *laissez-faire* type (mai lafiya) Palmer was firm, if discreet. Webster of Sokoto was quietly moved to Yola for his final tour in the North.[2] And with a D.O. who acted directly, i.e. not through the N.A., in an emergency he was severe while privately admitting that the man had had little choice in the circumstances.[3] Slowness or frivolity he particularly disapproved, and he made sharp distinctions between those he considered suitable or not for the Secretariat. Though he did not always hold to it in practice, his view of the proper relationship between Kaduna

[1] E.g. to Lethem, 13 January 1928, C.R.P.

[2] 'It is a pity we have such a "Mai Lafiya" in charge of the Province' (to Lethem, 30 March 1928, C.R.P.); he rejected the Governor's suggestion that Webster be sacked, however: 'There is no need to turn him out as H. E. wanted' (ibid., 22 June 1928).

[3] Sharwood Smith, the officer in question, was at first barred from further service in major Moslem emirates, but Palmer put the blame mainly on Webster (for the Gusau murder case, 1928, to be discussed in the following chapter), and after conducting his own personal investigation he set aside the original limitation on Sharwood Smith (27 March 1966).

and a Resident was the classic one: give senior posts to good men
only and then leave them to it. 'It is entirely inadvisable for the
Lieutenant Governor to . . . tell Residents . . . what they can
or should do . . . and if a Resident cannot act without instructions . . . and carry his Emir with him, he is unfit to be a
Resident at all.'[1]

Apart from the inclinations and capacities of particular
lieutenant governors and Residents as determinants of the
power relationship between them, there was also the possibility
of Residents having their own way on the sly. One Resident
Niger shortly after the Second World War had to deal with an
especially unsatisfactory Fulani Chief in a minor pagan emirate,
and he sought the Chief Commissioner's permission to remove
him. The suggestion did not meet with Kaduna's approval.
Undaunted, the Resident remembered methods used in the
Cameroons when he had been a junior there under Ruxton.
The hopeless Chief was packed off on an international tour
including the Pilgrimage to Mecca. In his absence reforms were
made in his council and throughout the N.A. Kaduna was
content with the spectacle of the Province's unruffled surface,
yet the Resident had achieved his purpose.

There were special factors such as long tenure in a single
post. Herman-Hodge was in Ilorin from 1920 until his retirement in 1933, and he understandably regarded the Province
as his personal satrapy. Of higher birth than the average officer
and delighting in a whimsical disdain for all higher authority
and for bureaucrats in particular, he was not above calculated
insults. When a train including the Acting Lieutenant Governor's private coach stopped at Ilorin on one occasion, Herman-Hodge boarded it to visit an old friend and pointedly
ignored His Honour.[2] It was just this sort of entrenched privilege
that roused Cameron's ire and caused him to limit the amount
of time an officer could serve in one place. Yet even after
Cameron's time the prerogatives of Residents were considerable. It was the Resident and no one else who gave permission

---

[1] Palmer drafted this himself and then, as a dig at Baddeley, had it sent to Lagos
over the signature of a junior officer (H. O. S. Wright, to the Chief Secretary,
31 December 1925). I thank J. H. Smith for calling my attention to this letter.
[2] The Acting Lieutenant Governor afterwards wrote, 'I'm standing no more
nonsense from him. He thinks we are afraid of his pen' (Browne to Lethem, 30
March 1933, C.R.P.).

for visitors to enter Bornu during most of the inter-war years.

If Residents were thus able to maintain considerable independence it might be expected that D.O.s, being much closer to their immediate superiors, would be on tighter reins. Such in fact was the official line: '. . . the personal element must more and more be subordinated to the machinery of administration rather than each individual officer attempting to perform his own particular duties in his own way'.[1] When officers were stationed at the same place as their superiors and when they were very junior it would seem only logical that they should have little or no independent authority. In many cases it was true that juniors and even those with the rank of D.O. did receive relatively close supervision and did see themselves as being in essence the agents of their Residents rather than masters in their own houses. One D.O. in charge of a division of Sokoto Province, who had previously held a commission in the armed forces, protested to the Resident that his orders were not specific enough, that he was given too free a hand, and was often forced to rely on his own initiative.[2] Another was unimaginative and literal-minded about orders from above. When his Resident upbraided him for repeatedly sending in unsatisfactory audit reports on the Native Treasury in his division, the D.O. simply took over the accounting, cash book, and vote service ledger himself rather than training N.A. officials and exerting discipline to see that the work was done properly. Lax or inept D.O.s had occasionally to be jacked up by Residents, especially if the latter were the sort who kept close tabs on the affairs of all parts of their provinces. Having given a new D.O. explicit instructions on the running of his division and a sermon on the sins of his predecessors, a Resident ended his letter ominously, 'I now wait with interest to see what you make of it.'[3] Subsequent messages indicated anything but satisfaction. Various officers were blasted for failure to tour enough, for complaining about N.A. deficiencies rather than attending to them, and for specific lapses. In all these cases the relationship between the

[1] Government of Nigeria, Sokoto Emirate, *Notes on Procedure*, 1932, p. 3. This document was put forward as a model for other provinces as well.

[2] Not surprisingly, this officer, who shall remain nameless, was retrenched during the Depression.

[3] Resident Sokoto, Carrow, to D.O. Gwandu, 8 August 1935, K.

Resident and his subordinates was determined not by objective difference in rank but by extraordinary vigour on the part of the Resident and by equally unusual shortcomings in his juniors.

More typical were situations in which D.O.s resisted their superiors and found various ways of asserting themselves. A Bornu D.O. went no further than writing to an officer who outranked both his Resident and himself, complaining that menial tasks were being assigned to him.[1] Weatherhead in Nupe received one order from the Resident and another, contradicting it, from his immediate superior. Hearing that the Resident was on his way to pay them a visit, he got out of an awkward situation by going on tour.[2] In Argungu a D.O. was criticized by Sokoto for getting political information from a government messenger thought to be in the pay of the Emir.[3] The D.O. continued to use this man and asked the Acting Resident where he got his information.[4] He went on over the ensuing weeks to supply Sokoto with detailed reports on rooting out corruption in the Emir's court and in the division generally, meanwhile still employing the agent to whom his superior had objected. Finally the Acting Resident admitted that the D.O. had 'a difficult task trying to clean an Augean stable—he is the man on the spot and should be . . . the best judge'.[5]

Another form of self-assertion was to do what one thought best and say nothing about it, in the meantime perhaps telling provincial headquarters what it wanted to hear. The Resident Bornu candidly advised a junior to learn what things to keep to himself and what things to pass on.[6] It was a matter of playing a game whose rules were known to all but were not universally acceptable. In Sokoto Edwardes showed that he either did not understand the game or was unwilling to play it. So with a D.O. in Niger Province during the 1930s, a likeable officer who somehow never got ahead, being either too proud to advertise himself or considering that sort of thing not worth the candle.[7]

---

[1] Patterson to Lethem, 11 May 1925, C.R.P.
[2] Letter to his parents, 6 June 1937.
[3] Prankerd, Acting Resident, to Sharwood Smith, D.O. Argungu, 7 January 1930, K. There was a case of mistaken identity in this instance, which came right in the end.   [4] Reply, ibid., 30 January 1930.
[5] 18 March 1930, K.   [6] Palmer to Lethem, 12 October 1918, C.R.P.
[7] Weatherhead, letters, 22 May 1937 and 2 September 1937.

A devoted junior observed that his superior concentrated so fully on running a good division that he could not be bothered to let headquarters know what he was up to. For those who knew and played the game, correspondence with the Resident could be almost a litany. 'How do you account for the increased population in your division?' 'A generally higher standard of living due to the success of our development scheme.'[1] In matters touching on policy everyone knew that the dogma was Indirect Rule. Appearances had to be kept up. If the local N.A. was weak the D.O. was running things himself, but this would not be altogether clear in official reports.[2]

D.O. independence was most marked in outstations where primitive communications left no alternative. Jema'a is now in Zaria Province, far distant from headquarters, but even when it was in Plateau with the Resident nearer at hand the D.O. was on his own virtually the whole time. 'Please remember', a Resident admonished unnecessarily, 'that I shall have to be entirely guided by your recommendations.'[3] In the inter-war years there was no all-season road to Hadejia from Kano. When the Emir died in 1925 the D.O., Walwyn, sifted the qualifications of various candidates, picked a new Emir, and told headquarters about it later, being careful to put his report in the form of a request for approval.[4] But even when they lived in the same Government Residential Area with the Resident and had an office next to his, some D.O.s were no less independent for all that. In Zaria a D.O., as a matter of routine, advised the Resident how he proposed to divide up the work of the division among its various officers. Seeing that the plan involved close supervision of all facets of N.A. activity by Europeans, the Resident replied that 'the whole idea seems to me to savour far too much of direct rule'.[5] This changed nothing. The D.O. knew the N.A. like the back of his hand and knew exactly what he wanted all officials to do in the furtherance of various plans for developing the Emirate. These went forward virtually with-

---

[1] Interview, J. A. H. Maund, 15 March 1965.
[2] A situation which continued beyond independence, according to British officers still serving in the North in 1965 (e.g. interview, P. J. Wallace, Zaria, 17 July 1965).
[3] Resident Plateau, Jos, to D.O. Kagoro, 6 November 1926, K.
[4] Secret File on Emirs, Hadejia, entry of 23 February 1925.
[5] Beck to Sharwood Smith, 24 August 1935, K.

out reference to the Resident or to his successor, although in all cases the appearances of subordination were strictly maintained. When, a year and a half later, the Emir died it was the D.O. who managed the succession, lock, stock, and barrel.[1]

The influence of personality was paramount and all-pervasive. If the D.O.s Gwandu and Argungu were sometimes rather closely supervised by the Resident, this was a function of their personalities in relation to his, and the relative autonomy of the D.O. Zaria, living on the same station with his Resident, is explainable in the same way. In general the system worked best when supervision was minimal, assuming that the D.O. was vigorous and capable. By the time an officer reached the rank of D.O. he had presumably proved his worth and gained enough experience to manage a division on his own. Interfering with him unduly or merely to demonstrate the constitutional powers of a superior was to short-circuit the system or at least to hinder it with unnecessary bureaucracy. Although their rank was not high, the D.O.s in charge of divisions were, as a group, the most important officers in the administration, from the standpoint of day-to-day governing. The best D.O., in the words of one who should know, 'by-passed or bulldozed obstacles'.[2] Although some were in weak positions owing to their own failings and although others curried favour for some such purpose as getting a flattering report on themselves, the average D.O. in charge of a division was his own man. Had it been otherwise the Northern Service would have been more bureaucratic and less powerful than it was and its influence on Africa would have been far less.

Over the years the system underwent certain changes that affected all its members and altered the nature of their work. Before the 1930s there was more continuity of posting and individual officers were more familiar with the local scene in many instances. There were fewer men to go round; provincial budgets were smaller; there was less paper work. The result was a relatively loose-jointed machine and a highly individualistic one. It delivered less power in these years than later on. Its impression on the people, while profound and lasting, was

[1] This succession, which will be dealt with in detail in the following chapter, is covered by correspondence between Zaria and Kaduna, 18 January 1937 ff., K.
[2] Sharwood Smith, 31 March 1965.

correspondingly less. In the earliest period of all—the pre-1918 years—the system was experimental to the point of being haphazard, and it had a remarkable sense of humour. Inevitably this was followed by steadily increasing bureaucracy and a greater reliance on precedent for its own sake. Better roads and motor cars gave officers a less distinct picture of the countryman, despite the persistent efforts of Residents to see that rural areas were periodically toured as always by juniors on horseback. After the lull caused by the Depression the number of administrative and other officers stood at an all-time high.[1] In spite of an increase in wives, generally thought to have been a discouragement to touring, and a rise in paper work, the capacity of the machine was greater as it turned more and more to schemes for economic and social development. Whereas a large number of Lugard's men and of the post-1918 crop had been soldiers, the average officer in later years came from the university. He would be a rash observer who made a neat generalization about the respective administrative styles and performances of the military and civilian streams. Probably it would be accurate to say that regardless of origin older men differed from younger ones in the usual way: they were more concerned with what had proved workable in the past and less inclined to try new things.

In other respects the genre of the system was constant throughout the British years. From start to finish there was tension between two disparate proclivities in the system: on the one hand, it tended to coalesce and to become something unto itself as bureaucracies do in more advanced countries; and on the other hand, it showed an inclination to disintegrate into separate and distinct units, each going its own way and united by little more than nominal, bureaucratic links to a common centre. In the middle and later years of those who rose to the top or who entered the upper reaches by lateral transfer we see the first tendency. These men tried to view administration in broad perspective and to reflect on what the whole thing was about. As their gaze turned away from local reality to problems of co-ordination and leadership they found themselves often at

---

[1] At its height in the mid-fifties the Administrative Service numbered about 230 men, being considerably below that figure during the inter-war years. The estimated population of the North in 1931 was 11½ million.

variance with brother officers who still looked downwards to the soil of Africa. In 1918 the Resident Bornu admonished a junior for his parochial outlook, for galloping about counting cattle and making intensive linguistic and ethnographic studies of small tribal communities.[1] He denied that there were important differences between provinces and held that it was nonsense to speak of 'Bornu methods' and 'Kano methods'. 'Unless you pull yourself up you will get the reputation for being a keen A.D.O. but not suitable for more responsible positions.'[2] Lieutenant governors had the job of rating Residents, deciding not only who was qualified to go higher but which man ought to be in which post.[3] There naturally came to be a preference for those who were safe, and this tended to put a premium on agreeableness and the avoidance of controversy. Insight and imagination may not have been thought dangerous but they certainly were not always emphasized by comparison with more pedestrian attributes. In any case, one dealt at this level with abstractions more than with Africans. Pulling together in an organization is easier and more natural for such people than it is for those who are scattered widely about the countryside, each being fully occupied with his own daily round of chiefs and lesser officials of the N.A.

The dichotomy between Europe and Africa, between paper and people, resided not only in Kaduna but also in provincial headquarters, divisional offices, and even within the minds of individual officers as they toured the countryside. For those who were rising in the system Africa tended to recede, to become more a matter of memory than of present consciousness. For others of different bent Africa went on occupying the centre of the stage. The officer who served out a normal career gave some thirty of his best years to it. The Government of which he was a part was Anglo-African and, for better or worse, he was enmeshed in it. An alien in a strange land, a temporary sojourner, he nonetheless had a powerful voice in the affairs of the community he lived in. History affords ample evidence of alien rulers responding to such situations by monopolizing power and

[1] Palmer to Lethem, 29 September 1918, C.R.P.
[2] Ibid., 12 October 1918.
[3] Cf. Alexander to Lethem, 28 February 1932, C.R.P., on Daniel, Herman-Hodge, *et al.*

victimizing their subjects. British morality ruled this out. Officers were therefore trapped between the stone wall of a culture that was closed to them and the pressures of having to live side by side with that culture. The white man in these circumstances, as Temple had good reason to know, 'undergoes a process of battering highly prejudicial to his mental and bodily strength'.[1] Men who were ordinarily of even temperament, moderate, considerate, open-minded, and helpful to their associates, often seemed to change character radically. Violent outbursts of temper were common. Many was the cadet who, arriving in his first station, was bundled off on tour without instructions and who spent his early years being kicked about by superiors who might have given him a minimum of advice and constructive criticism. All human institutions contain bloody-mindedness; the pressures of their interracial situation gave colonial governments more than their proper share of it. After years of catching African officials in the same acts of petty crime and deviousness and helplessly watching the sands of corruption and oppression sift back into the local institutions that one had only recently cleaned out, it is not surprising that a few officers would drink rather more than they would otherwise have been inclined to do. Whatever idiosyncracies one had were accentuated by Africa. Extremes of weather, servants who appeared to be deliberately dense, lashings of quinine, bad food, poor medical facilities in the midst of unusual hazards to health, loneliness, the unlikelihood of a normal family life— the wonder was that the Service performed as well as it did, and that so many officers had such strong attachments to Africa.

If over the years it was the second tendency in the system— the disintegrative and Africa-focusing one—that prevailed, the explanation is not far to seek. Aggregate British power was never enough for a tightly woven fabric of authority to be spread evenly and effectively over the whole Region. The hand of central government remained relatively weak to the last. The great impervious mass of Africa drew officers down to it and absorbed their best efforts and energies, leaving little extra for accountability to higher authority and to the outward-looking aspect of what is called colonialism. The men who *were* the system deferred and accommodated to Africa. The satis-

[1] Quoted from Temple, *Native Races and Their Rulers*, p. 59.

factions derived in the process were great. Ultimately it was the co-operation of D.O.s and chiefs and of their respective subordinates in the countryside that justified Britain's presence and built a mystique and structure of government that survived when independence came.

5

D.O.s and Chiefs

NONE of the essential characteristics of government in British Northern Nigeria was unique in and of itself, but the resulting combination was unlike any other in space or time. As in Tsarist Russia the government was an autocracy, but in Northern Nigeria the rulers were aliens. Unlike other alien conquerors, such as the Ch'ing, or indeed the Fulani, the British did not become absorbed into the conquered society. Like the Portuguese, the British were strangers in Africa, but their stay was brief and they did not merge their domestic and overseas provinces into a united empire or proclaim doctrines of non-racial, uniform citizenship. Unlike the French, whose territories adjoined Nigeria, the British made deliberate and extensive use of indigenous institutions and evolved hybrids that survived independence.[1] Comparatively speaking, Britain's view of her task in the North was remarkably objective and pragmatic. She manipulated the levers of power, made short-term plans, stayed socially aloof from the general populace and the local rulers alike, and then after half a century she went away.

We have seen that in the early years Anglo-African government was the child of British weakness and diffidence plus the relatively strong local regimes found in existence during the occupation. By the 1920s both sides had changed and new

---

[1] Political institutions in ex-French territories are more European than hybrid, and French rule had been more direct than British in that the French did not go out of their way to retain and build up local officials on the scale of British rule in Northern Nigeria. I am not aware of a comparative work that gets down to the grass-roots in a French and a British territory in the colonial period in a comprehensive way. The most enlightening brief discussion I have seen is in a book review by A. Rivkin in *West Africa*, 2565 (30 July 1966), pp. 857–8; see also Gouverneur Deschamps, 'Et Maintenant, Lord Lugard?', *Africa*, XXXIII (December 1963), and M. Crowder, 'Indirect Rule—French and British Style', *Africa*, XXXIV (July 1964). A highly interesting, brief comparison that includes Belgian as well as French and British rule is in W. R. Crocker, *On Governing Colonies*, London, 1947.

factors were present. The doctrine of Indirect Rule had made its appearance and was influencing some officers to take or avoid certain courses of action relative to the Africans. The Native Authorities had developed greatly. British and Africans alike had gained experience and progress had been made jointly, the two parts of Anglo-African government remaining separate, yet hooked together in all the important activities of daily administration. The direction, pace, and *modus operandi* of each division depended on the way in which the impulses and capabilities of its European and African officials blended in practice. The drill was common to all: a continuous confrontation of British and Africans on taxation, justice, the economy, the internal workings of the N.A., and on public works, education, and health. Regardless of personalities, the same themes were present everywhere. All N.A.s tended to backslide whenever one's grip relaxed. British ambivalence about de-Africanizing was always there, as was discontinuity of staff. Over the whole of the North reaction, conservatism, and localism fought against Regional uniformity and progress. Europe and Africa were both in motion, reacting to internal pressures and to each other, shaping and being shaped by the strong, weak, and indifferent personalities who held the reins of power from time to time.

The administrator and the Chief of 1930 and 1940 were like those of 1910 and 1920, yet subtly different. Virtually the same components of terrain, of life and of system were there. But, taken as a whole, the North was remarkable for the depth and permanence of the change that had come to it. The greatest watershed in its history had been reached and passed. Occasionally the major actors on both sides, European and African, thought about this and discussed it. More often they got on with mundane jobs and gave little thought to the whys and wherefores and to ultimate aims.

From earliest times officers laid down rules of varying formality that were to govern relations between Europeans and chiefs. Lugard was specific about this and his niceties hung on in places like Kano for a long time. A strict protocol and etiquette surrounded the regular weekly meetings between the Resident and the Emir of Kano, held alternately in the Residency and in the Emir's house. Should the Resident be away the meeting would be chaired by the D.O., but only in the Emir's house.[1] The Emir was received at the door of the Residency when he called there, never in the office. A native couch, covered with a rug, was made ready for him to sit on (not a chair). Strict punctuality was observed, it being unthinkable that either the Resident or the Emir should have to wait on arrival at the other's house.

Ruxton in Muri was still more specific:

Never lose your temper; always be dignified; never be familiar; always be courteous; never speak roughly or quickly; cultivate a low tone of voice; never give an order unless you know it can be obeyed, or if it can be obeyed and is not, that you have the power to enforce it; never jump to conclusions, but await events . . . don't write letters to Chiefs; don't rebuke a Chief in the presence of his people. . . .[2]

He went on to point out that prestige would accrue to the officer who comported himself correctly and that it should not be made 'a parrot cry by which to cover some high-handed action'.[3] European moral integrity in action would be the surest guarantee of respect from African officials. One must take time with little things like salutations and go slowly in interviews so that the native could 'collect his scattered thoughts'.[4] Chiefs should be escorted into headquarters and out again. Mats should be provided for Moslem officials to sit on. Europeans should never smoke in the presence of Moslems or allow dogs about. 'Hands should only be shaken with the Emir', and the African should give the whole of his hand, not just his fingers, the latter being a sign of contempt.[5] A native who enters your house with his sandals on is being deliberately impudent, and disrespect is also shown in the failure of a native to pull down his chin cloth. Europeans should not be present at sallas (*sic*) and should not enter mosques or fetish houses.

As time went on there were changes showing that the two races were getting used to each other and that there was less insistence on strict observance of protocol. In the mid-1930s the S.N.P. asked Residents what they thought of admini-

[1] Carrow, 22 April 1965, where he also notes that up to the 1920s in Kano there was no social intercourse whatever between British and Africans.

[2] 'Instructions for the Guidance of Newly Joined Officers', copied in the Muri Provincial Office in 1909 by H. M. Brice-Smith, C.R.P.

[3] Ibid.　　　　　　　　　　[4] Ibid.　　　　　　　　　　[5] Ibid.

strative officers shaking hands with all N.A. officials rather than with the Emir only.[1] The response was mixed. The D.O. Zaria noted that the Emir did not shake hands with his own N.A. officials and urged that progress of this kind should not be pushed too fast. Should chiefs be offered a chair when talking with D.O.s and should there be an occasional tea party for the Emir? There were traditionalists and progressives, often but not always on generational lines. A young A.D.O. in Zaria invited the Emir to his house for tea and waited in some trepidation for the Chief to arrive.[2] To his delight the Emir appeared more or less on time, attended by a single official. He sat on a deck chair, chatted happily, dipped his biscuits in his tea, reached for a cigarette without being offered them, looked at an album of photographs, insisted on his own being taken, and in general seemed to enjoy himself hugely. In the lesser Emirate of Hadejia it was not uncommon in these years for the Emir to stay to lunch with the D.O. after one of their regular weekly sessions in the D.O.'s house.[3]

The experience of working together on common tasks could bring about a considerable intimacy and meeting of minds. Seeing each other daily, the Emir of Yauri and the local D.O. soon developed a close working relationship, discussing matters frankly and speaking openly with one another. Asked for his advice and preference on whether to start work on a new road or finish repairs on an old one first, the Emir stated his opinion clearly and gave reasons which the D.O. found acceptable.[4] When the Emir of Gwandu received the C.B.E., an event that might have been expected to appeal more to the British than to the Africans, there was general pleasure and gratification, with both sections of the Birnin Kebbi community joining in without

[1] To Resident Zaria, correspondence 12 June 1934 ff., K.
[2] Giles, diary, February 1936. The A.D.O. was then living in Zaria city, not in the Government Residential Area.
[3] Emir's Interview Book, Hadejia, 28 December 1939.
[4] Yauri Book, 30 August 1930. (When I was visiting the Emir of Yauri in Yelwa during 1965 he was kind enough to lend me a book, in Hausa, kept by his father, the Emir Abdullahi, and by administrative officers stationed there in the years 1928–31—Messrs. Harris, Holme, Bulger, and Tupper-Carey. The book was kept at the Emir's residence and entries were made by him and by the local D.O. on a daily basis so that it provides a record of all administrative matters and a good deal on personal exchanges. I am grateful to J. H. Smith for arranging and to Mallam M. B. Gadzama for making the translation.)

respect to race or nationality.[1] The D.O.'s wife could not say who was more delighted, she and her husband or the N.A. official who brought them the news. In less pleasant matters both sides were capable of speaking out. The D.O. Yauri was quick to call the Emir's attention to little mistakes on his part and to prod him for what Europeans considered bad manners.[2] One Resident did not hesitate to do the same with the Sultan of Sokoto. Chiefs for their part would speak up in a spirited way when they felt strongly. Carrow tried to talk the Emir of Kano into allowing local broadcasting of B.B.C. programmes containing readings from the Koran. In this instance the Resident was actually relaying a request from young mallams in Kano who were in favour of the broadcasts:

THE EMIR. Oh, those young mallams have been getting at you, have they?

THE RESIDENT. I wouldn't say that. But why can't you agree? It seems a reasonable request.

THE EMIR (sitting up and looking determined). You know nothing whatever about the Holy Koran or the proprieties when it is being read. If you will keep quiet and let me speak I will explain things to you.

THE RESIDENT. Very well. I am listening. But I don't admit that I ever prevent you saying anything that you wish to, nor do I admit that I am so ignorant as you make out. However, go ahead and say what you want.

THE EMIR. It is not correct that just anybody should read from the Holy Koran. Only a properly qualified man of irreproachable character. London is miles and miles away. How do I know whom the B.B.C. employ to give these readings. He may be someone quite unsuitable and of bad character, in which case we should be wrong to listen.

THE RESIDENT (slightly shaken but still trying). I understand your point, but I can assure you that Waziri Churchill would never allow the B.B.C. to employ an unsuitable man to do these readings from the Koran. I have known you for many years, first when you were a district head and I was a junior A.D.O. Then I was D.O. when the Governor installed you here in Kano as Emir. And here we still are, old friends. I hope you will accept my personal assurance that I know an unsuitable man would never be employed.

[1] Letters to his parents, Weatherhead, 3 January 1944, and Mrs. Weatherhead, same date.

[2] Yauri Book, e.g. entry after that of 7 March 1929.

THE EMIR (a little doubtfully). Very well, I accept your assurance. But there is another point. Some of the boxes [loud-speakers] are in public and open courtyards. The words from the Holy Koran might be coming out of the boxes and most irregular things might be going on around—dancing, swearing, people walking about and so on.

THE RESIDENT (very confidently). But that is too easy. If at any time the readings are coming out and it is not convenient for those around to listen, then all that is necessary is for someone to put up his hand and turn off the little switch and the reading will stop.

THE EMIR (crushingly). What a suggestion! The Holy words are coming forth, and you suggest that someone should turn the machine off, thereby showing that he does not wish to listen! That would be worse than anything![1]

Shop talk was common. With the passing years D.O.s and chiefs learned to peer into each other's minds and to predict each other's reactions in well-worn circumstances. They achieved a certain closeness. If they were seldom able to relax completely in each other's company and to form the kinds of social relationships that each had with his own people, they were nonetheless capable of highly efficient communication. Living in different worlds side by side, they co-operated closely and continuously.

Weekly meetings were the original arrangement. The Zaria Political Diary of the 1930s shows formal meetings approximately every third day and this does not include less formal ones.[2] Entries in the Diary are a microcosm of ordinary subjects discussed and tasks performed: hereditary succession among district heads; the town water supply; manual labour in the elementary school; sanitation; 'Sheriff Mohamedu, an Arab of Timbuctou, to see the D.O. before seeing the Emir to ask for alms'; reform of a district and appointment of new village heads; complaints by A.D.O.s on tour that N.A. officials in Makarfi District are unsatisfactory; discussion between Emir and District Engineer (European) about N.A. apprentices in the Public Works Department; tax collecting; court cases and fines; *jangali* (cattle tax); N.A. Estimates for

---

[1] Carrow, 24 September 1965.
[2] I am grateful to the Acting Provincial Secretary Zaria, 1965 (P. J. Wallace, M.B.E.), for making available to me the political and touring diaries of the Division, covering the 1920s, 1930s, and 1940s. See entries of January 1931 ff.

the coming year; visit by the Emir and Nigerian Attorney General to Beit-el-mal; famine relief; visit by D.O. and Emir to a district whose district head is unsatisfactory; inspection of the Waziri's office by D.O.; Emir and D.O. conference with Veterinary Officer; checking of the N.A. cash; demonstration of equipment by Morris Motors for the benefit of the Resident and the Emir; the affairs of the near-by station of the Church Missionary Society; the prison; touring by the Emir to persuade the people to accept smallpox vaccinations; transportation for touring (the Emir favouring cars and the D.O. horses); and again and again, 'Emir told to warn Sarkin so-and-so that his work has not been satisfactory'.

In Hadejia, where there was only one British officer, the subjects were similar but the scale of activity was smaller and relations tended to be somewhat less formal. The N.A.s in both Hadejia and neighbouring Gumel, also under the D.O. Hadejia, were substantially inferior to Zaria's and references to disciplinary action by the D.O. were more frequent. 'The Emir agreed that Chiroma's tax work had been most unsatisfactory and stated that he had reprimanded him.'[1] The two emirs themselves were pushed constantly, D.O.s being less subtle about it than in major emirates. 'I informed the Emir [of Gumel] that I was not impressed by his efforts at investigating charges of extortion.'[2] Education had to be forced from above, for the average native, regardless of his class, looked on European schooling with suspicion. The introduction of new techniques in agriculture and of mixed farming in particular were resisted more often than not, as were health improvements and pressure for more equitable treatment of women. There was an attempt to introduce more representative forms in local administration so that the smallest communities would have, if not democracy, at least some say in their own affairs and a means of getting a hearing at the Emir's court. Some success was achieved in creating a basis of co-operation by bringing chiefs together. Chiefs' conferences and visits to major centres such as Kano, and eventually Lagos and abroad, were popular. Although most rulers did not at first grasp the objectives of meetings or have much notion of what would take place, the

[1] Emir's Interview Book, Hadejia and Gumel, 19 November 1934.
[2] Ibid., 19 February 1935.

gatherings did have the long-term effect of reducing parochialism. Young men with European education, whom D.O.s
forced chiefs to accept as members of their N.A.s, had a
similar effect in cutting into the stone wall of traditional
ways.

Yauri, an even smaller unit, had an extraordinarily vigorous
and capable Chief. His relationship with the local D.O. was
close, and no subject was too inconsequential for the two men
to discuss. At the D.O.'s suggestion, for example, the Emir
opened a chequing account at the nearest branch of the
Niger Company. 'This is not difficult. Just ask the Treasurer to
pay £10 to the Bank each month. The Bank will write from time
to time to tell you how much you have.'[1] The Emir had a taste
for European products, such as phonograph records, guns and
ammunition, biscuits, cigarettes, medicine, and shoes, and he
regularly sought the D.O.'s advice and help in buying them.
'Could you help me with that powder which you gave me . . .
during the last rainy season . . . it is good for catarrh . . . Oh,
I like it too much!'[2] The D.O. seized on opportunities for
introducing European ways of thought, the most common
being the unfamiliar notions of time and of planning ahead.
'Instead of purchasing 36 sticks of cigarettes, why not buy a
packet, which will last longer.'[3] In the administrative field the
problem was the classic one in situations of relatively un-
fettered if benign autocracy: an able ruler, a hopeless N.A., a
silent population. If the ruler was not restrained there would be
irresponsibility. If he was disciplined too much he would
become discouraged and obstructive. In either case the well-
being of the Emirate depended on one man, and what would
happen when he was gone?[4] The D.O. trod a tightrope, gently
restraining here, complimenting there, advising, urging forward, and counting on the new generation to supply future
office-holders who would help and at the same time check the
next Chief.

Because emirs as a rule do not write their memoirs we shall
probably never know much about how they regarded the

[1] Yauri Book, 23 August 1928.
[2] Ibid., 27 February 1929.
[3] Ibid., 30 March 1929.
[4] Cf. correspondence between Pitcairn, D.O. Gwandu (responsible for Yauri),
and Carrow, Resident Sokoto, 14 September 1933 ff., K.

administrators with whom the working day was shared.[1] When asked which of the D.O.s of the past he particularly remembered, the Emir of Gwandu unhesitatingly replied, 'The ones who worked hard and the tough ones.'[2] He and four of his councillors went on to name names and to speak animatedly of the characteristics and activities of a handful of D.O.s who had obviously left their mark in Birnin Kebbi over the past three or four decades. They had had no advance notice of the question; they seemed in the eagerness of their discussion momentarily to forget the presence of the questioner. One was reminded of college students talking about their preparatory-school masters. Types, as seen by the talkers, emerged clearly. There was the man of sympathy who was not strong; the unthinking martinet from whom it was necessary to conceal things; the shrewd man who saw but did not do; the man who waited for his leave time to arrive. But the most spirited talk was of those who had accomplished things, either through demonstration of that rare combination of qualities that sums up the paragon or, more likely, a single strong characteristic supported by human traits both good and bad that make it possible to live with him. Always, whether he had been liked or not, the remembered man was a driver, a mover, and shaker: 'he planted the trees', 'he put a road across the swamp', 'he reformed the Treasury'. When in England the Emir and one of his councillors had visited several former D.O.s in their homes.

The British, of course, had their own views of how they were looked on by the chiefs and N.A. officials. 'Africans do not respect people who merely wag their tails at them', said one, thereby supporting, from the other side, what had been emphasized in Gwandu.[3] Chiefs who could recall pre-colonial times were thought to resent the new order in so far as it curbed their power. Ibrahim of Zaria, wrote a D.O. who knew

[1] Administrative correspondence between chiefs and officers does give hints but does not address the subject directly. Published sources, such as the autobiography of the late Sardauna of Sokoto, Sir Ahmadu Bello, are not entirely above suspicion, being full of hindsight wisdom and self-conscious polemicizing. So are public statements by chiefs since independence, e.g. the remarks made in the Legislative Council by the Emir of Abuja, cited in R. Symonds, *The British and Their Successors*, London, 1966, p. 162.

[2] Birnin Kebbi, 25 August 1965. Among those also present were the Waziri and the Magajin Rafin.

[3] Sharwood Smith, 13 March 1966.

him well, had 'been a leading warrior in the Good Old Days [and] could hardly be expected to be very enthusiastic over Form D and Form Q, and the delegation of authority to what seemed to him the detestably modern and effeminate whipper-snappers of the Vizier's Office'.[1] Generational differences within British ranks had their counterparts among the Africans, and in some instances juniors on both sides shared complaints against their mutal seniors. It was not only the junior British officers who longed for the retirement of the 'masu lambobi' or military officers who held so many of the senior posts well into the thirties. On the other hand, senior members of N.A.s made no secret of their dislike for many young Africans who had been at government schools and for bureaucracy in general. When chiefs and British officers shared views growing out of common experience, such as having to put up with steadily mounting paper work, there was little room for doubt as to the Africans' real feelings. Similarly, estimates of African opinion made by reflective, experienced D.O.s with no desire to flatter their own culture have an authentic ring. The Fulani found the British erratic, thought Weatherhead, 'inflexible about what they considered unimportant [and] tolerant where they were not prepared to budge'.[2] 'They see us', mused Lethem, 'as people painfully addicted to order and fatiguing public works, as I think I have read was the attitude of our ancestors to the Romans.'[3]

Beyond this D.O.s had ample evidence of emirs' tastes in everyday matters. Like D.O.s themselves, most chiefs had pet projects and interests, like road-building, well-sinking, improvements in farming methods, and teaching. With the passing years such interests tended to be less exotically African and closer to one's own. Like the son of the Emir of Katsina who became Governor of the North in 1966, the Emir of Gumel in the 1930s adored polo. Automobiles were at first a curiosity to chiefs, then, as D.O.s saw it, a nuisance or even a vice. European education was resisted less, and there was not as much militancy in Islam in later years as there had been up to the 1920s. In hundreds of specific instances chiefs showed how they felt about ordinary administrative problems. When the Resident

---

[1] Giles, diary, February 1937 ff. [2] Unpublished MS., p. 319, C.R.P.
[3] To Alexander, 26 July 1931, C.R.P.

Sokoto was about to reappoint a certain junior British officer to
a financial post, the Sultan came to see him and pointed out
that the officer's notorious bad temper would make for inefficiency in the Native Treasury.[1] By the 1930s the chiefs and
the British knew each other well enough for such points to be
raised with confidence, and D.O.s could distinguish between
matters that chiefs took seriously and those they did not. The
more the two races worked together in the same administrative
machine, the more they tended to reach similar conclusions
about office procedure and the general desiderata of government.

For his part the British officer played a role that was concerned first and last with educating and disciplining. For the
average D.O. the day was full of pushing the N.A., including
everyone from the Emir down to village heads. The D.O.
Hadejia pounded his Emir on hospital improvements, the
sleeping-sickness campaign, inoculation of cattle, inspection of
goatskins, and on court cases, extortion by N.A. officials, and
the latest deposal of a village head. He compelled the Emir of
Gumel to accept as secretary a young mallam from the government school in Kano, imposed his own standards on the selection of village heads and even of the driver of the N.A.'s new
Ford. The Emir received a sharp reprimand because so few
cases were being brought to the N.A. court. Again and again
the division's two chiefs were ticked off, point by repetitious
point, and held to account. Having pressed for the establishment of a school at Auyo in Hadejia, the D.O. left the Emir to it
and found some months later that, as expected, he had done
nothing about it. When the Emir assured him that all was well
and that ten boys were ready to enter the new school, the D.O.
was unimpressed. 'Vague assertions are no good and names
must be produced; personally I am sceptical, considering [that]
Hadejia school itself can only be filled by force.'[2] In 1946, ten
years afterwards, his successor had to threaten to withhold N.A.
jobs from them in order to get the Emir's own sons to enter the
Kano school.[3]

Younger D.O.s were not as inclined as their predecessors had

---

[1] Carrow, 24 September 1965.   [2] Emir's Interview Book, January 1935 ff.
[3] D.O. Hadejia to Resident Kano, 22 March 1946, Secret File on Emirs,
Hadejia Office.

been to accept the *status quo* unquestioningly. Up to the 1930s D.O.s in Gwandu had lavished praise on the Emir Usumanu, one of the North's most energetic and able chiefs. Leaving him to his own devices had been the result partly of his recognized talent and partly of the inability of the small British staff to do much on their own. Reports on the Emir's performance were repetitive: 'a strong character, a progressive ruler and an admirable Emir', 'excellent, impossible to expect more from any Chief'.[1] But later on reservations crept in: 'Generous in his private dealings but . . . apt to be penurious as to public expenditure . . . hardly seems to realize that the talakawa [peasants] must no longer be burdened with "benevolences for the public good" . . . rather inclined to regard the N.A. as run for his personal benefit.'[2] Gradually the grip of alien standards tightened. Although it was done in the name of the N.A., the Estimates (emirate budget) were prepared by the D.O. in most cases, and senior officers gave chiefs to understand, politely but firmly, that there would be progress whether they liked it or not. Rule was indirect mainly in the sense that one's assistants were Africans. It was the D.O. who supplied the initiative and the continuing pressure. Implementation was watched as closely as possible, and many touring officers knew more about conditions in the countryside than did chiefs and other N.A. officials who were based in emirate capitals.

If the effectiveness of government by D.O. and Chief was limited by scarcity of men and money, its scope was nonetheless wide enough for it to be classed as virtually totalitarian. In the agricultural and commercial spheres, for example, the hand of government, however weak, was pervasively active. Medical officers, animal husbandrymen, and D.O.s supervised the slaughter of cattle and goats and the sale of meat. Planting, harvesting, and marketing of crops was subjected to ever-increasing government control, and it was the Government, in the 1930s, that started co-operatives. Public services such as railways were government-owned. When British commercial firms wished to advance money to farmers on unharvested crops such as groundnuts D.O.s provided regulation in the public interest. Codes governing labour in the mines were enforced

[1] Daniel, 31 December 1924; Backwell, Report for 1920, K.
[2] Diggle, Reports, 3 February 1926 and 7 January 1928.

by D.O.s in such places as the Plateau from the start. Since the people were passive and poor, there was no alternative to administrative initiative and management in all spheres, economic, governmental, and educational, from the village level upwards. Enlightenment, progress, freedom—everything had to be entrusted to the small Anglo-African élite in whose hands rested a monopoly of power and responsibility. There was a Rousseauian quality to one's job. On the one hand, D.O.s instructed emirs and their officials to gauge public opinion and to assure its free ventilation in such ways as urging village heads to speak up at the special meetings that were arranged for them;[1] and on the other hand, there was a conferring of tangible betterment from above. D.O.s and emirs co-operated in the eradication of sleeping-sickness and of crop rodents and in improvements in communications that would help raise farmers out of the pit of subsistence agriculture.

Looking back on their years in the North, officers disagree on whether there was identity of purpose among Europeans and Africans.[2] Most seem to feel that British and African mentalities were too far apart for this to have come about. They could gaze together at a stretch of new road and be glad for their respective reasons that it was there. They could separately resent Kaduna or Southern Nigerians. A progressive Chief and his progressive D.O. could feel common pride in the achievements of 'their' N.A. by comparison with others.[3] Each could partake of these kinds of thoughts and still keep to his own culture. What linked them was the hold of the everyday situation. Like masters and boys in school or officers and N.C.O.s in the army, neither could imagine a system that operated differently or circumstances that were greatly altered from those that had surrounded them in living memory. Momentum swept them along together, convincing them of the futility of resistance. Retreating to their separate worlds at sundown, each knew that the dawn would unite them again as it always had and presumably always would.

[1] Hoyle, Emir's Interview Book, Hadejia, 1 June 1936.

[2] 'What I am sure was special about the North was the identity of purpose and outlook between the D.O. and the N.A., from the Chief himself downwards' (Sharwood Smith, 22 February 1965).

[3] The Yauri Book repeatedly refers to 'our' police, treasury, lorry, resthouses, etc., whether it is the D.O. or the Chief who is writing.

In gauging the long-term effectiveness of Anglo-African government we may distinguish between two general types of situations which may be described as those of balance and of imbalance. Imbalance could be due primarily to attitudes, actions or inaction on the part of the British, including both Secretariat people and provincial administrators, or to scarcity of staff. In Zaria the major part of officers' time was taken by the affairs of Zaria Emirate itself, especially the heavily populated and well-farmed northern half, while other areas, such as Birnin Gwari N.A. and the remote southern districts of the Province, were chronically under-toured. At Muya in Birnin Gwari, only some thirty miles from Kaduna, an officer noted that he was the first European to visit the area in four years and that no administrative officer had toured it for over five years.[1] The annual report for 1931 on the Chief of Birnin Gwari remarked acidly on the 'complete lack of continuity and policy . . . [and the] lack of control and supervision without which any African Chief . . . would go astray'.[2] At Argungu in Sokoto Province staff discontinuity was clearly to blame for the depressing regularity with which corruption seeped back into the N.A. after D.O.s had cleaned it out. In the early thirties the slave who held the title of Galadima was removed by the D.O. from his position as a member of the Emir's judicial council, but as soon as the D.O. was posted elsewhere the Galadima was reinstated by the Emir.[3] A few years earlier the same D.O., when on tour in Bornu, had been treated with disrespect by a district head, and everyone realized that the district head's exaggerated idea of his own importance and immunity from European supervision was directly due to insufficient staff, discontinuity, and under-touring.[4]

An excessively doctrinaire view of administration lay at the roots of other unsatisfactory situations. In Jema'a D.O.s had been frustrated for years by a hopeless N.A. and had frequently urged that the ruling family be ousted and the whole administration revamped by British officers. At the very least, it was argued, the dynasty should be discontinued on the death of the

---

[1] R. M. East, 10 April 1943, Birnin Gwari Touring Diary, Zaria. The village is spelled 'Muiya' in this diary.
[2] Report dated 1 February 1932, K.
[3] Handing-Over Notes, Mellor to Tegetmeier, 23 October 1933, K.
[4] Lethem to Palmer, 12 July 1926, C.R.P., referring to Tegetmeier's experiences.

incumbent Emir. In 1926 the Resident Plateau forwarded to Kaduna the latest request from the D.O. Jema'a that the Emirate be dissolved and direct relations established between himself and district heads.[1] The Emir was ignoring him, obstructing the medical officer, embezzling the Native Treasury, and making a farce of local justice. Yet the Lieutenant Governor of the time, Palmer, wished to try all possible remedies short of deposal, and the request was denied.[2] Jema'a went on to the end of British rule very much a pariah among N.A.s and a trial for its luckless D.O.s.

Dogmas could so mesmerize senior officers that they were in effect tied to changelessness, even when chiefs and N.A.s wished to break free of tradition in some way. In 1937 the Emir of Hadejia, hardly the model of a forward-looking chief, wished to make one Shehu Makama a member of his council. The Resident Kano demurred on grounds that the man was an ex-slave and would be recognized as such by district heads and the people generally.[3] To this the Emir replied that times had changed, that there was now a more enlightened outlook on such things, and that the man was the most able of the candidates. But the Resident stood fast and insisted that the post be given to someone from an office-holding family.

Similarly it was the British and not the Africans who worried most about tradition in 1927 when it seemed possible that the brother and eventual successor of the Emir of Gwandu might turn Christian. The Emir's brother was Yahaya, district head of Kalgo and holder of the title Sarkin Gobir. The Resident Sokoto dreaded the prospect of a religious scandal and feared that dire consequences would result: the administration would lose an exceptionally able official; people in both England and Nigeria would say that the British were trying to convert the country; missionaries might be expelled from major emirates; and education would be set back.[4] The possibility was discussed of sending Yahaya away from the Emirate, perhaps to

---

[1] 31 October 1926, K.

[2] Resident Jos to D.O., 6 November 1926, K.

[3] Patterson to D.O., 14 December 1937, Emir's Interview Book, Hadejia.

[4] File, Emirs of Gwandu, 22 August 1927 ff., K. The Residents involved were Webster and Backwell, the D.O. Birnin Kebbi was Diggle, and the Superintendent of Education was Attenborough, whose talks with Yahaya brought the District Head's problem to the attention of the Government.

the school in Katsina. Finally the district head resolved the matter himself by deciding that his duty lay within Islam. Yet at the height of the Government's concern about the case the Emir calmly held to the view that what his brother did was his own affair and that the people would accept the conversion to Christianity if it came.[1]

When doctrinaire views were held by officers who inclined to an easy-going or lax administrative posture it was almost impossible that other factors could right the resulting imbalance. On taking over as Acting Resident Benue, Morgan was horrified at the state of Keffi Emirate.[2] The Emir, who had only recently been installed, was both inexperienced and corrupt, an unusually dismal combination. The administration was in the hands of a particularly venal clique of the Emir's younger relatives. An able waziri had been ousted because he was not of the blood. Worst of all, there was a complaisant D.O. who seemed to feel that interference with the N.A. constituted a violation of policy. To Morgan the indicated cure was a strong lead from the Resident so that junior officers would be educated in the ways of responsible and firm rule.

Yet the other extreme could be equally bad. In 1920–1 the D.O. Kano was an officer who had served in Southern Nigeria and in largely pagan emirates of the North and who had a strong dislike for Fulani chiefs, whom he regarded as obstacles to progress. A forceful man with a military background, he was convinced that what the country needed was ruthless purging of corruption through wholesale sacking of extortionist officials in the countryside. In his campaign to rid rural communities of unworthy officials he employed junior officers who, like himself, were new to the Emirate and who were further handicapped by lack of both administrative experience and knowledge of local languages.[3] On the D.O.'s orders these junior officers toured the Emirate, investigating suspected irregularities and holding on-the-spot courts which convicted and

---

[1] As in fact happened when the Alkali Jos became a Christian. To their credit all officers involved in the Yahaya case consistently saw the matter as one which Yahaya must be allowed to resolve by himself. 'Whatever the political consequences . . . he must be allowed to decide' (Alexander to Lethem, 10 November 1927, C.R.P.).

[2] To Lethem, 16 June 1927, C.R.P.

[3] Carrow and Noad.

summarily dismissed officials who were judged guilty. After some months' experience with this kind of rough justice the young A.D.O.s began to suspect that the whole campaign had been ill-considered and that what they had accomplished in effect 'was nearly to destroy the village administration'.[1] When after only a year in Kano the D.O. disappeared southward, never to return, it remained to his successors to reconstruct with N.A. officials who were certainly no more moral than those who had been removed and who were far less experienced.

Another pitfall for Europeans was excessive reliance on subordinates outside the N.A. In early years there had been no reasonable alternative to using various clerical and entrepreneurial assistants, first from other British colonies on the West African coast and later increasingly from Southern Nigeria. Some of these necessary go-betweens began modestly enough and later rose to positions of considerable responsibility and power. Audu dan Afoda, a Yoruba, was Hewby's groom when he was on the Benue with the Niger Company. Eventually Audu became a Political Agent and ended as Headman of Makurdi, the largest town in Tiv N.A., the capital of Benue Province, and an unusually difficult administrative unit owing to its mixed population. Such men were invaluable for their local knowledge and their ability to accomplish things that the British could not at first manage on their own. Weatherhead felt that no one in Nigeria understood the British so well as the messengers, 'the eyes and ears of a District Officer'.[2] Naturally, however, N.A. officials would see Political Agents and messengers as interlopers, objects of suspicion, envy, and resentment because of their influence with the Europeans. Moreover, the power of some Political Agents was enough to awe junior British officers. In Kano during the early 1920s one of these, who later became Chief Alkali of Kano, served the Resident as both Political Agent and Arabic scribe. He was 'a stern looking man with a heavy black beard', and he inspired respect and fear on all sides. One day, when an A.D.O. was hearing complaints from a group of peasants in his office, the Political Agent came in with a note from the Resident and proceeded forthwith

[1] Carrow, 11 January 1966.
[2] Unpublished MS., p. 320, C.R.P.

to upbraid the assembled peasants for not sitting in a sufficiently respectful way in front of the A.D.O.'s table. 'I had an uneasy feeling he might give the Resident an adverse report on my ability to enforce discipline and proper respect amongst the peasants.'[1] There was clearly a danger that such men would build up independent power for themselves and reach positions from which they could defy both the British and the chiefs and use one side against the other. In the 1920s Kaduna first issued a directive against the use of informers and then abolished Political Agents; but not before a certain amount of harm had been done in preventing more direct communication between D.O.s and N.A.s. For lazy or unimaginative officers, middlemen had too often been a crutch.

A more decisive factor in contributing to imbalance was the general sluggishness, conservatism, and egocentricity of the African ruling classes. Their numbers were far greater than those of the British and this enabled them to slow the pace of advance, to feather their own nests at public expense, and to oppress the people. In the early years corruption was a virtually immovable fixture. When the D.O. Borgu in 1919 had assembled enough facts to convict a local sarki and had publicly tried him with the full participation and agreement of the Emir, he found at the final moment that sacking the offender was impossible and that all he had accomplished was his own public humiliation.[2] The corrupt Chief had simply bribed the Emir, who advised the D.O. to give him another chance. Ignoring the Emir was out of the question, not only on grounds of policy but also because there was no one to put in his place and the British needed every chief they could find. In Hadejia there was still so much tax embezzlement by the late 1930s that the D.O. threatened to take the collecting function away from the N.A. completely.[3] The innovation of collective farms, a wartime measure by the British, similarly ran foul of office-holder corruption. The D.O. discovered that the Emir and his councillors were merely using the farms as a new device in the service of the age-old idea of self-enrichment.[4] After describing the

[1] Carrow, 24 September 1965.
[2] Cary, cited by Mahood, op. cit., p. 51.
[3] Emir's Interview Book, 21 December 1939.
[4] Ibid., 25 February 1943.

oppressive nature and extortionist practices of the Emir of Lapai, a D.O. on tour there in the 1930s summarized the circumstances of a hopeless emirate: 'The whole of the ruling class . . . are the same . . . they are Mohamadan Fulani ruling over pagan tribes with whom they have no sympathy or interest except in what they can get out of them.'[1]

In other cases lack of progress was due not to avarice or callousness so much as to the stubborn conservatism of a deeply traditional people. Following the reorganization of his Emirate in the 1920s and the appointment of more representative district heads in some places, the Emir of Kano could not bring himself to treat the new N.A. officials with the same courtesy and regard that he showed to old ones who were of the blood.[2] They were upstarts, mere Habe, and he refused to address them in accordance with protocol. The Emir of Hadejia proved the truth of the old adage about Africans and Asians who could tell which Europeans were chiefs in their own country and which were not. Two representatives of a British commercial firm were kept waiting in an outer room and after a brief interview were dismissed with an abruptness usually reserved for clerical staff and servants. 'His manner before the D.O. is beyond reproach, but with departmental officers . . . and even the second Political Officer when there is one on the station he is often barely civil.'[3] Resistance to European education was so strong at first that emirs sent the sons of slaves to school, pretending that these were their own offspring, and the original school for the sons of chiefs in Kano had to be closed. It was replaced by elementary schools in major towns, these being filled by a process of dragooning, with each district head being required to produce so many boys. Katsina College, started on Gowers's initiative, was still being stoutly resisted by some chiefs in the 1930s.[4] The Emir of Gumel explained to the D.O. that recruitment for the West African Frontier Force and the Police was difficult because young men of good family preferred to stay at home where they had status.[5] Novels printed

---

[1] Weatherhead, letter, 25 January 1936.
[2] Carrow, 12 February 1966.
[3] Confidential Political Notebook, Hadejia Office, 18 February 1935.
[4] Talks and correspondence with R. M. East have been exceedingly helpful to me in this regard.
[5] Emir's Interview Book, 14 September 1936.

in Hausa as a means of bringing gradual change through the indigenous culture were not successful at first.

Some chiefs were never really able to partake of the spirit of British administration, and they looked on its frantic perpetual motion with a dull passiveness and incomprehension. When discussing matters with D.O.s they could be pleasant and seemingly receptive, promising to do what was wanted at the first opportunity. But as soon as the D.O. had turned to other things they slipped back into the world of their own consciousness and later appeared to have no awareness that they had undertaken specific obligations. Usman of Hadejia was constantly plagued by D.O.s for not touring his Emirate enough. In 1941 the D.O., returning from one of his own tours, remarked to the Emir that he had just visited Auyo school and noticed in the visitors' book that the Emir had not been there for over two years. 'It was a good thing for his people to see him . . . and he should try to visit each district headquarters at least once a year.'[1] The following spring the D.O. was glad to hear that the Emir had in fact gone on tour, but 'perhaps next time he would be able to use a horse and visit some of the large villages away from the main road'.[2] Even his automobile ride along the main road had been the result of a talk which the Emir had had with the Resident, when Usman had been told that he must tour much more, that he must use his official council rather than rely exclusively on his favourites, and that he must watch the corn harvest with special care. A year later the Emir had not toured again and the Resident asked the D.O. for periodic reports on the subject. Usman explained that pressure of court work had made it impossible for him to leave Hadejia town. Unmoved, the D.O. suggested that Usman leave on tour immediately.[3] A month later nothing had happened, and the Resident Kano reported to Kaduna that drastic action would be necessary as the war effort required stimulation of groundnut production by all governmental and N.A. officials. 'He goes on tour today at my direct orders', reported the D.O.[4] The Emir, much chastened, was told that unless Hadejia's

[1] Emir's Interview Book, 9 September 1941.
[2] Ibid., 2 May 1942.
[3] Confidential Political Notebook, Hadejia and Gumel, 11 September 1941; Emir's Interview Book, 27 February 1943 and 28 April 1943.
[4] Confidential File, Emirs of Hadejia, Hadejia Office, 21 May 1943.

groundnut quota was filled in time his place at the coming Chiefs' Conference would be taken by the Emir of Kazaure. Although many chiefs still found the agendas of these gatherings mysterious and had to be patiently coached in advance by their D.O.s, the occasions were a great success socially and the threat of exclusion was a powerful weapon in British hands.

There were other causes of imbalance which each side, African and European, could respond to but which neither could control. Lack of progress, a seemingly endless condition of marking time, was often due to a basic characteristic of authoritarian governments in backward countries—their helplessness in the face of the people's conservatism and apathy. The imperviousness of the masses was a constant reminder to rulers and alien officials alike that governments are puny things. Hoyle and the Emir of Gumel did their level best to persuade the peasants of Gurri that physical examinations and possible treatment for sleeping-sickness were in their own interests.[1] Not even the village heads were convinced and the peasants made clear that they would leave the district rather than submit.

On the other hand, the authorities were also comparatively helpless in the face of the very tendencies to detribalization that Mary Kingsley had warned against in the 1890s. Mammon's lure was not a thing that D.O.s and chiefs could deal with very effectively. An Emir's official proclamation urging youths not to leave the 'respectable occupation of farming' for the town's bright lights was essentially pathetic and useless.[2] Yet when Mammon himself stumbled, society's defencelessness was all too apparent. The Depression struck Nigeria hard in the early 1930s. Retrenchment of administrative staff weakened the Government's hand and in education it penalized the North more than the South, which could fall back on mission schools.

The role of southerners in the North was another outside influence which could disturb the best-run emirate. It was basically a question of competition between half-educated or technically skilled southerners of low birth and northern aristocrats, at first secure in Islamic superiority and then increasingly pressed by the southerners' more relevant equipment for a

[1] Confidential Political Notebook, 4 March 1938.
[2] Emir's Interview Book, Gumel, 14 June 1934.

modern age that the North could not escape. The Emir of
Gwandu was bitter about the contempt which southerners felt
for northerners.[1] The Emir of Hadejia admitted to the Governor
that northerners had been wrong to resist European education,
which he now saw as a shield against southern threats.[2] Also he
feared southern domination in certain commercial fields, such
as Yoruba pre-eminence in fishmongering, and he was determined to resist it.[3] In 1943 there was strong objection by emirs
to the reporting of their Conference by Lagos journalists.[4]

Of all the situations of administrative imbalance in the inter-
war years, none was more significant than that of Sokoto
Emirate in the decade of the 1920s. Sokoto was not the largest
unit or the most populous, the richest or the most advanced.
But it had incomparable prestige, for its ruler, the only Chief
to bear the title Sultan, was also Sarkin Musulmi, or Commander of the Faithful. All other chiefs except the Shehu of
Bornu deferred to him officially and by tradition. In British
eyes Sokoto ranked with Bornu and Kano in the civil service
hierarchy, and with the departure of Palmer its Residency and
Kano's became the main routes to the chief commissionership.
What happened in Sokoto had an importance farther afield. If
Anglo-African government succeeded there, it could well
afford failures in minor places; if not, then the whole system was
called into question.

Mention has been made earlier of the attempt in 1921–2 of
the Acting Resident Sokoto, Edwardes, to curb corruption in the
N.A. and to bring reform in the interests of the local population.
It would be hard to imagine two more different men than
Edwardes and the officer for whom he was acting, Webster,
the substantive Resident. Webster was a mild and easy-going
administrator, a Hausa scholar and linguist. He preferred not
to interfere with the normal processes of African local government and he was loath to believe ill of the ruling classes.[5]

[1] Weatherhead, letter, 28 March 1944.
[2] Emir's Interview Book, 10 February 1943.
[3] Ibid., 25 February 1943.   [4] Ibid., 4 October 1943.
[5] In a letter to Lethem, 22 January 1931, C.R.P., he describes himself as being
fastidious about the outward appearances of N.A. accounting but willing to put
up with embezzlement as endemic. He confesses to being 'quite at sea' as to the
causes of unrest in Sokoto in the time of Muhammadu Tambari, 1924–31, when he
himself was Resident there most of those years, and he found it hard to believe
that the Sultan would be capable of the wrongdoing that eventuated in his

Edwardes, a few years junior to Webster in both age and service, was by temperament, interests, career performance, and outlook on Britain's role very close to being his superior's opposite.[1] Where Webster was meticulous, Edwardes was unconventional, even in such matters as dress. He appeared in the office wearing baggy trousers and a loose white jumper and when on tour he wore the great floppy boots of a cavalier. To more than one colleague he was 'the best of good fellows', a phrase that Webster's closest friends would probably not have chosen to describe him.[2] The Africans are said to have liked and respected Edwardes.[3] However, it is entirely likely that highly placed Fulani would have looked on him, and he on them, with suspicion or hostility. He was notoriously a friend of the peasants. To a junior officer who knew him in Bauchi he suggested that the best way of keeping in touch with ordinary people was to sleep at some distance from the rest of his party when touring, thus making it possible for peasants to approach him at night with their complaints, unseen by messengers, emirs' representatives, and servants, the bureaucratic and social outer wrapping that insulated many officers from the masses. Nothing would have been better calculated to outrage that sense of European dignity on which such as Webster insisted. Edwardes thought deeply about why he was in Africa and what his obligations to the Africans were. Webster's approach, although by no means unsympathetic, often seemed somewhat legalistic, as though he stood at one remove from the earthy essences of Africa and saw the common people as a problem that was not of direct concern to him. Both men studied Africa and enjoyed their time there. Webster's aloofness was more typical of the mainstream of civil service attitudes than was

---

departure from office. His view of qualities needed in a Sultan is hinted at in another letter to Lethem: 'I rather hope that the Sarkin Baura gets it . . . he is a dear old thing, if rather weak.' Webster's initials were G. W., and some of his colleagues referred to him as 'George Washington' Webster, a whimsical reference to the tall stories he told.

[1] I am grateful to E. L. Mort, who served with Edwardes in Bauchi, for much helpful information. Also useful are the Daniel letters, C.R.P., and Mahood, op. cit.   [2] Daniel, 18 May 1919, C.R.P.

[3] Of the two Hausa nicknames given to Europeans by Africans one was known and used openly. Edwardes's was 'mai munduwa', the man with the bracelet, not much help one way or the other. To his brother officers he was always 'Dolly' Edwardes.

Edwardes's passionate commitment to 'my people'.[1] Edwardes indulged in vigorous public works, such as irrigation and road-building, on a scale that was impressive for the 1920s; Webster, with many who began their service in the first decade, concentrated on maintaining law and order through the local Chief. Edwardes was profoundly interested in education and had well-developed ideas on Africa's future; Webster tended to think more of Fulani and Hausa history. Both were honourable, well-intentioned men. Observing their respective styles and daily work, one might have thought they had come from different planets.

In the autumn of 1921, with Webster away on leave, Edwardes wrote to the Lieutenant Governor giving him a disturbing report on irregularities uncovered by his 'personal secret service'.[2] Daniel, the D.O., had received similar reports. Edwardes was confident of a knowledgeable and receptive viewpoint in Kaduna, for Arnett, Acting Lieutenant Governor earlier the same year, had been Webster's predecessor as Resident Sokoto. On taking over as Resident in 1920, wrote Edwardes, Webster had changed Arnett's policy 'in the direction of extremely indirect rule'.[3] Finding everything in their own hands the Sultan and senior N.A. officials turned to wholesale milking of the peasants and extorting of N.A. funds. The Sultan himself, Muhammadu Mai Turare, secured a monopoly on the sale of potash by forcing traders to sell through his agents. Through a slave who was in charge of labour on the Zaria road he was also deriving considerable income from percentages of contracts let by the N.A. To Edwardes the whole picture was clear. At the base of society was a silent and helpless peasantry. 'We are not dealing with a sturdy race of freemen, conscious of their rights and tenacious of their liberties, but with a timid and ignorant peasantry, inured to oppression from the remotest times.'[4] The rulers for their part could see that there was no direct communication between the masses and the British, who dealt solely with the N.A., giving it full support and accepting its assertions without question. The result

[1] Mahood, op. cit., p. 10.
[2] 26 October 1921, K. Edwardes wrote informally, but Palmer treated his letter as semi-official. See also Edwardes Papers, C.R.P., 1921–2.
[3] To the Lieutenant Governor, 5 December 1921, K. Cf. Arnett Papers, 1922, C.R.P.
[4] Undated. This seems to have been written in December 1921 or January 1922.

was unchecked corruption and oppression. Edwardes asked for authority to proceed with discipline and reform, but realizing that Webster would not approve of his proposals, he sought assurance that an attitude of *laissez-faire* would not be resumed on Webster's return. He cited the Governor's recent policy statement in support of what he wanted to do and pointed out that Webster's methods were plainly in violation of it. As we have seen, this blatant impugning of the judgement of his superior, put forward in an official document, was Edwardes's undoing. All major figures in the hierarchy above him presented a solid front against a breach of etiquette that appeared to besmirch the whole Government. Edwardes did not of course mean any sweeping indictment, but his intentions had become as irrelevant as the abuses he was trying to correct. The Chief Secretary in Lagos, Cameron, thought that Edwardes's explanations were not full enough and that he should be reminded of his primary duty, influencing and guiding the N.A.[1] The Secretary Northern Provinces, Browne, made no comment and merely forwarded these views to Edwardes on behalf of the Acting Lieutenant Governor, Palmer. Arnett, whom Edwardes had suggested should come to Sokoto immediately to investigate, was silent. Instead the hapless officer found himself visited by the Governor, Sir Hugh Clifford, and the Lieutenant Governor, Gowers. Gowers found no evidence that peasants could not complain directly to political officers and he cited Webster's known capacity as a Hausa scholar.[2] When Clifford, Gowers, and Edwardes visited the Sultan together to interview the major figures, a final, if unnecessary, blow was struck at Edwardes's case. His primary witness, the Majidadi, burst into the room as the three officers were speaking with the Sultan and launched into an uncontrolled and almost insane rage, flinging insults at the Sultan and having to be forcibly removed. Clifford was unimpressed by the 'vague character of [Edwardes's] charges', and he deplored the officer's lack of judgement and ignorance of his Province.[3] Palmer, the Resident Bornu, was summoned to take over as Acting Resident until Webster's return and to write a report on

---

[1] Undated; in File 2870/4, K.

[2] Minute, 21 January 1922, K.

[3] To Gowers, 25 February 1922, K.

the case. To no one's surprise this parroted the Governor's findings. Webster returned in the following month and Edwardes was transferred. The Majidadi was removed from office and exiled to another province.

With Edwardes no longer there, administration returned to the state in which he had found it. Two years later, with Webster still in charge, the Sultan died and was succeeded by his son, Muhammadu Tambari. At first the electors chose Hassan, head of a collateral branch of the Sultanic family, but then changed and settled on Muhammadu. They later claimed that they had preferred Hassan but had been influenced by something Mr. Webster had said.[1] Webster himself remarked some years later that he too would have preferred Hassan but that Kaduna had queried the choice and that this is why Muhammadu was settled on.[2] In any case the new Sultan, like his father, could count on minimum interference from the British. The iron rule that everything must be done through the N.A. was carried to extremes. In 1928 a European was murdered near Gusau. The local D.O. moved quickly to investigate. In the course of the next twenty-four hours he visited the scene of the crime, interviewed many N.A. officials and local people, and drove all night to Katsina, known to be a refuge of bandits, to confer with the D.O. there.[3] Meanwhile he had sent messages to Webster in Sokoto explaining what he was doing and making clear that speed was essential. The Resident's reaction was that of a rule-book bureaucrat. The D.O. had acted wrongly in going to the scene of the murder without taking a representative of the Sultan with him, in using government rather than N.A. police, and in leaving the Province without official permission. To the downcast D.O., whose fate might well have been similar to Edwardes's, it seemed that this was 'Indirect Rule run mad'.[4] The Resident himself spent only a few hours at Gusau conducting his own investigation, while

[1] 'The Board was swayed, so they said, by a comment from Webster' (Woodhouse, Sokoto, to his sister, 1 February 1931), C.R.P.

[2] To Lethem, 11 May 1931, C.R.P. But a reading of the file on Muhammadu Tambari, K., shows Webster not to have been entirely consistent here. Cf. his letter of 23 July 1924 to S.N.P.

[3] Sharwood Smith, MS., pp. 188 ff. Earlier a gang of ruffians had murdered a Frenchman over the border, and Sharwood Smith assumed he might be up against the same gang, which had come from Katsina.

[4] Ibid., p. 199.

Palmer, the Lieutenant Governor, was there for three full days.[1]

Reports on the new Sultan were favourable at first, Webster describing him as 'quite excellent'.[2] Woodhouse did note that he seemed not to understand the need for progress very well, but Backwell wrote that, since the reorganization of his council, he had run an efficient administration and that he was a good judge of men.[3] Prankerd, Acting Resident in 1930, felt, however, that the Sultan left something to be desired and that in particular he was too much swayed by personal feelings. Earlier Lindsell, who was briefly Resident, had expressed doubts on the wisdom of the council's reorganization because under the new set-up district heads again lived in Sokoto, ostensibly to help the Sultan. This left the countryside to the tender mercies of slave tax-collectors as in pre-British times. In fact, as a subsequent investigation discovered, corruption and oppression had reached new heights under Muhammadu Tambari, who was found to be under the influence of sorcerers. Persistent rumours led to inquiries by British officers, who proceeded with caution in view of the still-remembered Edwardes débâcle. Reports came in also from near-by Gwandu and Argungu as well as from Kano. It was soon clear that the Sultan had perpetrated monstrous injustices, that he was practising usury on members of the N.A., and waxing rich by interfering in the free sale of corn in Sokoto market.

Late in 1930 the Resident recommended that Muhammadu Tambari be deposed. A formal inquiry, headed by Woodhouse, who was brought in especially for the purpose, established the Sultan's guilt beyond any doubt, although facts were at first difficult to come by owing to the impression received by the ruling classes generally that complaints would not be listened to. The previous Sultan's successful appeal to Clifford in 1922 was recalled, and it was widely thought that 'as far as the Government is concerned [a] Sultan's conduct is above criticism'.[4] The Lieutenant Governor, Alexander, accompanied

---

[1] It was Palmer's investigation that saved Sharwood Smith from punishment comparable to Edwardes's and resulted in Webster being posted to Yola for his final tour in the North.   [2] Report, 31 December 1924, K.

[3] Cf. Webster, 28 January 1925; Woodhouse, 18 February 1927; Backwell, 4 March 1929, K.

[4] Woodhouse to the Lieutenant Governor, Alexander, January 1931, K.

by the Resident, Backwell, and by Woodhouse, visited the Sultan in his palace in January 1931 to present a formal warning, and it was explained to him that the Governor and Lieutenant Governor would soon decide whether or not to depose him. Muhammadu Tambari was undignified and erratic. He alternated between denials and repentance. Three days later, before the British had reached a final decision, he abdicated. In February he eluded the guards who had been placed around his residence and fled to French territory.

So ended the worst instance of prolonged imbalance in the British period, then about to begin its fourth decade. No major figure, British or African, can escape responsibility. Clifford and Cameron come out at least as badly as Gowers, for Edwardes gave them an opportunity that appealed to precisely that bias against the Sacred North that they are remembered for. They not only let him down; they destroyed him and in so doing helped to perpetuate evils about which they philosophized in policy documents and in speeches to the Legislative Council. A wooden policy and an over-zealous attention to propriety were allowed to turn back the challenges of imagination, moral fibre, guts, and local knowledge. Webster was a disaster by default, it is true. But in his vapid, negative responsibility he was not alone.

The N.A. showed itself to be typical of all N.A.s in depending completely on leadership. Middle-rank and minor officials could do nothing if there was rottenness at the top. Drastic surgery followed by lengthy and close tutelage were the indicated remedies. It is noteworthy that during almost all of Muhammadu Mai Turare's rule and the whole of his son's, their cousin in neighbouring Gwandu gave his Emirate an exemplary administration and was strong enough personally to be able to survive the occasional weak D.O.

There was an element of happenstance in the failure of action by Residents and D.O.s throughout the decade. Webster apart, and he was often away, no one had the minimum combination of necessary qualities to bring about a return of balance and thus to regain even the precarious early levels of satisfactory administration achieved by such as Vertue, Malcolm, and Arnett. Edwardes and Lindsell could see what was wrong, but the former did not understand his own countrymen, the latter understood them all too well, and nothing was done. No one was able to go it alone as Hale Middleton did in Kano or Palmer in Bornu. It was essentially a matter of chance also that Kaduna left Sokoto to its own devices in these years. Webster was not interfered with primarily because Gowers had a loose hand on the reins and because Palmer, his successor, had a strong interest in other parts of the North. When Sokoto did force itself on his consciousness in the Gusau murder case he acted quickly and effectively. But it was late in the game. Whether the explanation is ignorance or neglect, the fact cannot be blinked that the premier Chief of the North was making a shambles of Anglo-African government in his Emirate during the whole of Palmer's lieutenant governorship.

In Sokoto the two essentials of maximum balance—a good administrative officer and a good Chief—were both missing. Had at least one of them been present the Emirate could have been reasonably well run. As it was, a resounding failure occurred. Yet, ironically, the best measurement of that failure is the success that followed it and the other examples of administrative balance in the North during the inter-war years. Like unbalanced ones, balanced situations were all compounded of fortuitous individual factors and no two were alike. Experienced officers who ran their units effectively had learned that administration was the art of the possible, a phenomenon of the here and now, and that extremes were to be avoided. It was a question of discovering what each situation consisted in and therefore what was wanted from above. Alluding to one aspect of the problem, Palmer remarked, 'if we can avoid making changes, matters tend to arrive at an equilibrium. I know at Katsina it was so—for several years they [the office-holders] were constantly trying to upset each other—in the end they gave it up.'[1] As he was speaking to a fellow officer it was unnecessary for him to add that the indispensable factor in achieving this was his own vigilance. Carrow put the accent on strong management from above. Having spoken of his general approval of the Emir of Yauri, he went on: 'A tactful officer . . . doing the work in detail, but ensuring that all is in the end understood by the Emir, might work wonders . . . [whereas]

[1] To Lethem, 13 September 1924, C.R.P.

general direction *ex cathedra* may effect little.'[1] And Sharwood
Smith put the two aspects together for the benefit of his
juniors in Zaria: 'excessive . . . missionary zeal should be
tempered by the realization that . . . attempts to cure on sight
a minor and ephemeral evil may result in damage to the social
or administrative structure . . . the authority of the Chiefs must
be supported and even if an individual has forfeited respect and
consideration, the dignity of his office should be maintained.'[2]

In Hadejia a D.O. showed what balance meant in minor
matters. He listened patiently to a tirade from the local Indian
doctor on the backwardness of the people in and about Mallam
Maduri. Hygiene, thought the medical officer, would have to
be forced in the people's own interests. Agreeing that pressure
had to be kept up constantly, the D.O. spoke, however, of the
limitations. Medical assistants were lacking, and regular
inspections would be impossible. N.A. officials themselves had
not yet been educated to the need for standards in such matters.
But a start had been made by building a hospital in Hadejia
town, and it was vital not to prejudice the development of this
still feeble institution. 'It has been an uphill struggle to popula-
rize the hospital and medical treatment among these backward
people who are antagonistic to all . . . progress and modern
conceptions of life. It would be most undesirable to destroy
confidence in the hospital and medical work by a too rigid
enforcement . . . [which in any case] would not make much
difference.'[3]

There were other ways of bringing progress. All over the
country N.A. offices were vacated regularly through death,
promotion, discipline, and other causes. Forward-looking D.O.s
posed conditions before making a new appointment, the long-
term effect inevitably being to favour British standards over
African. When the Emir of Gumel put forward an inexperienced
young relative as candidate for a district headship the D.O.
rejected the suggestion, promoted the most able of the serving
district heads, and gave the younger man a minor post on
probation.[4] Annual reports on chiefs always listed possible suc-

[1] Undated answer to letter of 14 September 1933 from D. O. Gwandu, K.
[2] Dated Autumn 1936, K.
[3] Eustace, Confidential Political Notebook, 30 July 1943.
[4] Ibid., 24 March 1935.

cessors and enumerated the qualities of each. Because of the Emir's advanced years and failing health Gwandu had more than two years' notice of an impending change in the 1930s. Speculation and jockeying for position were rife in the N.A., and there was continuous discussion among the British as to the problem of the succession. The Emir himself, like many authoritarians, had a blind spot where his own family was concerned and he wanted his eldest son to follow him.[1] The Resident Sokoto advised Kaduna, however, that every D.O. and Resident since 1920 had recommended Yahaya, the Emir's brother. Senior members of the N.A. were divided, but finally it became clear that the D.O. and Resident were determined on Yahaya. Although Usumanu was one of the best chiefs in the Region and although the Chief Commissioner himself asked the Resident if a son might not be preferable to a brother, Yahaya's extraordinary ability and character decided the issue. As in 1918 when Usumanu himself had been selected, local British officers were as forceful as they were progressive and there was no thought of allowing the Africans to choose an Emir who might fail to provide the kind of leadership the Europeans had in mind.[2] Merit was foremost, and traditional criteria were brushed aside if they pointed to someone who lacked it.

Two officers who in their rather different ways made outstanding contributions to balanced and progressive administration in the inter-war years were Carrow and Sharwood Smith.[3] Carrow, born in 1890, was the son of a comfortably off preparatory-school headmaster and was schooled mainly at home. He did have two years at Clifton, but entered the Navy at the age

[1] Emir of Gwandu, 1918–38, K.

[2] Cf. ibid. on Usumanu's own selection in 1918.

[3] Sir Bryan Sharwood Smith and Commander Carrow have pressed me on several occasions to reduce the number of references to them in this book and to describe them in a way that would not appear so laudatory. After considering the matter carefully I have decided against any change, and I owe it to them and to the reader to explain why. My attention was first drawn to these two officers by former colleagues and subordinates of theirs, both African and British. In due course my early information was added to by a wealth of official and private source material in Nigeria and in England and by voluminous written and verbal commentary. Sir Bryan and Commander Carrow provided background information and details, in response to specific inquiries of mine, and always in connection with events on which other information was available, such as files in the Archives at Kaduna. To tone down what I have written would only distort an appraisal which I believe to be accurate and balanced.

of fourteen. He distinguished himself in the First World War, winning the D.S.C., and was invalided out of the Navy with a complaint that did not preclude a career in the tropics. Carrow's service in the North, where he arrived in 1919, was untypical in that it was confined almost exclusively to two provinces, Kano and Sokoto.[1] In Kano his forceful personality, long service (1919–33, 1943–6), and vigorous administrative style made his name almost synonymous with that of the Province. In 1965 there was still a Carrow Road in Kano, and 'Kommanda Karo' was a name that was certain to get a response in the Provincial Office as well as in outstations such as Hadejia. As we have seen, he began under an officer who used bull-in-the-china-shop methods. This was lesson one to a man whose education was all practical experience. It taught him that martinet discipline without regard to practical effects can be merely destructive. Lesson two he imbibed in the years 1922–5 under Hale Middleton in the Kano Divisional Office. Its accent was on pervasive reform, carefully and intelligently planned, empirically, responsibly, and strongly carried out. Discipline certainly; hatchet methods, no. Hale Middleton, who had no social life and was a bachelor in these years, was oblivious to both evenings and weekends. He found that in early years scarcity of staff had left district administration and especially tax collecting drastically under-supervised and that inefficiency, corruption, and laxity were everywhere. Slow collections and muddled accounts invited extortion. Against intense opposition from the Emir downwards Hale Middleton forced all district heads to close their old accounts before starting new tax years, dealing with each case himself and breaking officials who consistently failed to measure up. Reform of the N.A. courts, Carrow's particular job, accompanied this. Hale Middleton had the classic attribute of the good bureaucratic superior, the ability to leave subordinates alone as long as they did their jobs. Carrow did his and he learned.

Lesson three was the Palmer reforms of the late twenties, by which time Carrow was Acting D.O. Kano Division and later D.O. and Acting Resident. A golden opportunity to build on

[1] He was at Ibi briefly before going to Kano in 1919, at Koton Karifi for three months in 1921, in the Secretariat at Kaduna briefly in 1928–9 and 1931, and he acted as Chief Commissioner in 1944 and in 1945–6.

the Hale Middleton improvements was provided by the death of the old, reactionary Emir in 1926. Full prior agreement to join in implementing further reform was a condition of appointment for the new Emir, Abdullahi Bayero, who was to rule for nearly thirty years. The remaining palace slaves were removed. An executive council was formed, consisting of the Waziri as legal and personal adviser, and two other officials, one an honest and able district head and the other a brother of the Emir who had been at Mr. Vischer's school for the sons of chiefs. In the 1920s these were startling and radical moves in a major emirate. They heralded gradual introduction of the notions and paraphernalia of local government as conducted in Europe. They suggested regular and systematic functioning, specific tasks, accountability, objective administration, instead of the personal whim that this part of Africa had responded to for as long as anyone could remember.

Lesson four, the shipboard lectures of Sir Donald Cameron, was followed by the spectacle of his own superiors giving emotional and politically motivated responses to Cameron's line. Carrow could see both sides: Palmer's correct emphasis on the need for a solid, traditional base and for bringing progress at a pace that Africans could follow; and Cameron's insistence on avoiding such excessive deference to tradition that there was no progress at all and society was left defenceless in a mechanized, sophisticated world. The issues were not all that sharp, nor did Carrow, with a decade of experience behind him, see his job in theoretical terms. But his own administration showed the effects of exposure to four very different men: the thoughtless D.O. who meant to reform and succeeded in destroying; Hale Middleton, the intense, determined, methodical builder-up, a latter-day Temple in his way; Palmer, the flamboyant and knowledgeable field marshal who made the Emir of Kano accept the rudiments of cabinet government but also made white women wear veils; and Cameron, who could see what was wrong but not what was right and whose ill-conceived attacks often failed of their objectives.

In running Kano and Sokoto Carrow made various impressions on his juniors and on outside observers. To one A.D.O. who did not stay long in the Service he was a tyrant.[1] A sub-

[1] See Crocker, *Nigeria.*

ordinate who eventually spent more time in Nigeria than did Carrow himself thought him tough, his methods sometimes smacking too much of the quarterdeck, but a driver who stamped his provinces with the mark of determined, forward-looking administration while at the same time inspiring juniors as no one else did. A younger officer whose personality and educational background were very different from Carrow's considered him one of the two or three best that the Service produced.[1] What the Africans thought may never be known. Members of N.A.s in Sokoto Province in the mid-1960s could name the dates of Carrow's service there without a moment's reflection and were quick to point out various accomplishments of his. One Emir, who had served him as an assistant in the groundnut production campaign, which, significantly, Carrow was given charge of during the Second World War, spoke of him with unselfconscious friendship and concluded, 'They [Carrow and two others whom he named] made me what I am.'[2]

Carrow does not take credit for rescuing Sokoto from the nadir of 1931. This was well under way when he became Resident there in 1933. It was for him to bring the N.A. up to the level of the best elsewhere in the North. His relations with Hassan, who succeeded Muhammadu Tambari as Sultan in 1931, were excellent. The contrast between Sokoto under Carrow and Hassan and the same place under Webster and Muhammadu Tambari should give pause to those who generalize about colonialism. On Hassan's death Carrow pulled down the dilapidated rabbit warren that lay between the gateway to the Sultan's house and his council chamber and had contributed architecturally to the Emirate's back-alley politics for decades. The move was characteristic. A Chief's residence should be sound and imposing and progress should not be impeded by nostalgia about the connections that an old wreck of a building had had with the past. Hassan, whom many considered a saint, was hard-working, unostentatious, and direct. It has been mentioned that he did not hesitate to oppose the posting of a British officer whose personality would create problems for the N.A. 'Old Sultan Hassan could be persuasive when he tried,' Carrow recalls, 'and I gave way.'[3] But all was not sweetness

[1] Giles, interview, London, 23 March 1965.
[2] Emir of Yauri, interview, Yelwa, 27 August 1965.   [3] 24 September 1965.

and light. The Sultan believed in the evil eye and would do
nothing to stop villagers from persecuting innocent old women
suspected of being witches, a matter that the British could
hardly cope with themselves. The gap between European and
African mentalities remained as always. In 1936 a technical
department officer complaining to Carrow about the non-
enforcement of a regulation that Kaduna had promulgated
and that Carrow had noted and then promptly forgotten. On
grounds of hygiene the regulation prohibited the growing of
high crops near dwellings. Badgered by the technical officer,
Carrow asked the Sultan to implement this. Hassan did so
without telling Carrow that the result would be a shortage of
grain at the end of the dry season. The shortage duly material-
ized and Carrow had no response when the Sultan said in
council, 'You owe us x thousand bundles of corn.'[1] Yet even
this failure of understanding points to an atmosphere of mutual
regard and openness that was utterly lacking in the twenties.
In restoring confidence throughout the N.A., both in Sokoto
town and in the districts, and in giving an example of honesty,
vigour, and efficiency, Carrow and Hassan worked wonders.

Sharwood Smith is nine years Carrow's junior. The compact
Yorkshireman still gives the impression of having to control a
superabundance of energy. He was just the wrong age for
Cambridge during the First World War and instead went
straight from Aldenham into the Royal Flying Corps. After
seeing action as a fighter pilot in France he was briefly in Germany and India. His Nigerian service began in 1921 and was
confined for the first six years to the Cameroons, where he
worked under Ruxton in those parts of the ex-German territory
that were attached administratively to Southern Nigeria.
Ruxton, whom Sharwood Smith greatly admired, viewed the
governing task from a firm moral base.[2] His perspective was
remarkable and he tended to moderation. Higher authority, if
it behaved in a tiresome way, should be got round inconspicu-
ously. On being posted to the North Sharwood Smith ran
straight into the Gusau murder case, which nearly ruined him

[1] Carrow, 22 April 1965.
[2] Ruxton remains something of a mystery. He was not over-successful as Lieutenant Governor of Southern Nigeria and he ended his life in a monastery in
England.

and which gave him, rather early on, a sense of proportion on
the complexity of one's relationship to immediate superiors and
to those higher up. If Ruxton had shown him how to do native
administration, Webster showed him how not to, and Palmer
added a postscript on the knowledge that Kaduna needed in
order to exert discipline without being unjust.

Sharwood Smith's first wife did not care for Nigeria. When
the marriage ended it was only natural that he who had loved
Africa on sight would throw himself even more intensely into
the life of whatever unit he was given to administer. In all the
documents that bear his mark he emerges as a participant who
is totally committed to the task. When he writes of an unsatisfactory situation calling for action, a thirty-year-old file, clothed
in archival dust, can spring to life again. Seeing him pacing
back and forth as he talked and almost never sitting down, the
Africans dubbed him 'Mai Wandon Karfe', the man in iron
trousers. Even as a junior officer Sharwood Smith was not a
man of whom it was possible to be unaware.

After a brief spell in Kano following the Gusau misfortune
Sharwood Smith went in 1929 to his own division, Argungu, a
posting he refers to as his rehabilitation. Here was scope for an
energetic man and challenge for a thoughtful one. The Kebbi
of Argungu were a difficult lot, independent and suspicious.
Never conquered by Sokoto in the nineteenth century despite
being its close neighbour, they had the pride of self-reliance, yet
they were aware of being despised as a lesser breed. Their N.A.
was as corrupt as any. Sharwood Smith realized that sympathy,
patience, and instruction were needed as much as discipline, if
not more. The place was anachronistic and pagan in outlook.
Brains were rare. One would have to work with whatever
material of leadership there was and be prepared to settle for
far less than perfection. The Emir did not really understand
that his conduct was reprehensible. What was crime to the
British was custom to him.[1] So with the N.A. Everyone bypassed
the native courts and the official *alkali* in favour of unrecognized
and secret adjudication. N.A. offices went to the highest bidder;
the estates of deceased landowners were tampered with; and,
as in Sokoto during the same time period, the court employed

---

[1] N.A. Confidential, Argungu, Resident Sokoto and D. O. Argungu, 4 November 1929 ff., K.

quack mallams who practised the black arts. An open inquiry would be futile and sacking the Emir useless, for no preferable successor was at hand. Though he gave in to the evils around him, the Emir was basically decent and well-meaning.

Sharwood Smith's handling of Argungu was a mixture of toughness and common sense. He devoted a good deal of time to gaining the Emir's confidence, meanwhile bringing home to him that a clean-up was unavoidable. On six of the worst offenders in the N.A. he assembled full details and in the Emir's name they were dismissed and sent away. Sharwood Smith considered the slave who held the title Majidadi a borderline case. Although he had a bad record, he was young and able and the N.A. could not afford to be cavalier with anyone who had talent. The man was warned and put on probation. Slowly the D.O. worked downwards from the top of the N.A., encouraging the capable and the straight, dealing quickly and firmly with others. When he handed over to his successor in 1932 Sharwood Smith was able to report improvement in the atmosphere at emirate headquarters. Communications with Gwandu and Sokoto had become easier. The D.O.'s passion for road building had decreased parochialism in rural areas as well. No one would yet compare Argungu favourably with the best in the North, but other D.O.s could build on Sharwood Smith's work. One lined the old town with trees. A new market appeared and a new residence for the Emir. Listening to an urbane and knowledgeable cousin of the Emir more than three decades later as he talked of the violence and hopelessness of life in old Argungu, one had difficulty imagining the place as it had been before.[1]

In his remaining posts before going to Kaduna as head of the Northern Government in the 1950s, Sharwood Smith never found two situations that needed the same combination of discipline and guidance. Gwandu, where he went after Argungu, was still basking in the reflected glory of its exemplary Chief. Usumanu was undoubtedly a pillar of strength, 'the main spring of the N.A. . . . without him there is . . . little else'.[2] But for

---

[1] The Emir's kinsman was a prominent district head. Pointing out the gravestones of his ancestors in the courtyard of the old Palace, now a museum, and speaking of the endless fighting with Gwandu that had claimed the lives of several of them, he remarked smilingly, 'We do not think of that sort of thing any more' (interview, Argungu, 4 September 1965).

[2] To the Resident Sokoto, 8 May 1933, K.

precisely this reason rural officials tended to be weak characters. The task was one of gently prodding an excellent but touchy Emir and keeping his loyalty while being less gentle with the rest of the N.A. Although road building and other public works went forward, these were discouraging years. The Depression kept expenditures down and one watched helplessly as the European staff was cut back.

Zaria was something else again. Providing the Emir with a really effective council was overdue, as was reorganization of district administration. Jealousy and intrigue still debased emirate politics, and the Resident under whom Sharwood Smith served as D.O. wondered if any possible claimant to the position of Emir could lift the N.A. out of its doldrums.[1] Sharwood Smith had his own ideas about this. In the meantime he himself attended meetings of the Emir's council and saw that officials were given definite responsibilities and held to them. The place must be made to move and the idea of systematic procedure instilled in the minds of feudal aristocrats who still thought of government in terms of taxes and privilege.[2] At Zaria Sharwood Smith lived on the same station with the Resident, as opposed to his two previous posts where his immediate superior had been miles away. Yet junior officers noticed that the D.O. was master of the situation and indeed that he virtually ran the Province, with the Resident serving as a kind of constitutional monarch. 'Nothing is ever done without or contrary to the D.O.'[3] When Sharwood Smith was himself on tour, juniors were bombarded with instructions, inquiries, and reminders that kept them jumping as much as when he was on the other side of the office wall. It was the same with N.A. officials. Everyone was watched, judged, driven, kept up to the mark.

Towards the end of 1936 the Emir died while visiting an army camp in Kachia District. Sharwood Smith was not only in close touch with events and ready with an emergency plan but was actually visiting the sick Chief and trying to persuade him to take medicines provided by the Army doctor instead of native potions thrust on him by his personal servants.[4] It was

---

[1] Backwell to S.N.P., 31 December 1935, K.
[2] Sharwood Smith to Resident, 2 May 1934, K.
[3] Giles, diary, 27 January 1936.
[4] File on the death of the Emir Ibrahim, 18 January 1937 ff., K.

L

the D.O. who now moved to set up a regency and produced the reports and recommendations on which the Resident's messages to Kaduna were based. Returning to Zaria, Sharwood Smith got the traditional electors together in his own house before taking them to the Residency.[1] The names of four candidates for the vacant Emirate were listed. As so often happened throughout the North, the electors did their best to absolve themselves of responsibility and to contrive a situation in which the British would choose. Sharwood Smith had already made up his own mind which candidate suited the needs of the moment. Two years of studying the N.A. assured that. But he was determined as usual that N.A. officials would take action themselves, guided by the clearest possible indication of government thinking. He explained that there were four criteria: the new Emir must be of royal birth; he must be acceptable to the people; he must be acceptable to the Government; and 'he must have the ability to do what had become a very difficult job, requiring much administrative experience'.[2] The first criterion represented no break with tradition and was therefore redundant as a guide. All the other three could be used to disqualify a candidate whom the D.O. might consider unsuitable. There was no doubt that the old Emir and some of his closest advisers would have preferred one of his own sons, a district head who had the title Dan Madami. But Sharwood Smith thought this man, though amiable, somewhat colourless and lacking in the necessary drive. Dan Madami was said to have spent a good deal of money to assure his own election. Ja'afaru, grandson of a former Emir, was theoretically ineligible, candidacy being traditionally confined to the sons of former chiefs, but he was popular with the people. This did not go unnoticed by the Emir, who sent him as district head to distant Zangon Katab on that account. The D.O. noticed Ja'afaru's popularity too and knew that it was based on his ability and integrity. Of the four major candidates only Ja'afaru had had the experience of working closely with the British as an office mallam.[3] He used a typewriter and kept his own district accounts, practices

[1] 7 November 1965 and interview, 26 October 1965.
[2] 7 November 1965.
[3] Cf. M. G. Smith, *Government in Zazzau*, London, 1959, pp. 234 ff. In fact the D.O. did not know about Ja'afaru's service as an office mallam, a possible drawback in the public view. He knew him only as a successful district head.

that were almost unique among district heads of the time. And only Ja'afaru satisfied the administration's four criteria. Although Kaduna fussed as usual about dynastic considerations, it was Ja'afaru who was introduced as the new Emir to a great crowd outside the Emir's residence. The introduction was performed by the Resident and it was the Governor who installed the new Chief later on. The guiding hand throughout had been Sharwood Smith's. His rationale had been straightforward: the vacancy was an opportunity to further modernize the N.A. by giving it a head who understood bureaucracy and the ends it was established to serve. Like Palmer in Kano a decade earlier, the D.O. had in effect made increased Europeanization a condition of appointment. A more glaring contrast with Webster's detachment at Sokoto in 1924 would be hard to imagine.

No one maintains that Carrow and Sharwood Smith had no faults and made no serious mistakes. Carrow's temper was a legend in his provinces and he himself makes no secret of it. Some of his juniors thought him too hard and so interested in driving forward that the pace might have been too swift for the average N.A. official to follow. Sharwood Smith's devotion to progress also drew fire from critics, some of whom thought him indifferent to tradition. As to the selection of N.A. officials, it was said that if he had to choose between an honest plodder and a hard-driving, efficient cad he would instinctively support the claims of the latter. His successors sometimes wondered whether there was not a bit too much of Sharwood Smith in the arrangements that he left behind, making it hard for subsequent officers to use their own notions and talents. Shortly after his departure from Zaria the new D.O. observed that there was entirely too much D.O. initiative and that the new Emir was not playing a big enough part in running the N.A.[1] No administrator, least of all the one who reaches high positions, will escape this kind of criticism. Those in authority are natural targets for the squeamish, the rigid, the unimaginative, and the disgruntled as well as for the objectively critical. In striking their respective balances between tradition and progress and between necessary evils and drumhead justice, both officers

[1] See File, N.A. Office Reorganization, Zaria, June 1937, K. It may be observed that at this point Ja'afaru had been in office only a few months.

were bound to displease a certain number of Africans as well as British, especially in a system that left so much to the individual. There can be no doubt, however, that the overall effect of their rule was to stir things up, to encourage progressive impulses in N.A.s, and to discourage blind reliance on tradition for its own sake. Things hummed in divisions run by men like Sharwood Smith and in provinces run by men like Carrow. Junior officers tended to feel that they were part of an organization that was moving forward towards something better. Chiefs and N.A. officials who could not accept the twentieth century were of course bitterly opposed to this kind of officer. So were the dishonest. Others, a growing number, co-operated with a willingness, even an eagerness, that must have indicated a general appreciation of what was being done.

Such chiefs as Yahaya of Gwandu (1938–55), Hassan of Sokoto (1931–8), Ja'afaru of Zaria (1937–59), and among the more minor ones Abdullahi of Yauri (1923–55), stand out as the African counterparts of the Carrows and the Sharwood Smiths. There is room for endless speculation about the motives of particular chiefs, especially with the handicap of grossly inadequate documentation on that side. There is no question about the genuine interest in development felt by such as Usumanu of Gwandu, who outdid many D.O.s in his resentment of the Depression and the cuts in British technical staff that were caused by it. A weakening of tradition's hold was sometimes unmistakable, as when Ja'afaru told the Chiefs' Conference in 1946 that he was not opposed to law reform, which some British assumed good Moslems might be. Directing his remarks to the British, he said: 'In the time of our fathers you abolished slavery, and we went along. If you wish to improve the legal system we will follow you in that too.'[1] By the 1930s a number of the more progressive chiefs showed that they could think in a regional rather than a purely local way. With inter-emirate warfare at an end, the idea of co-operating with neighbours was attractive. Financial or political motives were sometimes present, as when Gwandu and Yauri worked together to corner herdsmen who had always played emirates off against one another in evading payment of *jangali*. Furthermore, in such matters as road building, control of rinderpest, or an anti-

[1] Interview, Weatherhead, 16 April 1966.

hopper campaign, forward-looking chiefs like Usumanu of Gwandu and Abdullahi of Yauri found themselves closer to a D.O. or a veterinarian than to their own people. Chiefs of this kind had to some extent left the world of tradition and would never go back.

As for Yahaya, one is clearly dealing in his case with an exceptional man who would have stood out anywhere and whose actions stemmed from extraordinary personal integrity and conviction. The philosopher-king who has both power and an authentic feeling of responsibility is rare enough in any historical epoch. In the twentieth century, with its massive bureaucracies in big countries and petty tyrants elsewhere, the type is a curiosity. Yahaya showed his hand early by wishing to turn Christian, in the thought that that religion was morally and culturally superior to Islam. Such a notion would not have occurred to an opportunist or a reactionary. Carrow's first report on Yahaya observed that the new Chief was 'meeting difficulties with a spirit of "noblesse oblige" '.[1] D.O.s were astonished that in such a field as education the Emir would even bother to try, so great were the obstacles. 'Every new step is only made under pressure and compulsion . . . boys chosen to be trained as teachers deliberately fail the examination.'[2] Small wonder, then, that Yahaya, feeling as he did about progress, made common cause with D.O.s who saw the task in the same way. With Weatherhead he was a co-worker. White goes so far as to put the Emir in the first position and himself second: 'I was his chief executive . . . I would not think of going on tour until I had agreed my route with the Emir and he would tell me of matters into which he wanted me to enquire.'[3]

There were grey areas in every picture. In the 1940s a D.O. found much to grumble about in Abdullahi's running of Yauri. The Emir was using forced labour on his farms, confident that the British would not be too severe, for he was growing ground-nuts, the North's major economic contribution to the war effort. The D.O. was not hesitant about applying discipline, as Abdullahi was 'unwilling for Yauri to be in disgrace'.[4] Towards the end of Yahaya's reign, Sharwood Smith, by then Resident

---

[1] File, Emirs of Gwandu, 23 May 1918 ff., K.
[2] Weatherhead, 28 March 1944.   [3] Op. cit., p. 222.
[4] Weatherhead, 18 November 1943.

Sokoto, thought that the Emir was losing some of his celebrated
sense of proportion, mainly as a result of having been lionized
in Lagos.[1] The very excellence of some chiefs isolated them from
homely comforts available to mediocrities. They could have
their heads turned, and all but the most scrupulous would find
it impossible not to take advantage of opportunities for self-
enrichment opened up to them by their power and their superior
talents. But the D.O. was always there, a constant brake on this
familiar tendency of authoritarian regimes. Until the 1950s no
one on either side seriously considered the possibility of European supervision being relaxed, much less removed.[2]

The question whether Anglo-African government was in the
main more balanced than not—whether it compromised
sensibly between the need for imported improvements and the
ability of local society to digest these—is a subjective one and
cannot be documented one way or the other. A former D.O.,
whose service was mostly in the provinces but who spent some
time in Kaduna at the end of his career, recalls that a favourite
indoor sport was to trade opinions on the qualities and the
effectiveness of one's brother officers, individually and as a
group. This was done frequently, as it is in any relatively small
corporate body, and the rough consensus that emerged over the
years gives an interesting and relevant picture of what the
British themselves thought about the matter. There were
officers who had qualities that moved a division forward (perhaps 45 per cent had these qualities), officers whose units ticked
over quietly (perhaps about the same proportion), and officers
who presided over situations of backslide. There was great
variation, of course, in the individual attributes of D.O.s falling
into each group. But, one way or another, the successful ones
were likely to be respected and liked by N.A. officials and the
less successful ones not. By the 1940s all divisions had had their
share of good D.O.s, and officers with serious failings had either

---

[1] Report for 1950, K.

[2] When the Governor, Sir Bernard Bourdillon, asked the Emir of Yauri in 1943
what he thought of the possibility of African D.O.s, it was as though someone 'had
kicked over a hornets' nest' (Sharwood Smith, 17 April 1966). The Emir had in
mind D.O.s from the South. Sharwood Smith comments that this was stage one
in the Northern awakening (18 May 1967), and Weatherhead adds (25 June 1967)
that the Emir's reaction reflected his Anglophilia and mistrust of Africans in
general rather than of southerners in particular.

been sacked or shunted off into positions where they would do N.A.s no harm. Overall, there had been a slow, steady rise in N.A. capacity. By comparison with their predecessors of the first decade, officials were decidedly European in outlook, and this had gone so far by the end of the Second World War that it no longer depended exclusively on the presence of aliens.

Ultimately, balance was more likely than imbalance because the accumulation of changes and the momentum of the years made it less and less possible for a Webster or a Muhammadu Tambari to occur. Webster, who arrived in the North in 1901, was a phenomenon of his time. His administrative assumptions were due in large part to local conditions encountered by his generation in the first years. Recruitment as conducted by Lugard was catch-as-catch-can. Later the Colonial Office evolved a relatively high degree of system and cadets went through formal academic courses at Oxford and Cambridge. On arrival in his first post Webster had found a small Fulani aristocracy doing everything and the British nothing, he himself being only the second Englishman the locals had seen. The recruit of 1931, fresh from his lectures and full of untried Hausa, walked into a going concern, a sophisticated bi-racial complex, backed by decades of development and experience in which Africa had steadily, if unevenly, adapted itself to Europe's logic. The phase of groping, experimenting, and coming to grips had given way to increased system and better communications, to more European staff, professional and technical as well as administrative. Things had settled into a rhythm that gave more to Europe with every passing year. Although some D.O.s were less vigorous than Carrow or Sharwood Smith, the question of leaving the N.A. to its own devices or of closing both eyes to the naughtiness of a roguish Emir no longer arose. Aliyu of Zaria had fought the British and partaken fully of the normal pursuits of Fulani rulers in pre-colonial times. Ja'afaru could scarcely remember when there were no Europeans about, and he knew from his own experience what went on in government offices and what the British were aiming at. By the 1950s some would consider Ja'afaru too conservative. Aliyu had receded into the realm of the unimaginable.

The authoritarianism that the North got was responsible and efficient. It is hard to see how any government could have done more on so small a budget. There was no tendency for leadership to be demagogic, for the masses were inert, and when officers appealed to them it was not to obtain support for their own selfish ends but to teach the people how their lot could be improved. N.A. officials were expected to move with the times so that in due course they could work the levers of a state that their fathers would have considered both fantastic and contemptible. The ultimate finesse of Anglo-African government was that it moved at a pace that made this possible. While theoreticians talked of Indirect Rule, the D.O. decided what could be done by the Chief and the N.A. and what would have to be done by himself and his staff. The system concentrated on the finite, on today and tomorrow rather than next year. It did not exhort beyond the imagination of the ruling classes or invoke high abstractions. Though they came from different worlds, the D.O. and the Chief knew each other too well for that.

6

Touring

At the grass-roots, Anglo-African government was Assistant
District Officers touring the countryside on horseback. In this
way Europe reached out and touched the face of Africa,
watched its contortions and was watched in turn, tried and
failed and tried again for half a century to make the people
and their land change by an inch or two. Africa now saw the
bature close up, winced under the gentle lash of his strange
urging, went its stubborn way again as he rode off, and found,
later on and to its wonderment, that some of what he had
attempted was not entirely to be despised.

There were as many kinds of tours as there were hamlets off
the beaten track and A.D.O.s to send out from divisional headquarters. If we describe the situation throughout the North in
one year we must begin again the following year, by which time
divisions were in different hands, crises of crops and cattle had
arisen and been dealt with, and new plans had been made for
a road, an agricultural scheme, or a conciliar grouping of pagan
communities that had to be swept together by an A.D.O. who
usually did something else. One of the few constants in the
picture, from first to last, was the pressure of individual Residents and of Regional headquarters for more touring. Everyone,
hard drivers and *masu lafiya* alike, agreed that information on
the state of the rural areas was vital. If a D.O. could not say to
his Resident that officers in his division had spent at least half
the working month on tour, there had to be a convincing explanation. Beyond this there were no overall rules, for the two
aspects of the problem as seen by D.O.s—the regular and *ad hoc*
work to be done and the number and quality of A.D.O.s at
their disposal—were constantly shifting. Often the D.O. who
wanted his juniors to inspect and report but not to take too
active a part in rural administration preferred them to tour a
different part of the division each time. Conversely the hard

driver would assign A.D.O.s to fixed Touring Areas, each with a headquarters of sorts, perhaps a resthouse where the major part of an officer's equipment and provisions could be stored. The possibility of touring officers running their areas too directly as a result of coming to know them better did not worry these D.O.s, who felt that the advantages were worth the risk or that the issue was a false one. If the A.D.O. could go back again and again to check up on the same N.A officials, there was less likelihood of backsliding. District heads and lesser office-holders knew this full well. Even for districts close by divisional headquarters—nothing in Hadejia or Yauri was very far from the touring officer's residence—there was no such thing as too much touring.

Zaria Province in the 1930s and 1940s was normally divided into three Touring Areas.[1] The officer based at Zaria itself looked after the northern districts—Giwa, Makarfi, Ikara, Anchau, Soba, and Kubau. A second officer in charge of the southern area was based at Lere with, if possible, an A.D.O. at Kagoro. In the west, ideally, a third would tour from Kaduna, covering Birnin Gwari, Chikun, and Igabi as well as the Kaduna *sabon gari*. This meant that with luck officers could stay out on tour for many weeks at a stretch, seeing for themselves how the economy was progressing and sensing the mood of the people without having to get their information through

[1] See file on Touring by Political Officers, Zaria Province, K., e.g. D.O. to Resident, 8 August 1937. The present chapter makes use of Zaria Province as a case in point, drawing also on other provinces for examples of particular activities. This is justifiable, even though no two provinces were exactly alike, because Zaria was in many important ways a microcosm of the whole North. It had a large Hausa population and a major Fulani Emir. Its capital was a centre for railway activity, for commerce, and eventually for education. It had an important garrison. Its *sabon gari* was large and typical. The Hausa publishing enterprise *Gaskiya Ta Fi Kwabo* and the Gaskiya Corporation were based there. Experimental farms were in the Province, and experiments with co-operative societies were conducted there. Yet the Province also contained pagan units in great quantity, some under non-pagan chiefs or D.H.s, some eventually run by their own councils. Mining, farming of many kinds, and the pasturing of migrant Fulani all figured in the economic and social life of the Province.

The comments of former officers who have read this chapter in manuscript indicate a need for more stress on two points: (1) that senior officers also toured regularly, i.e. touring was not left to A.D.O.s and cadets; and (2) that there was more inspirational and constructive work done on tour than is perhaps emphasized in the chapter. One's aim here has been to characterize the tour rather than to give an exhaustive survey of its scope and activity.

the filter of the N.A. Conscientious officers were constantly reaching and being reached by the individual African. They heard complaints themselves, examined witnesses, checked the workings of native courts, and saw that inequities were put right without having to seek the advice of local officials. Inspecting crops, they talked with farmers about seeds, soil, weather, markets, and prices.[1] When a local *sarki* in a rich farming area south of Katsina did not respond quickly enough to the threat of crop destruction by locusts, an officer personally got together a force of 2,500 men and supervised their successful attack on the swarm of hoppers. The following year he swooped down on the village of Kungi in Birnin Gwari and arrested fifty villagers who had not paid their taxes. 'I don't think they will forget the last few days in a hurry.'[2] When a Hausa community refused to obey its village head he re-established discipline, prepared for the sacking of an ineffective N.A. messenger, and toured bush areas near by, making clear to farmers that they would have to pay taxes even though they had ceased to live in settled communities. A pagan in the mountains south of Kaduna sought out a touring officer to show him an infected foot, which the A.D.O. dressed and bandaged as best he could. Earlier, when chasing cattle Fulani, he got so far ahead of his N.A. touring companions that he had surprised the Fulani camp and was deep in conversation with them by the time his party caught up with him.[3] Near Yelwa an A.D.O. received a woman with a tax complaint and sent her on to the Chief only after hearing her story himself: 'Here is Iggi from Duku, who has brought a complaint that she was made to pay sixteen shillings—for what she can't tell.'[4] When N.A. officials near Rijau in Kontagora could not explain a severe drop in taxes, it was the A.D.O. who discovered the reason and did the necessary reassessment.[5]

Farming was so central to the well-being of the people that

[1] Zaria Touring Diary, Provincial Office, Northern Area, October 1942, Elliott.
[2] Zaria Touring Diary, Katsina (then part of Zaria Province), summer 1931 and autumn 1932, Talbot-Edwards.
[3] Private Touring Diary of L. C. Giles, Birnin Gwari N.A., 1935, on tour between Nassarawa and Kwingi in the Kamuku country. I am grateful to Mr. Giles for allowing me to read these highly informative diaries and for his valuable elucidation of particular points.
[4] Yauri Book, 21 December 1928, Harris.
[5] A.D.O. Rijau (Pott) to D.O. Kontagora, 3 May 1939, Pott Papers, C.R.P.

officers always concentrated on how the crops were doing and many became amateur agriculturalists. In early years the bringing of peace was a major achievement and allowed peasants to take up desirable land farther from walled towns and to build granaries in the open without fear of raiders. For some time thereafter, touring officers held a watching brief against the possibility of famine. Everyone knew that the peasant was in the habit of planting just enough to see him through from one harvest to the next. It was the classic situation of subsistence farming, accompanied by a generally fatalistic view of drought and locusts. While both the Agricultural and Administrative Services were small, there was little the A.D.O. could do beyond battling the hoppers and disciplining N.A. officials whose greed discouraged the planting of an excess that could be sold in the market. But gradually one turned to more positive things. If there were too few agricultural officers, at least they could supply seeds to touring officers and give them information on the success of crops in experimental farms. 'Planted a small plot of ginger' became a familiar entry in touring diaries.[1] In the thirties agricultural officers talked of a millennium that would be brought about through the introduction of mixed farming. With government help peasants would progress from hand cultivation to ploughs drawn by oxen whose manure could be used as fertilizer. A peasant so equipped, said the Agricultural Department, could use four times the acreage and would get twice the yield he had been getting with his short-handled hoe. Knowing that peasants were not used to managing livestock and that both staff for supervision and funds for equipment and animals were limited, administrative officers doubted that a millennium was within the Government's means. But the idea was good and bit by bit mixed farming spread. So did the people's willingness to fight crop blights that had been seen traditionally as acts of God. In the mid-thirties an A.D.O. noticed that Gwari villagers were attacking swarms of locusts on their own, without being prodded by Europeans or by their Chief. It was the same with co-operatives, started by the British a few years later. Questions about productivity were received with suspicion, the peasants assuming that they signalled an increase in taxes. Schemes for credit unions sounded

[1] Birnin Gwari, 21 May 1932, Talbot-Edwards.

'too good to be true'.[1] But once the benefits had been demonstrated, time was on the side of progress. A sceptical public
became gradually more amenable to trying new seeds and
methods and to notions of self-help, cash crops, and co-operation.

Touring officers came into direct contact too with cattle
Fulani, usually as a result of a forced march before dawn, with
the Fulani doing all possible to avoid having themselves and
their herds accurately counted. The experience could be a
lark. Riding eastwards towards Dogon Dawa at 1.30 in the
morning an A.D.O. was 'very contented to be on trek and
solitary again, trotting away in the cool air on my mad errand
. . . felt I should be rather crestfallen if the usual thing happened
and I didn't find a cow'.[2] At 6.00 he crossed a stream and can-
tered along a bit farther to a Fulani encampment (*ruga*) where
he found a few of the men to talk to but their cattle nowhere in
evidence. They were not especially communicative about the
numbers of their herd, nor did they want to go into Dogon
Dawa as he suggested to have the beasts inoculated against
rinderpest. They did not like the Waziri of Birnin Gwari, who
was travelling with the A.D.O. Relations with settled peasants
were normal—pasturing rights in exchange for milk and for
manuring of fields—but N.A. officials often turned in less tax
than they actually collected and in various ways made life
difficult. The British Peace intensified the pressure on land,
menacing the herdsman's very existence. Collection of cattle
tax (*jangali*) was more efficient under the British than it had
been before. Small wonder that the Fulani kept on the run.

Some days later, in the Kamuku country, the A.D.O. had
better luck. As he approached on his horse, a group of Fulani
boys employed the familiar tactic of stampeding their herd. But
the frightened cows led him straight to the *ruga*, where he surprised the main body of Fulani with virtually all their cattle.
They tried the usual excuses: they did not understand, their
leader was away at the market and therefore they could not
bring the cattle in to be counted. But soon they saw it was hope-

[1] L. C. Giles, 'The Hausa Village and Co-Operation', 1937, p. 82. I am grateful
to Mr. Giles for lending me his copy of this report covering surveys made by him
preparatory to setting up co-operative schemes. (Co-operative societies were
started in the 1940s.)
[2] Giles, diary, Birnin Gwari, 1935.

less and a fairly satisfactory count was made. All over the North
the same game of hide and seek was played. Full accuracy was
an illusion no one bothered to entertain. With fixed Touring
Areas, however, it became possible to identify the various nomad
groups, to learn the routes they took on their seasonal migra-
tions, and to keep reasonably close count on herds. It was
important that officers kept in direct touch so as to control the
venality or laziness of many N.A. officials. Yet officers could
carry efficiency too far, as happened when an A.D.O. in Kontagora inspected a *ruga* twice in quick succession and got such
accurate counts that the Fulani left his area permanently and
moved westward towards the Niger. With the whole country
becoming steadily more integrated, the problem was to make
civilization attractive to the Fulani so that they could come to
terms with it gradually. The situation in Yauri had become
sufficiently stabilized by the early thirties for herdsmen to be
generally content; *jangali* payments were adequate and Fulani
sought veterinary services on their own initiative.[1]

Dealing with settled communities, the A.D.O. was the Government's eyes and ears in the matter of society's general condition and development. He noted the effects of peace and order
in an ethnically heterogeneous country, especially the growing
interdependence of groups that had formerly lived apart from
one another or had met in violence. Hausa overlords in pagan
areas tended to intermarry and eventually to blend into local
society until a veneer of Islamic practice was all that distinguished them from the mass of the people.[2] Pagans meanwhile
adopted the Hausa language and indulged in more trade with
neighbours than they had done before. The process was helped
by the common denominators of European activity—road
building, regulation of commerce, pressure for higher standards
of public health and education. Even if they had wished to, the
British could not always influence what Africans borrowed—
one noticed that material conveniences were more easily assimi-
lated than abstractions like responsible government—but such
borrowings were relevant to the broad subject of changing

[1] Cf. Yauri Book, 26 January 1929 and 2 June 1930, Harris and Holme. See
also C. J. Hanson-Smith, 'Notes on the Sokoto Fulbe', 19 February 1955. I am
grateful to Mr. Hanson-Smith for lending me his copy of the report on his survey
made on secondment during the mid-1950s and including historical material.

[2] Zaria Touring Diary, 25 November 1931, Kennett.

public tastes and habits. When the A.D.O.'s own values collided head-on with some aspect of native custom, his knowledge of society's capacity for change could and did strengthen his resolve to help the process actively. Weatherhead released a penniless woman who had been imprisoned by a Moslem court for being pregnant though unwed. 'It appears questionable whether in this case Native Law and Custom does not conflict with the dictates of humanity.'[1]

It was more difficult when touring officers tried to prize open the lids of injustices that were fastened down by deeply ingrained prejudice in the exploited as well as the exploiter. Giles spent long hours lecturing N.A. officials of Birnin Gwari on their duty to peasants whom everyone still thought of as slaves.[2] The trouble was that many peasants, the Gwari for example, had never known anything but contempt and victimizing from their Moslem overlords and had no reason to think that the low esteem in which they were universally held was in any way exceptional. Bringing improvements to people who lacked self-respect and initiative was discouraging work.

On the Benue Letchworth saw all around him the dreary, familiar spectacle of petty intrigue and self-seeking and little evidence that anyone was thinking of progress and the public good. Taking direct action with whole communities was a possibility that had to be looked at in the broad perspective of patient decades. Meanwhile he picked at specifics that offered some promise of tangible results, such as watching the educated and privileged classes so as to spot the youth who would be 'worth a job later'.[3] But occasionally there was a chance to do something larger. Northwards in Niger Province were peoples who lived in inaccessible hill tracts where their fathers had gone to escape slave-raiders. In the Kashira area of what was to become the Kamuku N.A., Hausa traders did their business in daylight hours only and left ample time to reach near-by Gwari villages before nightfall. As late as the 1930s outsiders were continually molested, some by 'an elaborate process of torture involving hot oil'.[4] Whole communities were cunningly

[1] Zaria Touring Diary, August 1940, Weatherhead.
[2] Giles, diary, summer 1935.
[3] Notes on Nassarawa Emirate, 1936, C.R.P.
[4] Zaria Touring Diary, 19 November 1931, Talbot-Edwards touring near Kuki. And cf. Orr, op. cit., p. 56.

tucked away in heavily forested valleys and craggy hillsides. While the original purpose of taking refuge in such places was understandable, staying there was now economically and socially pointless, a threat to neighbours and a block to any sort of decent life for the inhabitants themselves. A.D.O.s in Niger and Zaria Provinces spent years coaxing people down from the hills into empty bush lands that could be cleared and cultivated.[1] The Gwari, too, seemed to be improving. Although they had little corporate sense and constantly defied touring officers' best efforts at communal projects, Varvill thought, on returning after seven years' absence, that feudalism was breaking down and outlying communities were in closer touch with bigger market towns.[2]

In the well-farmed and prosperous Hausa areas of the Zaria–Kano borders there was a similar problem despite a generally higher standard of life. Peace had made it possible to till the richest fields no matter how far they were from defensible communities, and this was a good thing for the farmer. But it depopulated whole villages and left some major towns in varying stages of decay, their markets unused, their ageing officials ignored, and deserted by the young. Deterioration of civic consciousness had reached a point where minimum administrative functions, such as tax collecting and local justice, were jeopardized. Roads fell into disuse, partly due to the abolition of forced labour and to farmers' not seeing road maintenance as an activity that would benefit them in the long run. Touring officers had various ideas of what might be done to make bigger villages attractive again. Improvement of markets was mentioned most often.[3] More wells could be sunk and shade trees planted.[4] The Government would have to think again about the salaries and perquisites of N.A. officials in outlying areas so that more able young men would see administrative jobs as worth having. A.D.O.s kept an eye out for literate boys capable of doing the work of the law classes in Kano and then going home again to become village *muftai*. Might there not be a 'financial

[1] A.D.O. Rijau (Pott) to D.O. Kontagora, 9 May 1939, C.R.P.

[2] Zaria Touring Diary, August 1940.

[3] Ibid., 7 October 1942, Elliott, touring Makarfi, Ikara, and Anchau.

[4] Ibid., March 1941, Weatherhead, touring Soba. Special mention should be made of the excellent work of geologists in well-sinking because of the profound and lasting effects of this on village life.

inducement to literacy', government-supported classes in which adults could learn to read and write Hausa?[1] Eventually model villages were established. They did well, although officers had misgivings about their dependence on British supervision. Would they survive a relaxation of the alien hand?

Some touring officers tried innovations that were unabashedly European. Boy scout troops sprang up in some of the larger rural centres, their leaders being carefully trained beforehand and broken in slowly so that the A.D.O. could watch their success at simple exercises like playing games with village boys and directing them in performing minor chores. At Lere an officer and his scoutmaster-in-training played 'grandmother's steps' with a gang of local boys, 'the proceedings getting steadily more uproarious [and all of us] . . . laughing ourselves helpless'.[2]

Like their superiors, touring officers were divided into those who did not conceive it a function of the administration to do much about stimulating the economy and those who saw the function as essential. Many administrators had their doubts about the United Africa Company, successor to the Niger Company, it being only natural that an organization concerned with profits would take a different view from that of the touring officer, whose business was law and order and the public good. African clerks in U.A.C.'s employ took advantage of ignorant peasants, underpaying them for groundnuts, which the Company bought in great quantity.[3] The protective response of administrators was automatic. More positively, some officers tried to use the Company to develop agriculture by promoting the sale of seeds on a larger scale.[4] It was a question of how best to strengthen the economic base. Railway work had dried up in Niger Province, for example, by the 1930s, and U.A.C. canteens were siphoning off what little the people had put by. New farming projects were seen as the alternative to stagnation. In hundreds of little ways, such as building a bridge connecting two

---

[1] Zaria Touring Diary, autumn 1942, Elliott, touring Ikara.

[2] Ibid., Lere.

[3] The Emir Yahaya of Gwandu reacted to this by ordering that peasants be compensated out of N.A. funds, and the D.O. responded by having N.A. scribes check the accounts of the U.A.C. clerks. See Weatherhead letters, 13 and 18 November 1943.

[4] Pott, report on Wushishi, to D.O. Kontagora, 24 June 1939, C.R.P.

M

communities that complemented each other economically, keeping roads open, and improving markets, officers did what they could to help trade. They were severe with chiefs and other N.A. officials whose self-seeking got in the way of freer development.[1]

In public health, both physical and moral, no touring officer had illusions about being able to do anything like as much as was required. But the periodic appearance of administrators in villages nudged their inhabitants into more wholesome practices year by year. A.D.O.s were often greeted by the sight of smoke rising off the village rubbish heap which had been hastily swept together and burned. This meant that the Emir's message announcing the officer's arrival had got to the village just before him. There was an extensive campaign against sleeping-sickness in the 1930s, including mass treatment of villagers and the clearing of streams. Gradually clinics appeared in major places and a number of epidemics were dealt with. If persuasion usually failed, demonstration sometimes succeeded. When there was an outbreak of smallpox in the thirties one village near Zaria accepted vaccination and escaped without a single fatality, while its neighbour refused treatment and was decimated.

Juju and fetishes were left alone at first because they were thought to belong in the category of native custom with which there was to be no interference, and because there were far too few officers to do anything systematic about abuses. Later, when staff grew, it was harder to stand aside. Not only was juju repugnant to the European mind—'hardly a faith to rouse aspirations to make the world a better place or life a nobler thing'—but increasingly it frustrated the plans that officers made for development projects.[2] Villages in Abuja Emirate refused to grow cotton because their juju was thought to be opposed to it.[3] Touring officers found it harder and harder to accept this kind of thing, especially when they knew from experience that the people did not care one way or the other and

---

[1] Sarkin Birnin Gwari was disciplined for making peasants market their cotton in his town rather than in Funtua, the natural outlet. See Zaria Touring Diary, 18 December 1932, Talbot-Edwards.

[2] Weatherhead, touring Lapai, letter of 17 February 1937.

[3] Ibid., touring Koro, letter of 2 March 1937.

that native custom was a cloak covering the selfishness of power-ful interests. When, however, superstition did have mass sup-port, officers had to decide whether opposing it would only aggravate the trouble. The administrator from Hadejia learned that magic powers had been ascribed to a stagnant pool at Auyo and that Moslem fanatics were flocking to the village.[1] More than 5,000 people had spent a night at the water's edge chanting the confession of faith and smearing themselves with mud. Not only common people but members of ruling families, such as a daughter of the Shehu of Bornu, were making pilgrimages to Auyo. The Emir of Hadejia affected to despise the affair, but officers suspected that he secretly sympathized with it. The furore was in part a protest against the new hospital which the British had opened in Hadejia. Finally, visitations to the magic pool reached such proportions that agricultural production in half a dozen emirates was suffering, social life was disrupted over a wide area, and there was a rising incidence of disorder. The touring officer from Hadejia preferred to let the spasm work itself out naturally, but the Resident Kano instructed that the area be cleared. This was not done very strenuously and in effect the affair did die a natural death after some months of fading attraction.

Had he lacked these kinds of direct contact with the land and people, the touring officer would have had to exert influence only through N.A. officials, from district heads on down to minor office-holders in the smallest villages. As it was, local knowledge gave the realistic and hard-working officer—if not his more easy-going colleagues—a sound backdrop of under-standing against which to view the functioning of the whole N.A. apparatus. Sometimes there was no alternative to taking direct action oneself, as a means of impressing N.A. officials with the standard demanded of them or because no one else was available at the moment. Nevertheless, one aimed at an N.A. that had enough self-confidence, knowledge, and skill to manage on its own. Even though no one had any thought of the Europeans going away one day, self-sufficiency was still the object of the exercise. The most important single facet of one's work was the inspecting, educating, and disciplining that

[1] Confidential Political Notebook, Hadejia Divisional Office, 1 April 1935 ff., Bubb, Findlay, *et al.*

constituted an officer's permanent relationship with the N.A.[1]

The nub of the matter was the interconnecting work of the touring officer and the district head. Apart from endemic economic and social factors, the order and well-being of districts rested on the degree and kind of co-operation achieved by these two, which in turn depended on their respective outlooks and talents. Some areas had such weak tribal organization and such inept leadership that early administrators did virtually the whole job themselves. In Tiv by the late 1920s the A.D.O. was still 'a cross between a priest and a district head'.[2] But farther north most districts had hereditary leaders who were members of entrenched Moslem families. Here British officers divided into conservatives and progressives and some spoke of themselves as 'right-wing' or 'left-wing'. While there was always great variation within the two categories, progressives usually disliked extreme deference to tradition, native and British, and wanted brisk forward movement towards a stronger and more modern economy, with all the administrative innovation that that entailed. They did not want to abolish chiefs but wished to revolutionize their thinking by persuasion and discipline, without provoking resentment or opposition. The other group, either by conviction or laziness, saw this as being presumptuous, impossible, or both.

District heads were key men because they linked remote chiefs to the mass of the people.[3] Popular ignorance and passivity ruled out pressure from below. Chiefs were tied to their central administrations much of the time and had to depend on D.H.s for the daily running of districts and for information on conditions in the countryside. Of all N.A. officials, D.H.s thus had the most independent power bases and the greatest capacity for good or ill. Chiefs were chosen as often as not from among their number. It is understandable that their tenure, their

[1] This point, which is massively documented in the official materials, was also stressed by the late Premier of the North, Sir Ahmadu Bello, in a letter to Sir Bryan Sharwood Smith, former Governor of the North, 23 March 1965. In this letter Sir Ahmadu refers to the proper focus of my research.

[2] Morgan, Resident Benue, to Lethem, S.N.P., 16 June and 10 July 1927, Lethem Papers, C.R.P.

[3] Cf. A. T. Weatherhead, 'Future Politics and Development of Nigeria', 15 February 1943, written in conjunction with Lord Hailey's Report. I am grateful to Sir Arthur for lending me his copy of this most informative paper.

indispensability, and the various combinations of knowledge, power, and capacity to help the people forward or not would bring about a complicated 'love–hate' relationship between them and officers touring their areas. The A.D.O., from his position of incorruptible outside authority, watched the D.H.'s performance closely and worked alongside him. If the two had had the same administrative standards, relations could have been easy and pleasant. In the nature of things this was hardly the case. The usual relationship was one of tension, mitigated by A.D.O. realism about the extent to which D.H.s could be made to toe the European line.

At the bottom of the district heap were such places as Illo, a pagan unit on the Niger in Sokoto Province.[1] Administered from Birnin Kebbi, Illo had always been 'the blacksheep district of the Division'. Its Chief, little more than a hereditary D.H. in effect, was a celebrated drunkard and embezzler. He was so sedentary that virtually no *jangali* was collected in his district. He robbed the peasants as a matter of course and had his agents systematically cheat them on groundnut payments. Every touring officer for over a decade had recommended his dismissal and the case against him was clear, even though peasants steadfastly refused to testify. The last straw was his failure to come to Sokoto for a hearing on the Resident's summons.[2] Soon thereafter the unit was amalgamated into Gwandu, whose D.O. was given powers to run it directly until its N.A. could be reformed. Illo thus showed itself to be beyond local redemption for the time being. The solution adopted was an admission that no amount of outside supervision could make up for the deficiencies of the ruling house and the passivity of the people.

Paki in Zaria Province offered a striking contrast as regards both ethnic composition and economy. Located roughly midway between Zaria and Kano, Paki was an almost purely Hausa community whose prosperous farmers were within easy reach of two of the North's most advanced urban areas. In 1936 the D.O. Zaria got wind of what appeared to be a case of extortion by the D.H., a high-born Fulani who held the title Magajin Gari. Workers on roads near Paki seemed to have

[1] Cf. Weatherhead, letters of 22 June and 4 July 1943, Birnin Kebbi.
[2] Ibid., 5 March and 11 April 1944.

received wages far below those listed on N.A. accounts. Accompanied by his messenger, an astute former Political Agent called Audu dan Gaji, an A.D.O. went to the area to investigate.[1] Previously the N.A. had been given a chance to uncover the trouble itself, the Waziri of Zaria being sent to look into the rumours. But he returned empty-handed, reporting that the affairs of the district seemed to be in order. On arrival in Paki the A.D.O. found that as usual no one would testify and as always it was hard to tell from paysheets on roadwork whether inconsistencies arose from dishonesty or incompetence. Patient investigation in three villages finally proved that the D.H. and his accomplices had pocketed about one-quarter of the labourers' pay, many of the men having been put down for work they had never done; other workers had not been paid at all because the D.H. had been too idle to apply for the money; the D.H.'s retainer had been harbouring thieves and had successfully prosecuted for slander three villagers who had accused him of this. Magajin Gari was now caught between growing resentment among his own people and a determined pair of British officers. As the investigation went on he was denied permission to come to Zaria to greet the Emir on the occasion of an Islamic festival. Paki's village head, hearing that police were on their way to arrest him, fled at night and escaped to Kano. Testimony flowed in as villagers saw that the game was up and that guilty officials would not be able to retain their offices. Those in charge of local justice were made to prosecute offenders whom, but for the European intervention, they would have ignored. To drive the lesson home, especially in the minds of other D.H.s, the punishments were severe. Magajin Gari and the district scribe were dismissed; the village head of near-by Kwari was imprisoned, as were the Emir's agent and a lesser official; Paki lost its separate identity and was joined to Ikara, then under the much-respected D.H. Sarkin Yaki.

There was a major difference, however, between Paki's punishment and the downgrading of Illo. The pagan unit had everything against it: an ignorant, poor, and quiescent population; a remote, inaccessible setting, cut off from divisional headquarters by the Niger and miles of roadless wastes; a benighted ruling clique. Paki's situation was meliorable. Given

[1] Giles, diary, 1936. The D.O. was Sharwood Smith.

the general prosperity and worldliness of her people and the fact that she was part of a major N.A., it was possible to correct and reinforce her local institutions without wiping the slate clean and beginning again as in Illo's case.

Other unsatisfactory situations dealt with by touring officers were variations on the same themes. Birnin Gwari was the exasperation of junior officers from beginning to end. 'These Gwaris!'[1] An A.D.O. who had given specific instructions to the Chief and his council left the town for a few days and then sent word that he was returning to see how they were getting on. No one met him. Storming into the Chief's residence he found that nothing had been done and 'the Emir and all his followers were reading the Koran'.[2] A once-vigorous clan of Hausa over-lords, they had never recovered from the smashing administered to their area by Mai Sudan late in the nineteenth century. The ruling house was careless of the people's needs and its government was 'a perfect example of nepotism'.[3] One of the Emir's sons was Waziri, another was D.H. Dogon Dawa, and another D.H. Kuki. The D.H. Gwarawa was a nephew, as was the D.H. Mazawoje. The Ma'aji was a son-in-law. Misappro-priation of N.A. funds—the Beit-el-mal being in the Emir's compound—was common and 'what do you do when the Emir himself is involved?'[4] The Chief, whose tenure antedated the coming of the British, was too old to control his household and the best he could do was repeatedly to promise improvements, meanwhile begging A.D.O.s not to tell Zaria of the misdeeds they uncovered. Some betterment might be hoped for when the Chief at last went to his fathers. In the meantime some officers felt that the British were at fault for not giving enough encour-agement to the Waziri, his son and presumed successor. Know-ing that the British did everything through the Chief, who monopolized power, the younger man resented not having a freer hand in his own district and he reacted by letting things slide. Finally, in 1936, the time came, confronting the Govern-ment with a dilemma brought on by their default of remedial action in past decades. Should they seize the opportunity of the

[1] Zaria Touring Diary, September 1931, Shirley.
[2] Ibid., 5 February 1932, Talbot-Edwards.
[3] Ibid., September 1931, Shirley.
[4] Ibid., 22 October 1933, Humphreys.

Chief's death to do away with or drastically alter an unsatisfactory N.A.?

Morgan, the Acting Chief Commissioner, had been Resident
Zaria two years earlier and felt from his experience of Birnin
Gwari that the ruling family were basically hopeless.[1] Therefore the Kamuku people living within Birnin Gwari N.A.
should be detached and allowed to join their brothers in Niger
Province, the rest of the N.A. being downgraded and perhaps
put under the financial wing of Katsina, then part of Zaria
Province. While the question was being debated the Waziri was
given the title Wakili, or regent, and warned that he and the
whole N.A. were very much on probation. An A.D.O. touring
the area admitted to himself that his own views were influenced
by his liking for the Wakili and his belief that, given a chance,
the new head of the N.A. would prove himself. He went on to
summarize the two main alternatives as they appeared to him.
If the unit were left as it was, good use would be made of staff
trained by administrators for over three decades. These included men who had been painstakingly lured into education
and agriculture as well as administration. Hausa colonies established by the British would continue to raise the quality of the
area, as would experimental farms. If, on the other hand, a
Cameronian solution were adopted, each tribal unit would have
more say in its own affairs, there would be fewer border squab-
bles and more administrative neatness: all the Kamuku would
be toured by an A.D.O. in Niger Province and all the Gwari by
another in Zaria. There might be a financial improvement as
well.

Ironically, the methods that Cameron had recommended—
studying the people closely to see what they themselves wanted
—turned up views that were often diametrically opposed to the
Governor's assumptions. Giles rode towards the westernmost
fringes of Birnin Gwari, to Kimbi and Randeggi in the hills
across the Kwingi River where officers had seldom gone. People
lived in twos and threes in the jungle or the bush. Villages
perched on rocky, wooded slopes decayed steadily as young men
left for greener pastures elsewhere. The simplest traditions of
even two generations back were hazy and no one could say
much about more ancient history. Lack of historical conscious-

[1] Cf. Reports on Chiefs, Zaria Province, 1935 ff., K.

ness was matched by indifference to the abstract notion that ethnic fellows should be united and society provided with a democratic base. What was real was the immediate complaint, the certain, proximate knowledge that the conniving village head of Randeggi would use a Kamuku federation for his own selfish ends and that the known shortcomings of Sarkin Birnin Gwari far across the horizon were preferable. They had been left alone under his weak and slovenly rule. Were the market place and the road not more important than anthropological symmetry?

When the Chief died in Birnin Gwari a delegation representing a majority of Zaria Kamuku went to the Wakili to ask that there be no change. The A.D.O. suggested a compromise whereby the Wakili would rule them but through a unified council of their own people. Even this much difference was disliked. Would such a link strengthen the hand of Dawakin Bassa over neighbouring Kuki and was it not better to be under the direct rule of a more distant and weaker authority? In the end an empirical solution was worked out that did not break violently with the past and that satisfied more people than not. Birnin Gwari was put under the financial control of Zaria, but it kept its own slightly downgraded N.A. The Kamuku stayed under Birnin Gwari and a council of six village chiefs was formed to represent their interests in such a way as to prevent any one of them dominating the rest. And then, said a touring officer, 'A great sleep . . . descended once more on the District.'[1]

Elsewhere A.D.O.s chipped away at encouragement, discipline, and minor improvements. Makama, D.H. in the Hausa district of Soba, was not completely hopeless, but his laxity in assessment made his area a haven for tax evaders. He himself had a poor record in collections from known residents. It was 'time the old dodderer went on pension'.[2] Meanwhile the two edges of the Anglo-African sword were used in an attempt to keep him at least minimally straight. While touring officers worked inside the district, the D.O. Zaria had the Emir send regular admonitions, instructions, and warnings.

Other D.H.s won consistent praise. Ikara, to the east of Zaria, was repeatedly mentioned with approval in the thirties

[1] Zaria Touring Diary, 23 October 1940, Weatherhead.
[2] Ibid., March 1941.

and forties. One aimed at keeping the pressure constant without losing sight of the fact that really good D.H.s were a great rarity and that maximum encouragement had to be given even to those who were barely acceptable. When a touring officer was rough on anyone above average he was likely to be rebuked by his more experienced superior. 'For Allah's sake don't be too fervent in your witch smelling. All these abuses must be stamped out, but the method is the thing!'[1]

Below the level of district headquarters one dealt with village heads and holders of lesser offices down to scribes, *muftai,* and members of clan councils. Communities were widely scattered and before the 1950s most could not be reached by all-season roads. A.D.O.s spent weeks in open country, riding through the endless bush of the North's high savanna and staying the night in some lonely resthouse or camping outside a village that could not boast even that much mud-and-thatch luxury. Officers travelled with a gang of carriers, one or two servants, a messenger, and usually someone from N.A. headquarters, an important title holder or a council member who represented the Emir.[2] Local officials would attach themselves while the party was in their territory. Owing to the heat of midday one started in the small hours, the servants going on ahead, and breakfasted at dawn with perhaps half the day's journey already finished. In country broken by valleys, ravines, and rivers the going was slow. One morning in the rainy season Shirley covered six miles in four and a half hours.[3] He was suffering from the recurrent fever that dogged everyone's tracks, and having to swim streams did not help that. But the trek could provide a feeling of comradeship with African companions by momentarily wiping out the differences of circumstances that otherwise kept the races apart. A junior officer and a local N.A. official who stripped beside the bank of a rushing stream and

[1] Sharwood Smith, D.O., to Giles, A.D.O. Giles diary, 1936, quoting a private letter. The A.D.O. had been investigating forced labour near Kachia. This involved an important D.H., who in the past had been of the greatest service to his pagans.

[2] An experienced touring officer who read this chapter comments on the importance of the Emir's representative, '. . . whose presence was a controlling factor on the behaviour and procedures of correct (or incorrect!) touring officers'. He goes on to describe the Emir's representative as 'the touring officer's shadow . . . through whom instructions and advice had to be carefully channelled'.

[3] Zaria Touring Diary, September 1931.

swam their horses across could forget, if only briefly, the line that divided the races.

Although the line remained, there did grow up between some officers and members of N.A.s a closeness of sorts that allowed for easy communication. In Sokoto A.D.O.s found officials still mindful of the glories of the jihad that had established their ancestors' hegemony throughout Hausaland. That pride could be appealed to in promoting the honesty and efficiency the British wanted, despite the strangeness in native eyes of many particulars in the European scheme of things. Elsewhere the personal qualities of certain office-holders lent themselves naturally to British drive even when the spirit and performance of the whole N.A. did not measure up to Sokoto's. An officer who toured with one prominent Zaria D.H. knew that the man's record was far from being untarnished; nevertheless, his character and his talent were remarkable. 'If only I could persuade someone like him to train me in knowledge of native life and mind, what a wonderful A.D.O. I would be.'[1]

To many an officer the days on tour were high points and everything else one did was apt to pale by comparison. Riding in the brilliant sunshine of early morning was exhilarating. Often there was scenery to grip the aesthetic consciousness of the most prosaic type. One rode through forests and up along ridges with magnificent mountain views stretching off to horizons that showed no human mark. If the crops were doing well villagers were content, and as the *talakawa* talked of the harvest there might be a word tucked in here and there about how people looked on the N.A. There were places where one could rest beside a waterfall or a rushing mountain stream. At night by the Tilley lamp nature's sounds were joined by the notes of an unseen flutist in a village beyond the trees.

There was time to think. Africa was reality to some and the newspapers from home were a bore. Even the closer Europe of provincial headquarters could seem remote and ridiculous from the vantage point of the tour. Near the hamlet of Udawa in Gwari country Giles was overtaken by a Dan Doka bringing dispatches from Kaduna and Zaria. Opening these and expecting to hear at least that war had broken out, he learned that 'officers proceeding on leave from Riverain Provinces may use

[1] Giles, diary, summer 1935.

the route via Offa and that Government Ordinance something
or other does not apply to intended wives'.[1] Weatherhead,
touring from Bida, found much to be irritated by and in spare
moments he devoured books by the dozen and wrote home for
more.[2] But he too grumbled over the irrelevance of what came
out from headquarters: 'Stacks of paper from . . . arch quill-
drivers . . . a long screed about estimates which [he and the
D.O.] had taken no notice of at all.'[3] Occasionally men thought
about what colonial government was supposed to be and,
rarely, they discussed it among themselves. Visiting Kafanchan,
Giles talked with the local A.D.O. about Lawrence's *Seven
Pillars of Wisdom*. What was the proper relationship between
aliens and natives? Could one work with Nigerian chiefs as
Lawrence worked with Feisal in Arabia? Was there a middle
ground between total aloofness and surrendering to Africa?
Did serving an adopted country really mean 'bartering [one's]
soul to a brute master' and becoming a 'yahoo man'? In
Lawrence's book, even though it referred to a different con-
tinent, there was 'much that makes the imperialist squirm'.[4]

All were likely to agree that England knew nothing about the
colonies and cared less. 'There is very little that the Government
Servant can write about that England wants to read . . . the
thing bores them stiff . . . one of the great eye-openers to the
home-coming wanderer [is] the complete indifference of modern
England to its Empire . . . [people] pass it all by with puzzled
politeness . . . "how *in*-teresting".'[5] Perversely this had its
wholesome side, for London ignored the bad along with the
good. Weatherhead raged against the irresponsible but voci-
ferous type of office clerk whom everyone found so irritating
and who sometimes took it upon himself to write complaining
letters to Kaduna. 'Mr. William Rufus Lawson of the Gold
Coast', a half-educated and half-Anglicized clerk, had written
an impassioned letter to the Lieutenant Governor denouncing
an officer.[6] This His Honour had referred to the Resident, who
passed it back to the officer himself. 'Fortunately the British

---

[1] Giles, diary, 16 August 1935.
[2] Letters of 22 July 1933 and 18 June 1937, from Bornu and Bida.
[3] Letters, 1 August and 11 July 1937, from Bida.
[4] Diary, Southern Districts, Zaria, 1935.
[5] Quoted ibid., 22 February 1936.
[6] Weatherhead, letter from Nguru, Bornu, 22 July 1933.

Parliament doesn't get excited about Nigeria or they would probably take him [the clerk] as typical of the voice of the people.'[1]

Gauging that voice was step one of the A.D.O.'s job in villages. Sometimes the real attitudes of the people to their village heads were not hard to discover, especially when people were uninhibited and prone to be insubordinate. Pagans with village heads from their own families occasionally turned them out of office when they incurred the community's displeasure. This contributed to situations of such disorder in early years that Moslem D.H.s were put in charge of many parts, and by the middle period the usual arrangement was one in which a D.H. drawn from the Emir's circle ruled over village heads who were locally recruited. A.D.O.s tried to see that D.H.s did not abuse the substantial power they derived from this system. The main problem was not that D.H.s were invariably inclined to tyrannize but that there was so little local resistance to misrule of any kind. Even in the more chaotic pagan areas there was minimum pressure from below, and village heads could only see themselves as agents of the D.H. Whether they were his co-religionists or not, most village heads were in the D.H.'s pocket.

Touring officers could do a certain amount by direct action, even with the D.H. in tow. Talk was endless. A village head who had only recently inherited his position was young, lazy, and drunken, with one of the most miserable tax-collection records in the Emirate. On two successive tours an officer railed at him, promising to see him replaced if he did not pay more attention to his work.[2] If it could be kept up this sometimes had an effect. Village heads and elders were for ever being scolded for 'hear-say census' and lack of system in keeping public records. After Kwaga's village head died and no one did anything about a successor, an A.D.O. hurried up the selection process so that the village would have someone in charge when tax time arrived. D.H.s were made to back up the authority of weaker officials at the local level. And, as with higher officials, one was always ready to compromise in the realization that perfection was impossible. When an A.D.O.

[1] Ibid.
[2] Zaria Touring Diary, 28 March 1932, Talbot-Edwards.

reported that the Emir had reinstated two village heads recently gaoled with hard labour for embezzlement, the D.O. agreed with him that there was no one else in their villages and 'the known is better than the unknown'.[1]

In their never-ending lectures and exhortations, officers could stress European standards and they could give strong support to that rarity, the minor official who showed genuine interest in his work. One village head in a Hausa District east of Zaria was extraordinarily effective, 'more like a European temperamentally', and everyone went out of their way to help and encourage him.[2] A major difficulty was that the traditional system of clientage did not respond to the urgings of rational government. Merit was secondary by comparison with loyalty to one's patron or superior. But for the nagging of Europeans it would have been virtually irrelevant. But as long as clientage was accepted as immutable, could touring officers do much more than scold? 'I wonder if the system of paying Village Heads a salary directly proportional to their population (really no different from the old system by which they took a proportion of the tax) and not according to efficiency is sound? Can we break the petty jealousies . . . and the constant ambition for each to enlarge the area of his authority . . . by the present system?'[3] The salaries of village heads were low, while below them many office-holders were paid still less or nothing at all. 'It has struck me . . . with reference to [village] mallams and Alkalai, that there is . . . injustice and inefficiency in the N.A. having no real staff list . . . in which merit or even mere existence could be recorded.'[4] The answer was as obvious as the trouble. With staff for touring and money from the N.A. treasury both strictly limited, the best that the A.D.O. could do was watch and, depending on the case, either praise or blame. Time and education would strengthen his hand. Meanwhile he concentrated on controlling abuses and, with brother officers in the professional and technical departments, on attacking the public ignorance, apathy, and helplessness that made them possible.

Riding back towards the bigger town that was his permanent

---

[1] Zaria Touring Diary, 11 September 1939, entry by A.D.O., Michie.
[2] Ibid., October 1942, Elliott, touring Anchau.
[3] Ibid.
[4] Giles, diary, touring Birnin Gwari, summer 1935.

base, the touring officer was bound to think of contrasts between
the snail's pace of changes in the countryside behind him and
tradition's more brittle surface in town. Much stayed the same
in urban areas as well: 'Clusters of marketing farmers . . . shrill-
crying girls and boys wandering in the soft dust of alleyways
selling beancakes . . . walls and towers soon to be magicked by
the streaming moonlight . . . grey-bearded scribes sitting outside their houses studying the law . . . the sour smell of indigo
blowing off the pale grey mouths of neatly plastered dye pits . . .
the saddlers and the kola sellers . . . the Fulani milkmaids . . .
the corn merchants . . . and rows and rows of men with shiny
chips of . . . antimony spread out before them in little heaps
. . . earrings and necklaces of coral . . .'[1] But the bustle of
bigger commerce, especially in the *sabon gari*, was more insistent with every passing year. The railways and the telegraph
brought the coast northwards. Lorries went farther and farther
into the bush, carrying people and goods and ideas back and
forth from the hybrid cosmopolis. There were soldiers and
traders from the South and Africans who did not dress as Hausas
dressed. The town was African still, but it looked outward, as
though the old ways were not good enough any more. Coming
back to it from a sleepy pastoral, the touring officer seemed to
be bridging two cultures. Surrounded by cars and blaring wire-
less sets he felt himself as anachronistic as the *talakawa* he had
visited on tour. 'Amid the smiles of the more sophisticated of
the inhabitants the A.D.O. rode into prim Kaduna on shaggy
horse and native saddle.'[2]

[1] Giles, diary, Zaria, autumn 1935.
[2] Ibid., Kaduna.

7

The British in Northern Nigeria

OVER the face of the North in the 1950s the rhythm of Anglo-African government went on as always. Every familiar aspect remained, the same ingredients were there, the same determining factors, the same attitudes and daily activities. One knew that a great change was in store, but somehow this often seemed to have little to do with everyday work.

The D.O. in charge of Jema'a reported on his unit very much as officers in the 1920s had done. The Emirate was still judged hopeless and for the same old reasons: 'The population are such unpromising material . . . the aristocracy . . . is more than usually apathetic and decadent . . . there has never been any real continuity in Divisional Officers.'[1] Zaria's southern districts still had a mixed bag of good, bad, and indifferent N.A. officials with all the usual attributes, and they were responding in a familiar way to the age-old opportunities and pressures of their positions. The D.H.'s messenger at Zonkwa, who was the *de facto* ruler of the place, 'ought to be shot but is well connected and well protected'.[2] The D.H. Kachia was a forceful and efficient traditionalist who did well if backed by the Emir, and otherwise not. The Jaba Chief was well liked but was far too reactionary and the complaints against him presented *in toto* the recognizable picture of a 'naughty old man'.[3] One of Kachia's councillors had been schooled at the Sudan Interior Mission. He talked rather a lot and his taste for public speaking was already bringing him into conflict with the D.H. Zangon Katab's new young scribe showed promise, and it was thought that he ought to be encouraged as 'one of the new breed' whom the district could make good use of.[4]

[1] Johnston to Resident Zaria, 25 May 1948; cf. Greatbatch, 19 June 1951, and Hibbs, 9 May 1957, K.
[2] Hodgson, Handing-Over Notes, Zaria Division, 27 February 1952, K.
[3] Ibid.
[4] Ibid.

Gumel Emirate far to the north was similarly ticking over with problems that would not have surprised touring officers before 1918. The Emir and the D.O. were exhorting D.H.s on *jangali* and agriculture; the prison mallam was corrupt, but clung to office through the influence of the Waziri to whom he was related by marriage; the Native Treasury, with five educated young mallams on its staff, showed improvement; the Alkali got a good report, but the two oldest members of the Emir's Council were thought to be beyond redemption, being 'literally sleeping partners [who] generally nod off during Council meetings'.[1]

Among the British there were still the familiar differences in outlook between desk men and touring officers and between seniors and juniors. An A.D.O. wanted more autonomy for the southern districts of Zaria, while the Resident thought that discontent in that pagan area had been exaggerated and that mission-educated minorities were stirring up trouble as they had always done.[2] Junior officers, who spoke of themselves euphemistically as forming a 'union' against their superiors, tended to be less satisfied with the performance of local N.A. officials than senior men were, and they stressed the needs of rural populations more than those of administrative efficiency.[3] Sokoto spoke to Birnin Kebbi in the mid-50s much as it had done thirty years before, about the lack of initiative from below, the slackness of N.A.s, and the need for a combination of delegating and discipline by touring officers. They must fasten authority on D.H.s and lower officials without losing control in the process. 'This is of course no new subject.'[4] One still hoped that when a chief died it would be possible to appoint a successor who would be an improvement, but this depended on the available candidates and on the views of those with whom they would have to work. The new Emir of Hadejia in 1950 was not the man the British preferred, being less efficient and progressive than his main rival. But he was popular with senior

[1] Town and District Book, Northern Divisional Office, Hadejia, entries of 1952–5, Russell *et al.*
[2] Cf. correspondence between Zaria Provincial Office and officers in the Southern Districts and between Zaria and Kaduna, 15 July 1953 ff., Greatbatch, Williams, Bryant *et al.*, K.
[3] E.g. J. H. Smith, Kauru District Touring Book, 25 January 1954.
[4] Acting Resident, Pott, to D.O. Birnin Kebbi, 25 July 1955, K.

N

members of the N.A., and the Europeans considered a compromise better than a situation that would be fraught with difficulty from the start.[1]

Elsewhere, notably in the more important emirates such as Bornu, Kano, and Sokoto, great strides were made in what were to be the final fifteen years of the colonial period. Colonial Development and Welfare funds at last provided the wherewithal for bigger projects that had always been beyond the Region's own capacity. The pace of physical change—roads, schools, hospitals, and agricultural and veterinary institutions—quickened. The *élan* of British officers and N.A. officials reflected this, and the introduction of politics made fundamental changes in the outlook of many office-holders and therefore in the relationship they had with the British locally. D.O.s in charge of divisions now dealt with certain N.A. officials not only as local office-holders, as before, but as sitting Members of the Assembly in Kaduna or as powers in the ruling political party.

Once the decision was made to prepare for early self-rule one might have expected to see a sharp break in the steady evolution of regionalism and local administration that had characterized the half-century of Anglo-African government. London certainly looked for dramatic changes, for the very idea of a completely independent Nigeria was new and it seemed logical to the outside observer that old instrumentalities would not serve the new purpose. The novelty of the aim of full self-government and the suddenness of its appearance need to be stressed. In 1928 Lethem, Acting S.N.P., pointed out that 'national and racial self-consciousness . . . must inevitably grow', but he made clear that no one's thinking went beyond a bit more local self-reliance and competence.[2] Lugard, writing from England, was precise about the aims that he thought relevant in these years. Dissociating himself from the ideas of Cameron, he put forward the view that 'Representative institutions and legislative councils are . . . unsuited to African peoples'.[3] So were European concepts of law and giving power to centralized

[1] A.D.O. Northern Division to Resident Kano, 6 June 1950, Secret File, Emirs of Hadejia, Divisional Office.

[2] To Residents, 24 January 1928, K.

[3] 'Note on the Present Position of Indirect Rule in Nigeria', 17 December 1928, sent to Lethem with Lugard's letter of 9 January 1933, C.R.P.

bureaucracies that had no knowledge of bush reality. What the North needed eventually was a council of chiefs. In an authoritarian society it was only they who could speak and act for the people as a whole. Precipitate self-rule in a country like Nigeria would mean a tyranny of semi-educated, semi-Europeanized political figures who were not representative of all the people. Cameron thought that there would some day be an upsurge of popular feeling, but he too considered ballot-box government unthinkable in Africa.[1] Self-rule was a distant objective, something highly unlikely to happen 'within the next few generations'.[2] In the meantime he agreed with the Secretary of State, Amery, that such places as Tanganyika and Nigeria would long remain parts of the British Empire. Even though the former territory was legally a Mandate of the League of Nations, the King's likeness should be put on its stamps, for the British had full sovereignty in fact.[3] In Northern Nigeria people always spoke of progress in terms of specifics— better roads, more efficient treasuries and courts, improved agriculture—and it was not until the 1940s that such an ultimate as self-government was bruited about. Even then chiefs, D.O.s, and the general run of common men had difficulty in imagining it.

No wonder, then, that the chiefs were surprised and shocked by the notion of a North without the British. Whereas in the South independence had been demanded by Africans, in the North it was announced by the British as a thing that the rulers would have to prepare for in a short space of time so as not to be defenceless in the face of Southern talents and ambitions. In 1900 strong chiefs and Islamic organization had given the Northern areas an advantage over the primitive societies and tribal anarchy of the South. By the 1940s something close to the opposite pertained: European commerce and education had poured into the void of Southern culture and had given the area a much greater degree of Afro-European self-consciousness and unanimity and far more competence in trade and European political organization than the North had. The North had

---

[1] Writing on both Tanganyika and Nigeria to Lugard, letters of 12 September 1925, 22 June 1930, 14 August 1930, and 11 November 1930, P.; cf. his letter to Oldham, 26 July 1925.

[2] To Lugard, 29 June 1928, P.

[3] Ibid., 8 November 1925.

changed greatly. But it had developed on its own lines, the lines of established tradition. The British period meant headlong Europeanizing for the South, and for the North the slower evolution of a cultural hybrid that owed more to Africa than was true of its Southern equivalent. The implications of this were plain to the British in the North, just as they had been at the time of Cameron's onslaught on their position. A federation that recognized regional differences and was founded on mutual tolerance might work. A highly centralized Nigeria, on the other hand, could only come about by one of two developments: a dictatorship of the South, or of the North.

The British called the tune to the extent of insisting that the North be protected by marching towards independence as an autonomous entity. This was logical to those who were conscious of the North's commercial, educational, and political backwardness *vis-à-vis* the Southern areas. 'I think', wrote Palmer in the early fifties, 'they had better split Nigeria back into . . . pieces.'[1] European conceptions of democracy were all very well in the South, he thought, but had little relevance in the North. Dr. Miller, the missionary whose work had often brought him into conflict with Northern administrators, blamed the the British for deliberately slowing the pace of Europeanizing in the North. But he too felt that the Region's undeniable weakness by comparison with the South had to be faced. 'This country will not be ready or fit for self-rule for 50 years.'[2]

Internal self-government would come to the North only a decade after this statement was made. Given the mode of Anglo-African administration as it had evolved, that government could only be a kind of super-N.A. It would be headed by educated and capable aristocrats whose ties to tradition were strong enough to bring them the support of the governing classes and whose experience of British rule had given them a sense of what was needed in the way of modern bureaucracy and economic development. In a word, the new politics of the North would be throughout the Region what that of N.A.s had always been at the local level: a moral and organizational expression of continuity with the past. It would be new because the British would not run it. It would be familiar because based

[1] 3 July 1952, P. And see Lord Hailey, *An African Survey*, London, 1956, p. 307.
[2] To Lugard, 16 July 1944, P.

squarely on the African and Anglo-African spirit and machinery that stretched back in an unbroken line to pre-colonial times.

This was by no means unforeseen. When asked what would happen when the British left, Yahaya of Gwandu made clear that he did not think the country ready, but that if self-rule did come, its local basis would be the chiefs and their N.A.s.[1] Early in the day an attempt was made by a minority to move away from traditional forms towards a political solution not unlike that taking shape in the southern parts of Nigeria. The attempt failed.[2] The failure was hardly surprising in that a vast majority of the Region's educated people were identified with the traditional rulers, most of them being employed directly by N.A.s. The experience did accelerate, however, the forming of the North's own political apparatus, which quickly won over-whelming power throughout the Region and with which the British worked closely straight through to independence.

Within the context of this seeming departure traditionalists did old things in new ways. Now, in addition to the House of Chiefs, an outgrowth of the Chiefs' Conferences, there was a House of Assembly in Kaduna. In the absence of an alternative, its members had to come from the same ruling groups that supplied staff to N.A.s, to schools, and to commercial firms. That the Waziri of Gumel should become a member was only to be expected, for no one else on the Emir's council could speak English.[3] Just as the Waziri was indispensable locally as the interpreter of circulars and instructions from Kano, so he was the logical representative for Gumel in the councils of Regional affairs. Some chiefs thought they saw an opportunity to extend the range of the time-honoured *douceur* in an effort to get higher sanction for a local misdemeanour. The Emir of Jema'a, annoyed that a touring officer got his son removed from a district headship, sent £5 to the Sardauna of Sokoto, by then Premier, with the request that the young man be reinstated.[4] More thoughtful chiefs tended to be at one with

[1] Stanhope White, op. cit., p. 223.
[2] D. A. Pott was kind enough to lend me an eight-page typed account of the N.E.P.U. failure in Kano, written by an administrative officer of some seniority and undoubted personal familiarity with the subject. I am not at liberty to disclose his name.
[3] Gumel Town and District Book, 1937–55, entry of 22 March 1955.
[4] Confidential file on Emirs of Jema'a, 9 May 1957, Hibbs, K.

D.O.s in recognizing that the main task was to strengthen N.A.s and that the North had little time to put its house in order. A.D.O.s could disagree on whether some of the young fire-brands in the countryside were genuine progressives with roots among the people or just opportunists. There was less room for doubt when a Chief of Ja'afaru's integrity spoke up. Admonishing D.H.s, he reminded them again of their duty to the people. At the same time he called attention to the specific activities of trouble-makers, giving chapter and verse on ways in which they had disrupted the workings of local administrations: 'Do not let irresponsible people lead you astray.'[1] Although more conservative in his last years, he proved himself an able intermediary as local discretion shifted from British officers to the N.A., now reporting more and more to an African-run Kaduna. African Ministers now went on tour as chief commissioners had done before.

While the details of politics in the immediate pre-independence years lie outside the scope of this inquiry, and the period after 1960 even more so, it is useful to project a bit by asking how local administration has stood the test of the British withdrawal and, later, the violent upheavals of 1966. Close studies of particular N.A.s are much needed, especially ones that bring out the viewpoints of the major African participants themselves and that do this in such a way as to avoid the polemicizing that so blurs our vision of African realities in the 1950s and 1960s.[2] When the voice of local Africa is heard on the events of these years we shall have an invaluable comment on the down-to-earth effectiveness of government in the colonial period.

After 1960 there was a rise in corruption and a decline in

[1] Emir of Zaria to D.H.s, confidential file, 1954, Provincial Office.

[2] I have been much helped by the remarks of D. M. Last, Ahmadu Bello University, Zaria, on the kinds of research that would assist in this regard. Abubakar Imam, then editor of *Gaskiya Ta Fi Kwabo*, deals with the subject in a general way in notes on a talk he had with Lugard, 'The Problems of Northern Nigeria As the Natives See It', 1943. I thank Sir Arthur Weatherhead for lending me his copy.

An interesting recent contribution to the literature in this regard is a paper by A. H. M. Kirk-Greene, 'Qualification and the Accessibility of Office', African Studies Center, University of California, Los Angeles, May 1967. Research by Professor C. S. Whitaker, Jr., of the University of California, Los Angeles, and by Professor John Paden of Northwestern University should also be noted. Unfortunately I had not been able to see the work of either as of the time this book went to press.

efficiency. Apart from these predictable responses to the disappearance of the master from the classroom, what can be
said about African management of the basically unchanged
Anglo-African machine? Did the power of the chiefs rise or
decline in relation to Kaduna's? What was the relationship
between the chief and the local representative of Kaduna, no
longer a Resident but a political man with cabinet rank and
charged with responsibility for policy matters while the more
mundane administrative ones were supposedly left to a provincial secretary? What was the new relationship between the
chief and the D.O., now a young African with some European
education, coming in most cases from the Middle Belt and from
a course in the Institute of Administration at Zaria? Some of
the things done by this new D.O. were the same. The officer at
Hadejia in 1965, just in from a tour on horseback, talked as his
British predecessors had done of *talakawa* who got out of paying
tax by crossing the border into Katagum, of famine relief, of
seeds and crops and sanitation problems.[1] He grumbled about
the Premier's recent visit with all its fanfare and officialism just
as European D.O.s had grumbled about junketing lieutenant
governors. But there were differences. He disliked touring and
preferred the town. Grass grew on the tennis court. One was
given a drink on the veranda, but not dinner. The D.O. knew
that the Emir had him shadowed, which was nothing new,
but he did not speak of the Emir as a man who would jump if
he cracked the whip. In Birnin Kebbi the Emir of Gwandu
referred patronizingly to the administrative officer, who was
seated at his right, as 'our young friend, the D.O.', an unimaginable description in the colonial time.[2] With the assassination of a strong Premier in January 1966, did the new head of
the Northern Government, the youngish son of the Emir of
Katsina, defer rather more to major chiefs than the Sardauna
had done? Would he be more likely, or less, to do away with a
stubborn potentate like the old Emir of Kano?

Local pride had a familiar ring. The African D.O. at Argungu,
digging out a sewer pile alongside his works crew, sounded
very like an Englishman as he spoke of the soundness of 'his'
treasury by comparison with the one next door that had just

[1] J. D. Bejide, Hadejia, 29 July 1965.
[2] The D.O. was M. S. Minjibir. Birnin Kebbi, 25 August 1965.

been disciplined by Kaduna.[1] Young Britons sent out by Volun-
tary Service Overseas spoke with unaffected pride of the talents
of their African superiors.[2] And senior British officers still
holding positions of major power and responsibility appeared to
feel easy enough in their delicate way-stations between African
Kaduna and African D.O.s.[3] Could they have felt so if there
had been more change than sameness? If by the end of 1966
there was more order than not in the North, does this not
bespeak a considerable continuity? Would it not appear, in
sum, that whereas Africans in the southern parts of Nigeria
had opposed and replaced the British in an almost revolutionary
way, in the North the quondam rulers, urged on by the British
themselves, had added a political dimension to their existing
traditional order but had otherwise gone on pretty much as
before?

These are subjects for Africans and Africanists. Here we must
summarize and pass judgement on what the British did in the
North during the half-century when the positions of ultimate
power were theirs. What difference did the British presence
make?

It is well to begin with the reminder that what happened in
the years of British rule did not necessarily happen because
someone planned it. We study evolution, not the smooth, logical,
consistent responses of players to the baton of some all-knowing
and all-capable maestro in his pit of power. This might seem
redundant but for the swelling torrent of literature, journa-
listic and scholarly, that has poured forth over the years of
the nationalist era in Africa. It is not only lovers of scapegoats
who have increasingly succeeded in finding the place and
person of blame for independent Africa's troubles. Many who
think of themselves as followers after objective truth have also
succumbed and have begun their allegedly empirical studies by
accepting at face value whatever rationalizations of the
British presence the rulers have put forward from time to time.
'This is what they said they were doing; therefore this is what
must have been done.' In fairness we must forgive erring artists
and chide the subject himself for talking too much during the

---

[1] Salihu Abdullahi, Argungu, 4 and 5 September 1965.
[2] T. N. Wells, Kano, and S. R. J. Powell, Zaria.
[3] St. Elmo Nelson, Kano, and P. J. Wallace, Zaria.

last sittings while his portrait was being finished. An acute observer of the British and colonial scene has remarked that self-conscious protestations tend to increase as physical power wanes.[1] We must try to ignore breast-beating explanation and concentrate on the record.

The ingredients of Anglo-African government were a relatively small number of British and a larger number of Africans who together operated the mechanisms of administration from 1900 to 1960. The British were actuated by the sense and sensibility of England in the early decades of the present century. Instincts were backed by the home society, by schools and universities and perhaps military units through which the future officers passed in their maturing years. The unspoken code of living that overshadowed any official line was fundamentally a matter of growing up among certain kinds of people, thinking certain thoughts, having certain expectations, and being aware of the sanctions that were available and might be used in case of deviation. There was no prototype D.O. or Resident, but common denominators were there. For all the individualism that formed so essential a stream in Colonial Service life, one came from an organized nation, a society whose worldly success in the eighteenth and nineteenth centuries owed much to corporate functioning. Co-operating in the pursuit of discrete aims was in the blood. Moreover, this sense of deeply ingrained standards and of pulling together as a matter of course was bound to be heightened in an atmosphere that epitomized something close to the opposite tendency. Men who might not have been especially strict at home often became sticklers for propriety in Africa. Integrity, in the objective sense of the word, was apt to harden in the face of what appeared to be an unconscionable egotism among the local people. An attitude founded on honesty, humanity, and justice seemed to confront the universal assumption that power meant licence to exploit.

Most officers felt that progress was a good thing, that roads and bridges would help trade and the agricultural economy. If this was not so pronounced in some of the earlier administrators, it was likely to be more common with every passing year. There were always opposing tendencies. In the minds of a substantial number of officers lurked a notion that Africa would not change

[1] V. S. Naipaul, *An Area of Darkness*, London, 1964, p. 207.

of its own accord or should not be made to or both. Some had a cultural reticence born of humility or doubt. Was Europe really superior in the moral sense? Even if it was, did Europeans have a right to inflict their ways on others?[1] And some who were not inhibited in this way saw Africa's huge mass as a dead weight that the small alien cadre could never move very far. It was wiser to accommodate than to push.

Yet officers who had doubts of these kinds were Europeans nevertheless. With their more forward-looking and vigorous brothers, they signified by their very presence the standards and therefore the discipline of Europe.

Ideologically British rule was static. It does not have that reputation with everyone, for Lugard did arrive with predispositions, and many people—the odd Secretary of State, most governors, some lieutenant governors—did pronounce in the policy realm. Taken in series, these dicta showed a progression from a rationalization of what more or less had to be done at first to some quite idealistic, or at any rate abstract, statements in the 1940s and 1950s. But what mattered was the day-to-day double-harness administration of D.O. and chief. It was not Bibles that counted but putting brick on top of brick. Progress cannot be understood outside the framework of precedent and momentum. Ideology is nothing if it does not guide the hands of A.D.O.s on tour and chiefs in council. In the North it was not

---

[1] Cf. C. E. Carrington, 'Rudyard Kipling and the Commonwealth Ideal', *Commonwealth Journal*, IX, 2 (April 1966), pp. 75–6.

The British sometimes describe themselves and are described by others as being personally and socially inhibited, unnatural, or psychologically stunted (cf. E. M. Forster, *Abinger Harvest*, London, 1953, p. 13). An extension of this criticism is that they passed their inhibitions on to peoples under their rule, thus doing the whole ex-British colonial world a vast disservice. The natural spirituality and unaffected social posture of hundreds of tropical communities, runs this argument, were warped to fit the tortured, socially alienated stance of modern bourgeois civilization in Europe and America. It is doubtful if this view takes into account the actual relationship between rulers and ruled and especially the degree to which the British were able to influence their subject peoples in this sphere. Financial procedures can be imitated by an African, for example, without his taking on at the same time the private paranoia of a European accountant. Children who receive clothes and school fees from their parents do not thereby automatically imbibe whatever is psychologically unwholesome in the father or mother: and the British–African relationship was far less intimate than the parent–child one. Moreover, we may ask whether Africa would be better protected today from the horrors of mass civilization if it had never received, via colonialism, the externals of European religion, bureaucracy, and commercialism.

ideology that did this but the persistent Britishness of the former and the slowly changing African-ness of the latter.

In the colonial period the North got leadership. The men who ran things had integrity; that is to say, a standard of operation which may not have been thought about or discussed but which in practice they did not depart from. British rule did not respond to the bias and hedonism of the mass as democratic governments must do. Some say there is no point in crediting the British with this since their aloofness from the native rulers and the masses made it inevitable. Any leader may follow his conscience when public opinion does not count. But the incorruptibility of the British may be dismissed as an automatic consequence of their apartness only if it is held that alien rule is always incorruptible.[1] Was it so with successive alien dynasties in China, with Islamic conquerors in India, with the Portuguese in Africa, with Hispano-Indian élites in Latin America? The British could have used their power in the North to enrich themselves, as some of their seventeenth- and eighteenth-century ancestors did in India. There was no power to stop them being oppressive either, if they had been the kind of people who derived pleasure from ruling in that way. In an age when both naïvety and cynicism about power are common, the Africans may be congratulated on their good fortune in receiving a benign rule.

The other main essential on the British side was poverty. For the first few years the Government could barely maintain itself in existence and was unable to do more than contemplate the flanks of African society. Slowly a hybrid tax structure was built and wasteful practices were severely cut into. In the ensuing decades the revenues of Government and of N.A.s steadily expanded. But the determining factor was the Region's own wealth. Even as amplified by European technology and contributed to by commercial firms, the economy had always to go forward at its own pace. Deficit financing, administrative hire purchase, and all the largesse of national and international aid programmes lay undreamed of over a distant horizon.[2]

---

[1] Cf. Lord Radcliffe, *The Reith Lectures*, v, London, 1952.

[2] It is well to remind ourselves, too, that this kind of spending, which has become a fixture of international relations since the 1950s, was not characteristic of the metropolitan countries themselves in the years before the Second World War.

With twice as much money the British might have been able to enforce higher standards of efficiency, either by putting more European officers into the field or by training native ones. As it was, their poverty kept the numbers down and brought about that much less change.

Thus the Briton was an underpaid schoolmaster in an over-populated school. He lived in the house and took a full part in its life, without ever crossing the line. He knew the boys well and liked them and he sympathized with their problems. His discipline was unyielding and fair, and it was as constant as sun and rain.

About the Africans one must speak with much more diffi-dence. Continually in these pages it has been necessary to note the lack of dependable information on their views. One knows what arrangements were made from time to time and what the British wanted to do and tried to do. Specific actions of chiefs and other members of N.A.s have been described. But an apprai-sal of African feelings, the basic outlook that underlay these actions, remains outside our capacity. Occasionally a major figure would show by his behaviour as well as his words that his fundamental attitude was nothing more nor less than what it seemed on the surface. Yahaya of Gwandu put in too many years of hard work with too many different British officers for there to be much doubt that he was just what he appeared to be. His sense of responsibility would have been recognizable in any cultural setting. On the other hand, the Chief of Birnin Gwari, who antedated the British and remained in office through to the mid-1930s, simply could not change in any essential way. He was clearly a child of the earlier time, and no amount of plead-ing or threatening could alter what went on in his head. In varying degrees most N.A.s showed a similar changelessness, having to be continually prodded and dragged along and slip-ping backward again whenever the pressure relaxed. In the opinion of one former D.O., the average African of the ruling class was affected by British morality hardly at all. It was as though the Europeans had performed functions rather like those of the old household slaves, leaving chiefs in ceremonial and privileged positions, cut off from responsibility and from real contact with the people.[1] Many of his brother officers will

---

[1] J. H. Smith, 14 April 1967, Durham, North Carolina.

think this an extreme view; but they would doubtless agree that morally and spiritually most office-holders remained traditionalists.

What did change was the whole broad context in which chiefs and N.A.s operated. It has been observed how the British gradually realigned administrative structures, introducing European concepts of order and system in finance and compelling Africans to work the mechanisms of bureaucracy. For all their failings, N.A. officials became habituated to a far greater degree of regularity in administration and law than their forebears had known. Meanwhile education and the steady growth of the money economy had remade the atmosphere in which administration worked. No matter how much trauma the Region would still have to go through in the latter half of the 1960s, it was already clear, as of independence, that the old order had been undermined. There would be no going back. The question was not whether traditional attitudes and ways could be preserved but what combination of African and alien parts the new society would be made up of.

Perhaps the most profound and important change in African viewpoints has come about by indirection. E. L. Mort, who had a long and distinguished career in the Education Service, speaks of the original relationship between British and Africans as one of master and man and, growing out of this, the slow rise in African minds of a determination to be equal.

At the time of the First War and after, schoolboys absorbed western ideas in the classroom but remained African in habits and outlook and did not apparently want to be anything else. But during the last war I was conscious of a steady pull between the ultra-conservative ideas of some of my African staff and a desire among boys for non-African standards—wearing shoes indoors and out, a decided preference during the holidays for clothes of European style, abandonment of traditional salutations, discarding of old Hausa names . . . all these things spoke of a revulsion against what must have appeared as the marks of servitude and a determination to rise above them.[1]

It was only by enduring this humiliation—whose unintentional nature made it no easier to bear—that the young would shift their gaze voluntarily away from the age-old standards of

[1] Letter, 4 June 1966.

their fathers to those of their fathers' masters. Only by starting up the European ladder could new generations of Africans assert equality with those who occupied its highest rungs. It became a matter of choosing, sometimes unconsciously, to follow a culture that had shown itself politically and technologically superior. Traditional Africa had few convincing answers to the blatant fact of European pre-eminence.

In 1950 the Bauchi Provincial member in the House of Assembly made a speech that sharply criticized British laxity and called for N.A. reform.

We cannot afford to stagnate; we must go forward . . . the chief must understand that he has no right to his place and power unless he renders proper service to the State . . . one of the biggest defects of the system is the complete ignorance of everyone from top to bottom about his rights, his obligations and his powers. This ignorance must somehow be removed and the people made to realize that they too have a share in their own government . . . the Natural Rulers [i.e. the chiefs] in the North should realize that Western education and world conditions are fast creating a new class of people . . . that this new class must exist is certain, and the Natural Rulers, whom the North must retain at all costs, should, instead of suspecting it, try to find it proper accommodation.[1]

The future Prime Minister went on to speak with strong disapproval of 'the twin curses of bribery and corruption' which had such a grip on office-holders that 'the ideals of disinterested service' were crowded out entirely.[2]

It may be observed, firstly, that these were precisely the ideas, both positive and negative, that forward-looking administrators had been hammering at for decades. Some, like Edwardes, might have demurred over the part about keeping the chiefs at all costs, although probably not if they could be made to toe the mark of good government. Secondly, Sir Abubakar, as he later became, was speaking as few African leaders would have spoken only a few years earlier, or, indeed, even at that point in time. The standards he appealed to may have corresponded to those of the model Islamic state in some degree. But they had virtually no reference to administrative practice in pre-British Hausaland. For one of the new breed of Northern leaders to chastise the British for not being progressive enough was to

[1] Hon. Abubakar Tafawa Balewa, 19 August 1950.   [2] Ibid.

demonstrate that traditional standards were losing the battle. Mallam Abubakar appeared to be more royal than the alien king.

As the core of the speech made clear, however, most members of N.A.s possessed no such enlightened views. The slow progress of Anglo-African government reflected a general sluggishness among the Africans and a British tendency to accept this as a basic condition that would only change gradually over a long period. If the British were not especially imaginative in the realm of ideology and if their standards were comparatively rigid in everyday administrative practice, that rigidity was a condition of African forward movement. Had the British constantly sprinted on ahead, to put it another way, there would have been confusion in African ranks and not the natural and organic wish to imitate that Mort refers to. Within the familiar, unchanging framework of British discipline and encouragement African self-consciousness developed at its own pace.

The central dilemma of Indirect Rule versus Direct Rule was in practice never resolved. One school of administrators worried about the dire consequences of interfering too much. If they exerted too rash a discipline the Africans would lose interest or become discouraged and would not learn by their own efforts and mistakes. The opposing school looked with horror on the quagmire of corruption and inefficiency in N.A.s, a standing affront to British sensibilities and a mockery of colonialism's claim to be a civilizing force. Policy and consensus aside, however, the two schools were mixed with good and bad chiefs into the *pot-pourri* of living, moving administration. Like Fulani government before it, Anglo-African government had a wholeness and genre of its own. This was apparent enough to its African and British participants, especially at the local level, but it has often been missed by outside observers. The phrase 'Indirect Rule' accounts for much of the obscurity and confusion, conveying an impression of political apartness and lightness of touch that conflicts with what actually happened. There is no room in it for Palmer's reorganization of Kano Emirate in the 1920s, for Sharwood Smith's insistence on the appointment of Ja'afaru, for Giles's clean-up of an unsatisfactory rural district, for Yahaya's co-operation with Weatherhead and

White, and for generations of young *Turawa* on horseback
chasing cattle Fulani and listening to the *talakawa*. The fact
that Africans and British lived apart socially is another reason
why the oneness of their government has escaped notice or has
been denied. On most stations there was considerable distance
between the Government Residential Area and the Emir's
residence and N.A. offices. Abubakar Imam told Lugard in the
1940s that social separation kept the British from understanding
the Africans. 'The Europeans like us, I know, but . . . they do
not mix with us.'[1] He called for interracial dinner parties and
sport. But in doing so this remarkable broker between the two
races was not speaking for a majority among his own people.
Neither side was ever really comfortable at the after-hours
gatherings of the other. Nor did a lack of truly profound understanding preclude administrative cohesion in the colonial period.
In fact, mutual recognition and tolerance of the cultural gulf
dividing Englishman from African was one of the regime's
firmest bases. The two could function coincidently at all levels
from provincial headquarters to the smallest hamlet without
pervasive insight into every nook and cranny of each other's
character, and without seeing one another at home or in the
club.

The administration was a bi-racial phenomenon whose two
interconnecting parts changed over the years as they responded
to each other and to the evolving society around them. The
British at first deferred to Africa, greatly and by necessity. As
their power grew they instinctively asserted their own conceptions of what government ought to be and do. The Africans
learned new skills. Some of them, especially the young, moved
away from traditional values towards those of the British. By
the 1950s the governmental machinery had developed substantially. In general it was working well, being familiar
and basically acceptable to both races. If it was not a carbon
copy of local government in England, neither was it much like
Fulani regimes of the pre-1900 period. The overall effect of
Britain's presence in the North was to transform taxing sul-
tanates into local units whose functions were regularized and
uniform and hundreds of whose staff members were experienced
in the rudiments of bureaucratic procedure.

[1] Note 2, p. 176, above.

The British have criticized themselves and have been criticized by others for not doing enough to develop the economy. It is true that large expenditures from the home treasury were not made until the end of the colonial period. Economically, British rule was on a subsistence basis, with progress being determined by the fiscal capacity of each local unit as augmented *ad hoc* from central funds. Nevertheless, there was more prosperity than there had been before. Peace and order assured a favourable atmosphere in which local commerce and the activities of larger firms from abroad could advance normally. Woodhouse was not praising imperialism, but merely noting a fact, when in 1931 he remarked on the altered face of Gusau in his time. 'How this place has changed since I first trekked up this way on horseback at the end of 1922 . . . first the cotton people established themselves . . . in a small way and were building a big ginnery when I passed through in 1927. Since then has come the railway extension—116 miles from Zaria . . . close on the heels of the railway came . . . various trading firms . . . the native town is nearly doubled by an influx of *hoi polloi* from the Southern Provinces, clerks, shop boys, store-keepers, buying agents, artisans . . . whom it is not too easy for the local Hausa District Head to supervise . . .'[1] In a time when Africa was not part of the world it is arguable whether her own people considered the British deficient in this sphere.

Similarly it said that the Europeans undercut tradition without promoting democracy.[2] We may ask whether democracy is ever introduced from above—by indigenous rulers, not to mention alien ones—or whether it has to grow over a long period and in response to the demands of self-conscious, resourceful, upthrusting classes. However this may be, the effect of colonial rule was not to make the masses substantially less docile. Rather it gave them a taste for order and for the things—roads, wells, bigger markets, cash crops—that become possible only when order is preserved. Negatively the people developed a greater capacity for discontent in the face of misrule than they

[1] Letter, 5 July 1931, C.R.P.
[2] Cf. Sir Arthur Weatherhead, review of A. H. M. Kirk-Greene, op. cit., in *The Journal of Administration Overseas* (April 1966), pp. 135–7. Cf. Sir John Maynard, *Russia In Flux*, New York, 1941, p. 300, discussing the Anglo-American obsession with democracy. For a rather different view, however, see Hugh Tinker, *Ballot Box and Bayonet*, London, 1964, pp. 1–2.

had had before. This would be a factor that any future government of the Region would have to reckon with.

By the same token the ruling classes were not made more honest and responsible by their experience under the British. Certain instincts and habits frowned on by the British seem to have dried up. Since independence there has been little talk of the Moslem's duty to wage holy war. The hands of thieves are not amputated. Most people reacted with embarrassment to the Islamic evangelism of the late Sardauna of Sokoto. But the morality of leadership, which could not be tested until the Africans were on their own, seems to have undergone no great change. The corruption that led to the coup of January 1966—or was at any rate one of the factors that produced it—suggests that the North's new and inexperienced leaders failed this test. We will now learn whether the survivors have become aware of the price of corruption and will steer clear of the excesses that brought their predecessors down. Responsibility in government is partly a matter of finding out what irresponsibility costs.

It is doubtful too that the British period saw much change in the deep-seated improvidence of the Africans, their disinclination to plan ahead or to take the future into account in any serious way. Linked to this, which experience could well change, has been a tendency not to accept responsibility for their own shortcomings or to profit from mistakes. At the time of the British conquest adversity could be ascribed to Allah's disfavour. During the colonial years members of N.A.s complained with great regularity that they were misunderstood or subjected to unfair treatment by British officers. In the years just before and just after independence some African officials continued to blame the British for whatever went wrong. 'The truth is,' said the Nigerian Supreme Commander recently, 'there is so much pretence in our society, so much posing. We like to appear better than we are but we do not always work hard enough to do better.'[1] In the protests, violence, and recriminations of 1966 and after, we discern clearly enough the marks of petulance and immaturity. There has been rather less evidence of a cold, hard determination to face up to the thankless task of running a government in a poor and inexperienced country.

[1] Lt.-Col. Gowon, at a national conference in Lagos, September 1966, reported in *West Africa*, 17 September 1966, p. 1070.

The British did two things above all others: they faced the facts of the local culture, and they gradually altered those facts. Had their approach been merely deferential, a type of rule that was literally indirect, there would have been little or no progress. All the innovations that set today's North off from the Fulani–Kanuri one—education, better communications, increased productivity, regional uniformity and unity, a virtual abandonment of inter-tribal and inter-emirate warfare—came about as a direct result of British initiative or as a close consequence of the Pax. Left to themselves the Africans, like the Hadhrami of South Arabia up to the late 1930s, would have borrowed a Europeanism here and there but remained otherwise unchanged. Had the British ruled by themselves, on the other hand, forcing the pace of change and ignoring or manhandling the country's natural rulers, there might well have been a good deal more progress, especially of the economic kind. But such gains would surely have been made at a high cost in social shock, and it is doubtful to say the least that in that case 1960 would have found the Region prepared to stand on its own feet at all. When independence comes a brilliant economy is of little use unless local skills are adequate and some political stability is possible.

Gaining perspective on the particular combination of order and progress that Anglo-African government gave to the North is difficult because of the bewildering speed and ferocity of events since the beginning of 1966.[1] Following the assassination of the Premier, it appeared that the flimsy outer wrapping of artificial politics was torn away, leaving the chiefs and their N.A.s as the Region's main bases of order. One reaction to the discrediting of the politicians and the weakening of Kaduna's hold has been a rise in the power and prestige of traditional institutions and a reversal of such liberal steps as putting European-educated men on the councils of chiefs. This is regrettable for it represents the opposite trend to one that added much to

---

[1] Particularly so since it is hard to separate the question of Britain's record in the North from the question of federation and the difficulties experienced by federal Nigeria in the period 1960–7. The two questions must be kept separate, however: early independence in a federal context was not foreseen and aimed at during the greater part of the colonial period: judging Britain against a standard of a successful federation, therefore, is to presume an ideal which neither the British nor the Africans, by and large, presumed until very late.

N.A. strength and resilience before. But the survival of traditional power does show, as it did after independence, that the
chiefs and emirate administrations had local roots. If in the
future they do no more than bridge the gap between the stability
of Anglo-African government and the new stability now being
painfully groped for they will have served a vital purpose. In a
situation of deepening confusion any oasis of the familiar, the
calm, and the constant is much to be prized.

Beyond that, the N.A.s of the colonial years have their own
record. Given the existing African material and the small
numbers of the British, it was a remarkable performance. No
more can be asked of any government than that it provide an
order wherein tyranny can be challenged and a degree of movement that avoids stagnation without harming those traditions
that the majority esteems.

The D.O. was an empiricist, not a dreamer. He steered a
middle course not because he had puzzled it all out and arrived
at an abstraction of the Good, like Aristotle's Golden Mean, but
because he was an Englishman in Africa. Anglo-African government was what he and the N.A. did together. It was what
happened when his qualities and values were applied to an
African mass which, for all its sluggishness, would move forward
if approached with sympathy, patience, and skill. Its essence
was accommodation. The best officers learned that intolerance
and blind vigour were apt to end in personal frustration and
administrative ineffectiveness.

One morning in the mid-1930s the Resident Sokoto and the
Sultan were preparing to go on tour together as they regularly
did.[1] Although their relationship was excellent, there were the
usual small problems that arise when travelling companions
come from radically different backgrounds. The Resident would
have dearly loved to take his dogs and do a bit of shooting en
route. But dogs offend Moslems, and in this instance one was
accompanying the Commander of the Faithful himself. 'Aren't
you going to bring your dogs?' asked the Sultan, knowing full
well what the Resident's habits were. Surprised, the Englishman hesitated. 'Put them in your car with your boy,' suggested
the Sultan, 'and you come in my car.' The little caravan drove
out on the road towards Wurno, where the Sultan's ancestors

---

[1] Carrow, 6 January 1966.

had often gone to escape the tedium of Sokoto and to learn what their enemies, the near-by Gobirawa, were up to. The heat and the dust were bothersome as always. Still, their Hausa conversation was brisk enough at first. Both had recently married and had met each other's wives. The Resident had been invited into the harem at the Sultan's country place, where he had called on a Sunday afternoon. Again the breach of Moslem etiquette had surprised the Englishman, by this time a veteran of some fifteen years' service in the North. The Sultan's marriage was his fourth, however, and had only been arranged to heal a political schism in the Emirate. 'I met your new wife,' he had said, 'so why can't you come and see mine.' But as mile followed bumpy mile both men wearied of talk and each secretly wished for the privacy and comfort of his own place. At last the African spoke up. 'I know you don't like it, but I must chew a kola nut. I am dying for it.' It was true that most British found the kola habit unattractive, with its stained teeth and spitting. 'Go ahead', replied the Resident, much relieved. Here was an excuse to indulge a vice of his own that he knew to be distasteful to Africans. 'But if you are going to chew a kola nut, then I'm going to smoke my pipe.' As they continued on their way, recalled the Resident more than thirty years later, they were both at peace with themselves and with the world.

Sources

The following lists are representative only. Surveys and bibliographies of wider compass, or books containing such bibliographies, include: M. Hiskett, 'Arabic and Hausa Sources for the Pre-Colonial History of Northern Nigeria' (seminar paper, Oxford University, November 1965); *The Cambridge History of the British Empire*, III, 1959; J. E. Flint, *Sir George Goldie and the Making of Nigeria*, 1960, and *Books on the British Empire and Commonwealth*, 1968; H. M. Wright, 'British West Africa', in R. W. Winks (ed.), *The Historiography of the British Empire–Commonwealth*, 1966; M. Perham, *Colonial Government*, 1950, *Lugard*, II, 1960, and *Native Administration in Nigeria*, 1937; J. Fage, *An Introduction to the History of West Africa*, 1955; J. S. Coleman, *Nigeria*, 1960, and 'A Survey of Selected Literature on the Government and Politics of British West Africa', *American Political Science Review*, XLIX, 4 (December 1955); F. Carnell, *The Politics of the New States*, 1961; A. Hazlewood, *The Economics of Under-Developed Areas*, 1959; T. Hodgkin, *Nationalism in Colonial Africa*, 1956.

I. UNPUBLISHED MATERIAL

A. PRIVATE PAPERS*

L. C. Giles: Touring Diaries, Zaria Province, 1930s.

Sir Bryan Sharwood Smith: Typescript of memoirs; paper, 'The Northern Nigerian D.O. in the Period 1928–1935'.

Alhaji M. Tukur, Emir of Yauri: Administrative Diaries of the Emir Abdullahi of Yauri and British officers, 1928–31.

Sir Arthur Weatherhead: Letters, 1930s and 1940s.

B. OFFICIAL PAPERS

1. Administrative Offices, Northern Nigeria:

    Touring Diaries, Kano Division, by districts, 1920s to 1940s.

    Secret Files. Emirs of Hadejia, 1906–50.

    Confidential Reports on Emirs and District Heads, Hadejia, 1919–33.

---

* In addition to papers listed below I was fortunate in having access to certain letters which have not yet become generally available to scholarship and which cannot therefore be identified as to source.

Interview Books, Emirs of Hadejia and Gumel, 1935–45.
Intelligence Reports, Hadejia, 1926–32.
Confidential Political Notebooks, Hadejia and Gumel, 1935–45.
Handing-Over Notes, Northern Division, Kano Province, 1930s.
Town and District Books, Hadejia, 1950s.
School Ledgers and Visitors Books, Gwandu, 1914–53.
Files on Emirs of Yauri, Gwandu, 1938–50.
Political and Touring Diaries, Zaria Province, 1931–54.

2. Nigerian National Archives, Kaduna:

Secretariat Files: Correspondence with officers of the Provincial Administration, 1906 ff.
Confidential Notes on Indirect Rule (correspondence among Residents), 1907–8.
Correspondence between the Governor and the Secretary of State, Native Administration Policy, 1930.
Assessment and Ethnographic Reports, by Districts, Divisions, and Provinces, 1907 ff.
Records of Katsina College, 1919 ff.
Visits of Chiefs to the United Kingdom, 1927 ff.
Correspondence of Chiefs, 1930 ff.
Liaison between Administrative Officers and Departmental Officers, 1920s to 1940s.
Files, by Provinces, on Native Treasuries, Courts and Public Works, and on Education, 1908 ff.
Annual Reports, by Provinces and Divisions, 1900 ff., and Reports on reorganization of units.
Confidential correspondence among officers, Kano Province, 1921–32, on touring, conduct of Chiefs, role of slave officials, Chiefs' Councils.
Confidential Reports on N.A.s, Sokoto Province, 1909–35.
Correspondence between Kaduna and Residents, Sokoto Province, regarding the Sultans of Sokoto, 1909 ff.
Confidential Reports and correspondence on Chiefs, Sokoto Province, 1909 ff.
Confidential correspondence on Chiefs, Zaria Province, 1909 ff.
Correspondence between Kaduna and Residents, Zaria Province, 1910 ff., on District and Village administration.
Files on relations with Church Missionary Society, Wusasa, Zaria, 1932 ff.

C. PAPERS OF THE COLONIAL RECORDS PROJECT, OXFORD UNIVERSITY

Sir Gordon Lethem: Correspondence, 1911–33, with his family and with officers in Northern Nigeria and England (principally with Messrs. Palmer, Ruxton, Tomlinson, Patterson, Woodhouse, Tegetmeier, Alexander, Webster, and Browne, and with Lord Lugard); Provincial Annual Reports, 1931, with comments by the Acting Lieutenant Governor; assessment reports.

C. A. Woodhouse: Diaries and letters, 1908–32, mainly Kabba and Sokoto.

Sir George Tomlinson: Letters, 1906–21, Sokoto, Zungeru, and Lagos.

H. S. W. Edwardes: Letters, memoranda, and reports, 1914–24, Bauchi, Sokoto, Kontagora, and Munshi.

F. de F. Daniel: Letters, 1912–35, Lagos, Jebba, Kano, Katsina, Argungu, Gwandu, Sokoto, and Ilorin.

H. M. Brice-Smith: Reports and notes, 1909–27, Kano, Muri, and Minna.

T. E. Letchworth: Reports, 1936–49, Benue and Kabba.

Sir Arthur Weatherhead: Memoirs of Northern Nigerian service, 1930–60.

Sir Richard Ramage: History of the Katagum Division, compiled 1925–9.

E. J. Arnett: Private correspondence and other papers, 1906–25, mainly Kano, Kaduna, and England.

D. COLONIAL OFFICE

Staff Lists
Civil Lists
Gazettes
Blue Books
Maps

II. PRINTED SOURCES

N. U. Akpan, *Epitaph to Indirect Rule*, London, 1956.
E. J. Arnett, *Provincial Gazette*, Zaria, 1920.
—— *The Rise of the Sokoto Fulani*, 1922.
—— *Sokoto Gazetteer*, 1920.
H. F. Backwell, *The Occupation of Hausaland 1903–1904*, Lagos, 1927.
H. Barth, *Travels and Discoveries in North and Central Africa*, 5 vols., London, 1857.

Sir Ahmadu Bello, *My Life*, London, 1962.

R. L. Buell, *The Native Problem in Africa*, 2 vols., New York, 1928.

Mary Bull, 'Indirect Rule in Northern Nigeria, 1906–1911', in K. Robinson and F. Madden (eds.), *Essays in Imperial Government*, Oxford, 1963.

Sir Alan Burns, *Colonial Civil Servant*, London, 1949.

—— *History of Nigeria*, London, 1942 edn.

Sir Donald Cameron, *My Tanganyika Service and Some Nigeria*, London, 1939.

Joyce Cary, *Mister Johnson*, London, 1939.

David Caute, *At Fever Pitch*, London, 1959.

J. D. Chick, 'Some Reflections on the Political and Administrative Functions of Provincial Authorities in Northern Nigeria', *Journal of Administration Overseas*, v, 2 (April 1966), 89–96.

E. Chilver, 'Native Administration in the West Central Cameroons, 1902–1954', in K. Robinson and F. Madden (eds.), *Essays in Imperial Government*, Oxford, 1963.

J. S. Coleman, *Nigeria*, Berkeley and Los Angeles, 1960.

W. R. Crocker, *Nigeria*, London, 1936.

—— *On Governing Colonies*, London, 1947.

M. Crowder, 'Indirect Rule—French and British Style', *Africa*, xxxiv (July 1964), 195–205.

Major Denham, Captain Clapperton, and Doctor Oudney, *Narrative of Travels and Discoveries in Northern and Central Africa in the Years 1822, 1823 and 1824*, London, 1828.

Gouverneur Deschamps, 'Et Maintenant, Lord Lugard?', *Africa*, xxxiii (December 1963), 293–305.

R. M. East, *Akiga's Story*, London, 1939.

—— *Stories of Old Adamawa*, Lagos, 1934.

J. E. Flint, *Sir George Goldie and the Making of Nigeria*, London, 1960.

A. F. Fremantle (ed.), *Two African Journals and Other Papers of the Late John Morton Fremantle, C.M.G., M.B.E.*, printed for private circulation, London, 1938.

Sir William N. M. Geary, *Nigeria Under British Rule*, London, 1927.

L. C. Giles, 'The Hausa Village and Co-Operation', typescript, 1937.

S. F. Graham, *Government and Mission Education in Northern Nigeria*, Ibadan, 1966.

Lord Hailey, *Native Administration in the British African Territories*, Part III, London, 1951.

C. J. Hanson-Smith, 'Notes on the Sokoto Fulbe', typescript, 1955.

J. D. Hargreaves, *Prelude to the Partition of West Africa*, London, 1963.

P. G. Harris, *Sokoto Provincial Gazetteer*, 1938.

A. C. G. Hastings, *Nigerian Days*, London, 1925.

A. C. G. Hastings, *The Voyage of the Dayspring*, London, 1926.
Hon. H. B. Herman-Hodge (pseud. Langa Langa), *Up Against It In Nigeria*, London, 1922.
T. Hodgkin, *Nationalism in Colonial Africa*, London, 1956.
S. J. Hogben and A. H. M. Kirk-Greene, *The Emirates of Northern Nigeria*, London, 1965.
M. H. Kingsley, *West African Studies*, London, 1901.
A. H. M. Kirk-Greene, *The Principles of Native Administration in Nigeria*, London, 1965.
—— 'Qualification and the Accessibility of Office', African Studies Center, University of California, Los Angeles, 1967.
—— 'Traditional Authority and the New Leadership Cadres', Conference on Education and Political Development, Committee on Comparative Politics, Social Science Research Council, June 1962.
C. Larymore, *A Resident's Wife in Nigeria*, London, 1908.
D. M. Last, *Sokoto in the Nineteenth Century With Special Reference to the Vizierate*, Ibadan, 1964.
Lord Lugard, *The Dual Mandate in British Tropical Africa*, London, 1922.
—— *The Political Memoranda*, 1918.
Lady Lugard, *A Tropical Dependency*, London, 1905.
J. P. Macintosh *et al.*, *Nigerian Government and Politics*, London, 1966.
M. M. Mahood, *Joyce Cary in Africa*, London, 1964.
C. K. Meek, *Land Tenure and Land Administration in Nigeria and the Cameroons*, London, 1957.
—— *The Northern Tribes of Nigeria*, London, 1925.
C. K. Meek, W. M. Macmillan, and E. R. J. Hussey, *Europe and West Africa*, London, 1940.
W. Miller, *Reflections of A Pioneer*, London, 1936.
A. F. Mockler-Ferryman, *Up The Niger*, London, 1892.
D. J. M. Muffett, *Concerning Brave Captains*, London, 1964.
S. F. Nadel, *A Black Byzantium*, London, 1942.
Nigeria, *Conference of Chiefs of the Northern Provinces: Summary of Proceedings*, 1938.
—— *Conference of Residents, Northern Provinces, 1937, Summary of Proceedings*.
—— *Kano Survey*, 1950, by B. E. Sharwood Smith.
—— *Political Conference Agenda*, 1909.
—— *Report on Local Government in the Northern Provinces of Nigeria*, 1950, by K. P. Maddocks and D. A. Pott.
—— *Sokoto Emirate Notes on Procedure*, 1932.
—— *Sokoto Survey*, 1948, by B. E. Sharwood Smith.

Sir Rex Niven, *How Nigeria is Governed*, London, 1950.

Sir Charles Orr, *The Making of Northern Nigeria*, London, 1911.

Sir Richmond Palmer, 'Some Observations on Captain Rattray's Papers', *Journal of the African Society*, XXXIII (January 1934), 37–48.

Dame Margery Perham, *Lugard*, II, London, 1960.

—— *Native Administration in Nigeria*, London, 1937.

S. S. Richardson, 'Decolonization and the District Officer', Comparative Administration Group, American Society for Public Administration, 1963.

C. H. Robinson, *Hausaland*, London, 1897.

R. Robinson, J. Gallagher, and A. Denny, *Africa and the Victorians*, London, 1961.

Royal Institute of Public Administration, *Development of Local Government in the Colonies*, London, 1955.

J. T. Saunders, R. L. Turner, and D. Veale, *Report to the Nuffield Foundation on a Visit to Nigeria*, London, 1946.

R. L. Sklar and C. S. Whitaker, Jr., 'Nigeria', in J. S. Coleman and C. G. Rosberg, Jr. (eds.), *Political Parties and National Integration in Tropical Africa*, Berkeley and Los Angeles. 1964.

J. H. Smith, *Colonial Cadet*, Durham, N. C., 1968.

M. F. Smith, *Baba of Karo*, London, 1954.

M. G. Smith, *The Economy of Hausa Communities of Zaria*, London, 1955.

—— *Government in Zazzau*. London, 1959.

—— 'Historical and Cultural Conditions of Political Corruption Among the Hausa', *Comparative Studies in Society and History*, VI, 2 (January 1964), 164–94.

C. F. Strickland, *Report on the Introduction of Co-Operative Societies into Nigeria*, Lagos, 1934.

C. L. Temple, *Native Races and Their Rulers*, Cape Town, 1918.

O. Temple and C. L. Temple, *Notes on the Tribes, Provinces, Emirates and States of the Northern Provinces of Nigeria*, Lagos, 1922.

J. S. Trimingham, *A History of Islam in West Africa*, London, 1962.

—— *Islam in West Africa*, Oxford, 1959.

C. S. Whitaker, Jr., 'A Dysrhythmic Process of Political Change', *World Politics*, XIX, 2 (January 1967), 190–217.

S. White, *Dan Bana*, London, 1966.

K. Younger, *The Public Service in New States*, London, 1960.

Index

ABADIE, Capt. G. H., xiii
Abdullahi, Emir of Yauri (*see also* Yauri, Emir), 105, 142–4
Abdullahi Bayero, Emir of Kano, *see* Kano, Emir
Aborigines Protection Societies, 17
Abubakar Imam, 176, 186
Abuja, 26, 110, 156
Adams. Sir Theodore S., xiii, 57, 85–6
Aden, 29
Administrative officers (*see also* District Officers; Residents, etc.), 51, 55–6, 63–4, 73, 82–101, 150, 162
  Africa, attitude to, 43–4; co-operation with Africans, 51, 103–46, 172
  Africans as, 7, 41, 76, 111, 153–4, 162, 177–8, 182
  British remaining after independence, 83, 96, 178
  changes in system, effects of, 97–8
  function of, 71
  Governors and Lieutenant Governors: *see those titles*
  health, 45, 100
  home thoughts, 43, 44
  institutional propriety, 88–91, 93
  'Instructions' for newly joined officers, 39, 104
  military officers as, 98, 111, 179
  offices, British ritual retained in, 83
  parochial outlook, 99, 109, 138
  personality and character, 41–2, 85, 98, 100
  postings, discontinuity, 45, 77–8, 81, 93, 97, 103, 115; long tenure of senior officers, 39, 93, 97
  prestige of postings, 84, 88–90
  recruitment, 55, 98, 145
  reports, writing of, 85–6
  retrenchment, 122
  shortage, 31, 51, 73, 97
  strength, 98
  touring by, *see* Touring
  typical day of junior officer, 44–5
  women, and, 43
Afoda, Audu dan, 118
Africans:
  Administrative service, in, *see under* Administrative officers
  awareness of their surroundings, 10
  complacency in the North, 73, 80, 185

desire for equality with British, 183–4
  relations with British, 43, 103–46, 182–90
  social separation from British, 186
  views and opinions on the British, 7, 110–11, 118, 135, 182–6
Agricultural officers, 55, 150
Agriculture (*see also* Farming), 7, 50, 68, 143, 147–51, 157, 162, 165, 177, 179; development, 48, 108, 147–51, 155, 172–3, 187; D.O.s supervision of, 113, 149–50, 171; marketing of crops, 113, 149, 155; prohibition of high crops near dwellings, 136
Aid programmes, 181
Alexander, C. W., xiii, 69–70, 76–8, 85, 89, 92, 111, 128; cited, 99, 117
Alien rulers, 2, 10–11, 99–100, 181, 187
Aliyu of Zaria (*see also* Zaria, Emir), 46–8, 145
Alkalai, 117–18, 137, 168, 171
Amalgamation of Nigeria (1914), 42, 55; Lugard report (1920), 61
America, 11–12, 180, 187
Amery, L. S., 173
Anchau, 148, 154, 168
Anglo-African government, xii, 25, 52, 67 *passim*, 178–90
Anthropology, intense, 73, 76, 80
Arabia, Arabic, 7, 88, 166, 189
Archer, Sir Geoffrey, cited, 39
Archives, 7–9, 40, 56, 132, 192–4
Area studies, 4–6
Argungu, 26, 41, 46, 95, 97, 115, 128, 137–8, 177–8; Emir, 84, 95, 137–8
Aristocracy, 122, 139, 145, 170, 174
Arnett, E. J., xiii, 47–8, 91, 125–6, 129
Artisans, 23
Asia, Asians, 10, 13, 120
Assassination of Premier (1966), 177, 189
Assessment, 28, 30, 32, 44, 51
Assistant District Officers (A.D.O.s), 42, 87, 89, 99, 118–19, 134, 171, 176; 'cross between a priest and a district head', 158; invites Emir to tea, 105; touring by, 86, 107, 147–69, 180
Assistant Residents (rank), 42
Attenborough, J. P., 116